6-10

THE PROFILER

THE PROFILER

MY LIFE HUNTING SERIAL KILLERS AND PSYCHOPATHS

PAT BROWN

WITH BOB ANDELMAN

voice

HYPERION NEW YORK

Copyright © 2010 Pat Brown

All rights reserved. No part of this book may be used or reproduced in any manner whatsoever without the written permission of the Publisher. Printed in the United States of America. For information address Hyperion, 114 Fifth Avenue, New York, New York, 10011.

Library of Congress Cataloging-in-Publication Data has been applied for.

ISBN: 978-1-4013-4126-8

Hyperion books are available for special promotions and premiums. For details contact the HarperCollins Special Markets Department in the New York office at 212-207-7528, fax 212-207-7222, or email spsales@harpercollins.com.

Book Design by Renato Stanisic

FIRST EDITION

10 9 8 7 6 5 4 3 2 1

For All Victims and Their Families
Who Have Never Received Justice
and Are Still Waiting for Answers

CONTENTS

ACKNOWLEDGMENTS

I would like to thank each and every person who believed in me, my message, and my mission.

In particular:

My sister Joyce, who was always there for me and never questioned my decisions;

My parents, who quietly supported me;

My children, Jennifer, David, and Jeremy, who never complained about the time I spent away from them to do this work;

My dearest friend, Terry Pazmino, who listened to me year in and year out;

All my friends in Maryland and Minnesota, who kept me sane;

My assistant, Donna Weaver, whose tireless volunteer work for the Sexual Homicide Exchange kept the organization alive;

The victims and the families of victims who came to me for help and have never given up their quest for justice;

The detectives who have brought me in and been willing to give criminal profiling a chance;

The television networks, news programs, and hosts who often invite me to educate their audiences about the pressing issues of crime and let me share my views on the notable cases of the day: Nancy Grace, Jane Velez-Mitchell, Larry King, the *Today* show, *The Early Show*, *Fox and Friends*, Montel Williams, and the many other shows on CNN, MSNBC, Fox, the Discovery Channel, and Court TV that have me on, time and time again;

My coauthor, Bob Andelman, for helping me bring all these cases together in a coherent manner;

My agents, Jane Dystel, Miriam Goderich, and Michael Bourret, who had confidence this story should be told;

And, of course, the editors at Hyperion Voice, Barbara Jones and Elizabeth Sabo, who acquired my story and brought this book to the public.

My deepest gratitude to all.
—Pat Brown

Working with criminal profiler Pat Brown has been a unique and rewarding experience for me on a professional level. I'd also like to acknowledge her patience and support during the early days of putting *The Profiler* together. Thanks for sticking with me, Pat.

Thanks, too, to my agents at Dystel & Goderich Literary Management, Jane Dystel, Miriam Goderich, and Michael Bourret, for recommending me to Pat, and to Barbara Jones and Elizabeth Sabo for making this one of the best and most professional experiences of my career to date.

I'd also like to acknowledge the hard work and long hours of Becky James, who has transcribed my book and magazine interviews for almost twenty years.

And finally, to my wife, Mimi, and daughter, Rachel, for waiting "just a minute more" for me to finish work for the night.

—Bob Andelman

NOTE TO THE READER

My recounting of the events that took place in each of these crime stories is based on my personal interviews with victims' family members, friends, and others as well as discussions at times with law enforcement personnel, and, where possible, the review of available files. My findings should only be considered as my hypotheses of how the crimes were committed and who may have committed them based on all the information available to me, my educational background, and my experience in profiling. When I identify a specific person as a possible perpetrator, it is to say that I think police should take a second look (and in some cases, a first look) at that person. As I have always said, profiling can be a powerful investigatory tool, but I am not the prosecutor nor am I the jury. Profiling is not an exact science, and with imperfect information and the passage of time it is not possible to give you anything other than my hypothesis in each of these cases.

PREFACE

What *is* criminal profiling?

It's a combination of analyzing the physical and behavioral evidence, reconstructing a crime from the beginning to the end, and coming up with the most scientific determination possible with the information available.

A lot of it is common sense—or at least it seems that way *after* the crime is solved. But coming up with the right answer requires more than instinct or good guessing; it requires examining the scene and the evidence scientifically, unemotionally, and without any biases.

It is a matter of applied logic that comes from a combination of innate skill, training and education, and years of practice. Learning never ends: learning from doing, learning from others, even learning from one's own mistakes.

Becoming a criminal profiler is a process, not a moment in time. Study, experience, and practice allow a criminal profiler to grow into a Sherlock Holmes of the modern day, improving one's skill, case by case, murder by murder. Whether one trains through the FBI, a police department, college, or on one's own, the learning process is a journey. As time goes on, our skills are honed and we become criminal profilers of worth.

Before I take you behind the profiling curtain, I want to emphasize my support for the detectives working these difficult cases and the struggle of law enforcement to get killers off the streets. What I present in this book represents the cases that came to me because they were unusually difficult to analyze or fell to an investigator with a lack of training or experience, or politics derailed the investigative efforts. The wonderful detectives who brought me in did so because they understood that sometimes an added expert can make the difference between a case being solved and a killer walking free. Many of the cases that I have been involved in are not included in this book because I signed an agreement with law enforcement not to disclose any information or because I felt inclusion would be damaging to the case.

I hope this book helps you understand the tough investigative issues detectives, profilers, and victims of crime face and that you will be encouraged to work together with your communities to fund and support all who fight to make our lives safer.

INTRODUCTION

The only witness to the crime wasn't talking.

By the time I spoke with the mother of the victim, the case had gone cold. A beautiful young woman had been murdered three years prior, strangled in her apartment where she lived alone with her African gray parrot. When the police arrived, the scene was tranquil—nothing in the apartment had been touched except the resident; she lay dead on the living room floor.

There were four possible suspects in the homicide: two men she was dating, an ex-husband who lived out of town, and someone as yet unidentified, perhaps a maintenance man or a fellow apartment dweller. The key to the identity of the killer was known only to the silent witness: the African gray parrot.

After the police released the crime scene, the heartbroken mother boxed up her dead daughter's possessions and carried the boxes and the parrot to her home. She stored the boxes in the garage and put the cage with the parrot in her bedroom. As she drifted off to sleep, she was jolted to full consciousness when she heard a horrified voice crying out, "What are you doing here? What are you doing here? Awwgh!!" There was no one in the room with her but the parrot.

The mother told the story to the police, but her claim that the parrot was mimicking her daughter and the subsequent attack was met with skepticism. The mother insisted she was telling the truth, that the parrot kept repeating the same thing over and over. No one believed her, and as the days went by, the parrot said the phrase less often, until he no longer remembered it.

It was an odd story, something one might think a Hollywood scriptwriter came up with. But it interested me, so I checked the veracity of the parrot with a bird expert. It turned out that African grays are adept at picking up words and sounds, especially older, more experienced parrots, as this African gray happened to be. Such a parrot also tends to repeat statements that are made with great emotion and sounds that are unusual. The expert concluded the victim's parrot might well have repeated the last event that occurred in the young woman's life.

If the parrot was credible, then the suspect was most likely the ex-husband. The victim would not have been surprised or alarmed to see either of the men she was dating nor would she have reacted so dramatically to seeing a resident or worker from the building. Only the ex-husband would have elicited such a response.

It was too late for the parrot to testify. The killer would never see the inside of a courtroom. I was starting to realize, early on in my career as a profiler, that unlike television crime dramas that give us all a feeling of satisfaction by the end of the show, in real life, justice is a rare commodity. Something needs to be done to change this reality and part of that "something" is criminal profiling.

PART I

THE BOARDER

CHAPTER 1

ANNE
THE MURDER

No one had ever been murdered in my town.

The community's first house—*my* house—was built in the 1700s on rolling Maryland farmland. Many interesting things happened here over the centuries, but the town had never experienced a violent homicide.

Anne Kelley, a brilliant government intern from the Midwest, would have the unfortunate honor of being the first.

I WAS OUT of town until Sunday. When I returned that morning, I was at home for only a few minutes when the horrific news reached me. The phone rang and it was my best friend, Terry, who lived just a couple blocks away.

"Did you hear?" she asked, incredulously, dismay in her voice.

"Hear what?" When I had taken the turn onto Sixtieth Street, nothing seemed out of place. There were no fire trucks or ambulances on the street. The town appeared serene. The only activity was a slight breeze, which hardly affected the oppressiveness of the heat on that early sultry summer day, the third of June.

"A young woman was found murdered in the stream by the softball field."

"WHAT?"

"Oh, it's just awful. One of the men playing softball in the league game this morning chased a ball across the path into the water and found a woman's naked body floating right at the edge."

I felt sick. My first thought was that it might be someone I knew, an area resident, a friend, or the mother of one of the local children.

I took a deep breath. "Do they know who she is?"

"No, not yet. I heard she was young, maybe in her late teens or twenties. They found her clothes and a Walkman; it seems she was jogging. The police figure she was killed yesterday, probably at dusk, because no one saw her there during the daylight. She doesn't seem to be a town resident."

It was a tiny relief to hope she was not someone I knew.

I hung up the phone with a nagging, uneasy feeling that I was somehow more connected to this situation than I should be. For a minute, I placated myself with the idea that it was just the shock of hearing about such a tragedy that made me feel this way. Or maybe it was the fact that this gruesome murder happened right at the ball field where I spent so many happy hours cheering on my son and his baseball team. But it wasn't that kind of feeling; it was something more eerie. Something was not quite right in the house; a malignant spirit was residing with us now, and it wasn't the ghost previous residents claimed they had seen on the third-floor landing. I made lunch for my kids and tried to distract myself. The children ate their sandwiches and went out to play. As I put the dishes in the sink, our latest boarder, Walt Williams, came down the stairs from his room into the kitchen. The feeling of anxiety increased.

Walt. It has something to do with Walt.

YEARS LATER, I would dig out the picture of Walt Williams that I had once shown to the police and stare at it. It was the photo I took on a church trip to Six Flags in the suburbs of Maryland just outside of Washington, D.C. The snapshot was dated May 13, 1990. Walt, a twenty-four-year-old African American, was dressed in blue-checked shorts and a white, short-sleeved T-shirt. He was holding the hand of an adoring, giggly prepubescent girl who looked to have a crush on him. He was grinning smugly, looking away from the girl, his chin up in the air. He seemed either arrogant or goofy, depending on how you read the picture, with his boyish face and slight pudginess.

My children were in the picture, too, which made me cringe a bit; my eight-year-old daughter, Jennifer, with her frizzed-out, fly-away hair, courtesy of the gene blend of her blond mother and Jamaican father, and my son, David, age six, who looks rather Hispanic, causing Latinos to state matter-of-factly, "Oh, your husband is from Mexico!"

Walt, our new renter of one week, made the trip to the amusement park rather reluctantly. Although he expressed initial enthusiasm when asked to help chaperone the church teens, that morning when my husband, Tony, and I were ready to depart, he made himself scarce. He had not come down for breakfast nor had I seen him in the hallway.

"Walt?" I called up to his room above the kitchen. "Are you coming?"

"Oh." I heard a muffled voice through the door. "I was sleeping."

I was not one to let people who had made a commitment off that easily.

"Well, hurry up. We leave in ten minutes. We're waiting on you."

My husband rolled his eyes. He hadn't been enthusiastic about Walt's moving in, but it was that or take on a second job to pay the bills. He never liked the idea of anyone living in the house who wasn't family, but he tolerated our cash-paying international students. Tony was more uncomfortable with the idea of Walt living with us because he thought a working man of his age shouldn't have to rent a room. He also thought Walt was way too old to be obsessed with Dungeons & Dragons and comic books.

"Well, he is kind of immature," I offered during our discussion of the new boarder, the present beau of my girlfriend Kim. A few weeks earlier, Walt had applied for a mail room job at her company, and she was the person in human resources who reviewed his application and hired him. Now she was dating him and she asked if we would rent him a room. Walt was looking for a new place to live; he wanted to attend our church and be closer to Kim's home. Kim was a soft touch, the kind of woman who always tried to help people improve their lives. She told us he didn't do drugs, didn't drink alcohol, and didn't smoke. He was honorably discharged from the air force and had a good work record. We really needed the income from the rental room, as I was a stay-at-home mom, so I agreed to go ahead and interview him. He came across as a pleasant enough fellow, and because my husband and I were in the process of adopting Jeremy, a six-year-old boy from the Delaware foster care system, we also had to have Walt fingerprinted at the local police station. He consented without any hesitation, so we decided to let him move in.

"He's weird," Tony said a few days later. "He doesn't talk with a guy the way guys talk with each other. Actually, I think he avoids me." I had to agree with Tony that Walt wasn't a "guy's guy," the kind who gets along in groups of males, drinking beer, talking sports, and going golfing or fishing together. He was more of the gamer type. Walt *was* different from the majority of men his age, but this was one reason I was willing to give him a chance. Rather than being into partying, bars, and one-night stands, Walt had come across as more of a religious sort with strong morals—kind of a Boy Scout. The other reason I may have convinced myself not to be too hard on him was that since fingerprinting became a requirement for any new tenants, our Chinese graduate student applicants found the required trip to the police station too strange and they vanished. We needed money, the room was empty, and beggars can't be choosers. Besides, I figured many people were a little "different," but that didn't make them bad. My friend Kim liked him, and she was levelheaded.

The day at Six Flags was lots of fun for the teens, but when I looked around, we seemed to be one chaperone down. Walt had vanished.

"Have you seen Walt?" I asked Tony.

"Nope."

We decided to do a quick tour of the park, but we never came across him. None of the other chaperones from the church had seen him either.

Twenty minutes before our planned departure time from the park, Walt suddenly popped up near the exit. Speechless, Tony and I could only stare at the apparition in front of us.

Walt now stood before us dressed in long black pants, a black see-through net shirt, and a black headband. From his left ear dangled a silver skull earring. His hands were encased in fingerless black gloves. He looked completely inappropriate for a teen church outing, creepy even, and the fact that he had disappeared and exchanged one outfit for another was unnerving.

I lacked the courage at that time to question Walt extensively to get to the bottom of his strange behavior. Instead, I only asked, "Where were you all this time?" He just smiled, swung his backpack up over his shoulder, and ignored the question as two giggling church girls ran up to him, grabbing his arms.

Tony and I gave each other a "What is up with this guy?" look. Then we shook our heads, gathered the kids, and headed to the van. Driving out of the parking lot, I pulled down the sun visor on the passenger side to "check my hair" and glanced at Walt's reflection in the mirror. He sat with his arms crossed, immobile, between Jennifer and David in the backseat, ignoring their discussion of the rides. He had disconnected from the rest of us in the vehicle, his eyes shaded by the dark sunglasses. There was definitely something not quite right about this guy.

Unfortunately, he was now living in my house and he had rights. The law does not permit homeowners to protect their families by evicting renters just because they feel they are a bit peculiar. I couldn't evict someone without cause and Walt had not broken any house rules. I told myself that I was focusing too much on his quirks instead of his attributes. Walt was friendly, often quite chatty, and he wasn't a complainer. We actually had some things in common; we both had studied karate, we both wrote fiction, and we both liked going to the movies. We enjoyed a number of pleasant conversations and Walt was never rude toward anyone in the family. He had not acted inappropriately with the children and they were never alone with him anyway, so this was not an issue. I figured I would just keep an eye on him, and if he sent up any real red flags, we would ask him to move on, giving him the proper notice the law required.

I DIDN'T MAKE a special project of analyzing Walt's behaviors and thinking patterns; I didn't have to.

Over the two weeks after the church outing, more and more negative aspects of his personality came to light. I would later learn these characteristics were often representative of psychopathic traits. If Walt had kept to himself, I might never have interacted enough with him to have formed any opinion of his character, but because he was a gregarious sort, he liked to talk and did so almost every time he saw me. Worrisome mannerisms and behaviors kept appearing.

Walt liked telling stories about incredible things that had happened to him.

"I actually left the military early," he told me one day as he was getting himself a bowl of Cheerios.

"Really? Why? What happened?"

"Well, I was in Grenada for the operation the United States conducted down there." He poured milk on the cereal.

Grenada? I could hardly remember the conflict.

"It was wrong, us invading them. So I asked to leave the air force and they let me go." He made it sound like such cooperation by the military was a regular occurrence. Walt gazed past me as if he wasn't expecting a response.

"They just let you go?" I asked. "I didn't think they let anyone go just because they decided military life wasn't a joy ride."

Walt acted as though I hadn't commented and he changed the subject.

"They just hired some new girl to work in our mail room. She's pretty cute."

The next day he stepped into the kitchen while I was preparing dinner and offered a new explanation for his separation from the air force.

"Actually, I left the military because I had to shoot a bunch of the Grenadians and it really depressed me. I don't like violence." I raised an eyebrow, but he abruptly turned and left before I could ask questions again. I found his stated dislike of violence rather ironic considering he was obsessed with Arnold Schwarzenegger movies and watched *The Running Man* again and again during the short time he lived in my house. He liked to pretend to be Arnold as well.

"I'll be back!" he would announce, striking a pose, hands on his hips and head turned sideways.

A week later, he had a new ending to the story.

"I got shot in the leg and that's why the air force released me," he told me. He seemed to be searching for an explanation that I would actually believe.

"Oh, I see," I said, and I didn't push for further information. My acceptance of this version seemed to end his need to talk to me about his short military career.

Though Walt professed a desire to avoid violence, he appeared to have problems with violence finding him. One night, he told me that he was attacked on the way home by a knife-wielding stranger who stabbed him in the thigh. He claimed he had been jumped while walking down the bike path that ran the two miles between Kim's house and mine—he carpooled with her from work to her place and then covered the remainder of the route home on foot. Walt told me he had already sewn up the cut himself. I glanced down at his upper leg but he was wearing jeans that covered the "damaged" area. I saw no rip in the cloth and wondered about the veracity of this story, which didn't quite ring true.

"Why did he attack you?" I asked, skeptical.

He shrugged. "I don't know." Then he went back to his room.

A few days later, Walt claimed he had been assaulted again, this time by a homeless man at a bus shelter. He said he was forced to punch the man. By the end of the week, another tale: he subdued a man who wanted to fight him in a bar. I commented rather dryly that my husband had never experienced all this criminal behavior; that Walt, at five eleven and 220 pounds, should have been less of a target for assault than Tony, who had the smaller build of a West Indian soccer player.

THERE WERE OTHER odd stories. On my only visit to Walt's room since he moved in, I noticed a framed photograph of a lovely young girl displayed on his nightstand. She wore a black graduation gown and a gold chain with a cross hung around her neck. Clearly, the photo was a high school yearbook picture.

"Who's the pretty girl?" I asked.

Walt sighed.

"She was my high school love, Tiffany. We were going to get married, but on prom night, while I was waiting for her to show up at the dance, she got into a traffic accident. Her car was hit by a truck and she got decapitated."

He looked at me sadly; then he added, "That's why I haven't had sex since."

After quickly picturing the headless girl in my mind, my next thought was that this man had not had sex since he was seventeen years old. I counted the years, seven of them. And he had been a military man, albeit for a short period of time. I found the likelihood of this self-imposed celibacy hard to swallow, especially since I had come to realize he was not particularly religious (in spite of his recent church attendance) and he talked often about how women were always coming on to him, calling them "sluts," "bitches," and "whores." He even commented that a number of women he had gone out with weren't interested in sex with him because they were closet lesbians.

He had other peculiarities. The all-black clothing Walt had changed into while at the amusement park had become his regular uniform. When he came home from work, he would morph into his "costume" and disappear out of the house for hours, returning home long after dark. He relished stalking about at night pretending he was a ninja.

"I'm the Avenger!" he informed me, clearly envisioning himself as an invincible gladiator, some superhero straight out of the comic books he loved. I soon discovered he knew nothing of karate outside of making *"HA!"* noises and striking a stance with bent knees, a fist, and a knife hand. He was like a child who never grew up.

It was during the third week of his stay in my home that Kim told me she was considering breaking off her romantic relationship with Walt.

"He's beginning to really creep me out," she confided. "He makes people at work uncomfortable with his bizarre behavior and his ridiculous stories, which none of us think are true. He avoids doing work and makes excuses for not getting tasks accomplished. He usually blames someone else for his poor work performance. Some of the women think he's stalking them." She reached into her pocketbook, pulled out a ring with some kind of jewel in it, and shoved it at me. "He told me he bought this to celebrate our one-month anniversary and that it cost him over a thousand dollars! Supposedly he has to make payments on the ring for the next six months!" She grimaced. "I was mortified that he had spent so much money on a present for me when we had been dating only a few weeks. I tried to refuse to accept it, but Walt acted all insulted and insisted I take it. As soon as he left, I began thinking that maybe he was lying about the cost of the ring, that it was really a piece of costume jewelry."

I looked at the ring, but I was no expert. Save my engagement and wedding rings, I never wore any jewelry in those days.

Kim continued. "I took the ring to a store to get it appraised. The jeweler told me it was definitely not real and probably worth about fifty dollars." She shook her head. "I have to get away from him. I am going to tell him I don't want to continue dating when I see him on Saturday."

As she left the house, she turned and apologized to me. "Sorry I pushed you into renting to him."

I told her not to worry. Everything would work out just fine.

Little did I know how my life would change.

That night, after tucking in the children, I lay in bed with Tony, staring up at the ceiling in the dark. I felt pretty much like Kim and her coworkers.

"Tony," I said, "we need to give Walt notice on the first of July. I don't think I want this guy in our house any longer than he needs to be here."

Tony surprised me by arguing against getting rid of him. "Why? What has he done? We'll lose the rent money if we evict him and we probably won't be able to find someone else to take the room." Even though Tony was not exactly fond of Walt, the pain of losing the income was now apparently worse than putting up with his strange behavior.

I struggled to explain. "I think there's something wrong with him. I don't think it's wise to have him around."

Tony grunted. "I think you're exaggerating things." He turned over and went to sleep.

Maybe he was right. I wasn't a psychologist. I wasn't trained to diagnose mental disorders. Walt hadn't done anything or said anything that was threatening or scary. I probably had overstated his eccentricities. I would attempt to see the positive side of him and not judge him so harshly.

THE NEXT FEW days went by without incident and I was feeling better. Okay, nothing to worry about after all.

On Thursday night, Walt came downstairs and handed me a sheaf of papers, stapled together at the corner.

"My new short story," he said proudly. "I'm going to try to get it published. Maybe you can tell me where to send it." I was a published author, if just once, having been paid one hundred dollars for my submission to *Humor* magazine, a short-lived publication.

I looked down at the single-spaced typewritten material. At the top of the first page was the title, "My Silent Enemy," and underneath it, "by Walt Williams."

Walt retreated to his room and I sat down on the couch and started reading. His composition quickly made my skin crawl. The story was about a man with two personalities. One was an avenger stalking "filth and vermin" in the local park—"his slayground." The second was a frightened man walking through the dark in the same park, hearing footsteps coming behind him. When he turns quickly to see who is following him, he sees no one. Then he wrote, "Death wore my face. Death used my name. I was my silent enemy."

All my thoughts about something being wrong with Walt rushed back to me with a vengeance as I read his work. I never did discuss it with him. I kept the story and one copy of it eventually ended up in police evidence. I didn't realize then that this tale was to be a harbinger of the events to come just a few days later.

Walt had now been living in my house for nearly three weeks. On Saturday, the day Kim planned to have her talk with him, I took the kids to Virginia to spend the day and night with a friend of mine who had children of the same age. When I got back the next day, I planned to call Kim to see how her talk with Walt went.

Then, on Sunday morning, I got the phone call about the homicide.

THE NEWS OF the murder still ringing in my head, I stared at Walt standing in front of me.

"Hey! Hey!" He grinned. "I'm going off hiking with the church."

I looked at his clothing. He wasn't wearing his usual daytime outfit of shorts and a summer shirt. Instead, he was in blue jeans and a long-sleeved dress shirt, which seemed overdressed for the hot June day. Maybe he was protecting himself from thorns and branches, I reasoned.

I looked him in the eye. "Say, did you hear about the murder on the bike path that happened last night?"

"Yeah, I heard about it."

"Isn't that dreadful? The poor girl!"

Walt made no comment.

"Were you on the path yesterday?" I tried to make it sound like I was kidding him a bit.

Walt looked away, crossed his arms, and then looked back at me with a cold stare. "Yeah, but I cut across the stream behind the bowling alley on Kenilworth Avenue and got my feet wet."

Then he turned abruptly and left the room.

I tried to process what I had just heard. Did he admit he was on the path yesterday? Did he actually claim he left the path and waded through the water to cut over to a road that would take him out of his way and make his walk longer? Did he really say he was in the same stream where the body was found? Did he really seem to have no reaction to the grisly murder, show no compassion for the victim, or even be spooked about the fact that she was murdered on a path he walked daily? Wasn't he worried he could become a suspect or could have been another victim? Yet he didn't seem to be fazed by the event or his proximity to it.

It was a long day of stewing and gnawing doubts. Could it be?

Nah, come on, it couldn't be. Okay, he is weird, very weird, and he has issues. This doesn't make him a killer. Of course, there was that story about the "slayground." Could he have been hunting "filth and vermin," "sluts and bitches," acting out his Avenger character? No, you are overreaching. Stop it.

IN THE EVENING, Walt returned to the house and went up to his room. An hour later, Kim called.

"Can you go check on Walt for me?" she asked.

"Why? What's wrong?"

She gave me a quick rundown of her talk with him during his visit to her home on Saturday afternoon. "I told him I wasn't ready for a committed relationship and would prefer to be friends. I tried to give him back the ring and he got very upset. He huffed out of the house."

I held my breath and then asked what time he had left.

"Early evening, about seven p.m."

I felt a moment of relief that he hadn't left later, closer to night-fall. Good, if he walked directly back to the house he would have already been home before the murder went down. Then the unfortunate thought came to me that maybe he didn't come directly back. Maybe he stopped at a store, or hung around near Kim's house awhile, thinking about going back and trying to talk her into giving him another chance.

"Anyway," Kim went on, "I thought I should call him to be nice and make sure he was all right, but when I was talking to him just now, he sounded really disturbed. I asked him if he was all right and he didn't answer. I thought he might be suicidal because he told me he tried to commit suicide before. I asked if he was going to do anything bad and he said, 'You don't know what I've already done.'"

I felt the room reel just a little. The early feelings of unease returned with the force of a hammer. Oh, please, do not let this be true.

"Can you check on him?"

I made myself sound calm. "Sure."

I knocked on the door and called to Walt. "Hey, everything all right up there? Kim is a little worried about you."

He answered in a chipper voice. "Sure, I'm fine."

I went back to Kim. "He's fine." I felt I sounded a bit sarcastic, as my attitude toward Walt was definitely going downhill.

Kim breathed a sigh of relief. "Oh, good. I would hate to think I pushed him over the edge. Okay, thanks, I'll catch you later."

I couldn't tell her my thoughts. I didn't want to burden her right then. And I didn't want to sound nuts. I didn't know what the heck I was really thinking, or what I should do. What if Walt really was a psychopath, a rapist, a serial killer? I wanted to believe I was wrong, and I told myself I was.

I put the children to bed and went to lie down myself. But I couldn't sleep. I kept thinking about the innocent girl lying in the water, naked and still. I felt ill and I felt guilty. I should do something. What if she were my child? How would I react if I thought a citizen was hanging on to information about who might have killed her? For God's sake, I would scream, "Go to the police!" I thought about my safety and my children's safety. I wondered what would happen if he knew I suspected him. Would he come after us, kill us all? I wondered what others would do. Would they decide they didn't really know anything and convince themselves not to contact the police?

"Tony!"

I slugged my husband in the left arm. "Wake up!"

He rolled over.

"What is it?"

"I think Walt may have killed that girl."

Tony groaned. "Oh, come on. Don't be ridiculous."

"No, I mean it. You don't like him, you said yourself he's weird. Well, you were right. He is," I insisted. "Kim broke up with him on Saturday and he took the path home from her house."

"So?"

"Tony? Don't you think it just might be him?"

"Lots of people are on that path. I run on that path. Yeah, Walt is a little bizarre and I don't like him, but I can't believe the guy is a murderer." He rolled back over, away from me. "Go to sleep," he muttered.

Great. Thanks. Easy for you to do.

Somebody killed that girl. Maybe I was out in left field with my suspicions about Walt, but on the other hand, if I was right, wouldn't it be better to be safe than sorry? I would rather be a little embarrassed that the killer turned out to be someone else than feel guilty that I let a murderer walk away without even bringing him to the attention of law enforcement. If he was the perpetrator and he killed again, how would I live with myself?

I spent the rest of the night trying to decide how to handle the situation. Do I just go to the police and tell them Walt is some kind of mental case? Do I try to learn more before I do that? Do I search for evidence? This wasn't a Hollywood movie and no scriptwriter was handing me a sheet with directions for the next scene. I had to go with my gut, and I decided that while Walt was at work, I would review all I knew. Maybe I could get more information on the psychology and behavior of serial killers and see if he even fit the description. Then I could search his room for proof of my theory, for true physical evidence, and see if any existed. If by the end of the day I felt fairly convinced I was right, I would go to the police.

The next morning, Monday, Walt rose at his usual time and left the house. He walked past his car with the expired tags and vanished around the corner. I wondered if he was going back to walk along the path where the murder had taken place and show up unannounced at Kim's. Yes, this sounded like something he would do, and Kim would probably go ahead and let him ride to work with her.

As the day dragged on, I watched the news and learned the name of the murdered woman: Anne Kelley. She was an intern chosen for her smarts, a graduate at the top of her class who came east for a job opportunity many others wished they had gotten. She was extremely bright, enthusiastic, and friendly, and naturally, everyone loved her. She was twenty-two years old, petite, and the short, wispy hair framing her face gave her a look of childish innocence. I almost wish I hadn't seen her picture because now she became a real person to me. Each time I shut my eyes, her face would appear before me. When she was attacked, I wondered, how many seconds did it take her to realize that everything she dreamed of was never going to come true? That this was already the end?

And who ended it for her? Who could do such a thing to this sweet girl? I thought about Walt's recent behavior and went over and over it in my head. *Was he a killer?*

By afternoon, I needed solid answers. I piled the kids into the car and went off to the library. Those were the days when most people did not have access to the Internet and I was one of them. I had to do my research the old-fashioned way—by going through card files and finding books on the subjects I wanted to know more about: rapists and serial killers.

During the next two hours, my children enjoyed their books of imaginative stories and humorous animal misadventures while I read about women being hacked into pieces and other sorts of terrible and unimaginable crimes. I learned that almost all men who commit sexual violence against others are psychopaths, people with no empathy for others and no remorse for the heinous crimes they commit. And while not all psychopaths are serial killers, all serial killers are psychopaths. In my readings, I came across Robert Hare's psychopathy checklist, a quick way to evaluate someone's likelihood of possessing this destructive personality disorder. It came with a warning not to analyze anyone yourself, that such an evaluation should be done only by a professional. I felt Hare was tossing out that piece of advice much the way every exercise book tells you to see a doctor before beginning their regimen, so I ignored it.

I started making checkmarks on the list based on the little I knew about Walt from his three weeks in my life:

- ✓ **GLIBNESS/SUPERFICIAL CHARM**—Yep, he was cheerful, gregarious, and lacked depth.
- ✓ **GRANDIOSE SENSE OF SELF-WORTH**—He bragged about many things that were unlikely to be true, or that I knew were not true.
- ✓ **PATHOLOGICAL LYING**—No doubt about that.
- ✓ **CUNNING/MANIPULATIVE**—Kim told me that she and her coworkers found him manipulative in the workplace and clever about getting around certain tasks.
- ✓ **LACK OF REMORSE OR GUILT**—He always seemed to think he was right, everyone else was wrong, and he never seemed to feel bad about anything he did or didn't do.
- ✓ **SHALLOW AFFECT**—I could see no depth of feeling other than occasional flashes of anger when he didn't get his way. He didn't seem to care about much, including Kim; he seemed to be play-acting most of the time.
- ✓ **CALLOUS/LACK OF EMPATHY**—He seemed indifferent to the horrible murder of the jogger.
- ✓ **FAILURE TO ACCEPT RESPONSIBILITY FOR OWN ACTIONS**—He never apologized or took responsibility for things he screwed up; he blamed others for pretty much everything that went awry in his life.
- ? **PROMISCUOUS SEXUAL BEHAVIOR**—Well, he hadn't had sex in seven years, if one believed him, so I couldn't put a mark there yet.

Walt fit almost the whole list and I hardly knew him. But, I argued with myself, maybe he was just a psychopath and not a killer; he just might be one of the annoying but nonviolent sort—a user, a con artist, an embezzler, or a thief.

I looked at actual descriptions of serial killers. I read that they tended to be psychopathic, male, underachieving (Walt was a twenty-four-year-old male who worked in a mail room and rented a room in my house), troubled in relationships with women (Kim didn't last long before she ran away), and to have a bent toward violent ideation. Frequently, there is a precipitating event that makes them feel like losers, causing them to want to commit an act of violence to regain a feeling of power and control. Walt was dumped just before the time of the murder. . . .

I closed the books I was reading. I gathered up the children, helped them check out what they wanted to read, and drove home. I told them to go play, opened the door to Walt's room, and started up the stairs. I carried along a pair of kitchen gloves. I needed to find out if there was any real evidence in his room that would support what I was now fairly certain to be true. I needed something more than theory to take to the police. If I just told them about Walt's behavior and my conclusions, I didn't think they would believe me. I needed proof.

Walt was a bit of a slob, and he didn't have very many possessions. I put on the gloves and worked my way around the room. I didn't find much of interest. Then I came to the trash bag by the top of the stairs. There were pizza boxes on top and I memorized how the two of them were stacked so I could put them back the same way when I was finished with my search.

By this time, I was starting to get nervous. It was late in the day and Walt could walk in at any moment. I ran down the stairs and looked down the driveway. He wasn't out there. I hurried back up and started in on the trash bag. I moved the pizza boxes carefully to the floor. Underneath them was a pile of magazines, at least two dozen of them. As I pulled them out, I saw that every single one was pornographic. I laid them in a stack.

Then I looked back in the trash bag and I saw a shirt. I lifted it out. It was damp and the back of it had been shredded, as if caught on briar bushes, the kind found at the edge of the stream where the girl's body was found. I held my breath and reached back into the bag. Next, I pulled out a pair of jeans, wet, but in good condition. Why would someone throw his jeans away? Why were they wet? They weren't dirty, but rather they seemed to have been washed, but not dried. Even if Walt really did wade across a stream on some whim not connected with the murder, why would he toss perfectly good jeans?

Next I found tennis shoes, again wet, but in perfect condition. I thought again of his story about getting wet in the stream. How many people threw away their tennis shoes because they got caught in the rain one day or stepped in a puddle? Then I came upon three very curious items. The first looked very much like a knife, or a letter opener filed down to a very sharp point. I wasn't familiar with weapons, but knew right away that it would be dangerous if used on a person. Next I found a package of condoms—two were still sealed up, but the third one was used and placed back in the wrapper. I found this peculiar. I knew that Kim wasn't having sex with Walt. And he had claimed that he hadn't had sex since he lost his beloved prom girl. Beyond that, if he did have sex with someone, who puts the used condom back in the package rather than simply tossing it? And why throw two brand-new condoms away?

Then I found what I considered the most mysterious piece of possible evidence: a clump of mud wrapped in plastic. A clump of mud? Wrapped in plastic? I tried to think of what innocent situation would call for someone to wrap mud in plastic. I had no good answer, but I felt fairly certain that the mud was from the stream bank.

I was now closing in on the bottom of the trash bag. I saw a piece of pink paper and picked it up. It was a receipt for a ring. The price was forty dollars. I laughed. Forty dollars—the lying dog. Then the reality of the situation returned. I ran down the stairs again and looked out the front door. No Walt, but time was slipping by. I hurried into the laundry room and found an empty box. I brought it up the stairs and put all the "evidence" into it: the pants, the shirt, the shoes, the knife, the condom pack, and the mud wrapped in plastic. Oh, and a few of the magazines and the ring receipt. Then I ran back downstairs and grabbed some newspapers to stuff the trash bag; since I had taken so many of the items out, it looked rather deflated. When I had filled the bag out satisfactorily, I placed the pizza boxes back on top. I surveyed my artwork. By now, I had forgotten what I told myself to remember, and I could only hope the boxes were placed correctly.

I ran back down the stairs, tossed the gloves under the sink, and carried the box to the trunk of my car. I went back in and collected Walt's story and the photo I had of him. Then I waited, counting the minutes until my husband got home. Finally, he drove up.

"I have to go to the police station. I found evidence, real evidence in his room!"

Tony looked at me skeptically.

"I'll explain when I get back." I wasn't up to trying to convince him before dealing with the police. "Do me a favor and boot Walt. Tell him he's late with the rent and be a jerk about it. Please, I just want him out of here and I don't want him to think I suspect him of the murder."

Tony gave me that look again.

"Please, just do it for me?" I didn't feel like arguing. "I have to go."

I HAD NEVER been inside a police station before. I had no idea of what to expect and I felt terribly uncomfortable. By the time I asked to see the detective in charge, I babbled like an idiot with the box in my arms to the officer behind the glass window. He listened to me, stone-faced, and then pointed to a row of plastic chairs on the other side of the room, saying, "Take a seat and one of the detectives will talk to you." Ten minutes or so passed and a tall, muscular police detective walked out and asked if I had something I wanted to tell him. He didn't invite me back to an interview room. I had to ask him if we could go to his office, as I needed to speak with him about the recent murder in town. He motioned me into the hallway and I followed him to one of the rooms. He went around to his side of the desk, settled himself into his chair, and gestured for me to sit down on the other side. I took the seat, setting the box on the table.

"So," he said, crossing his arms on the desk. "You have some information about the Kelley murder?"

"Yes, I have a new renter in my house and he's been acting strange. I brought you some stuff I found in his trash that I think may be connected to the murder."

He peered into the box and then settled back into his chair.

"What makes you think he's guilty of anything?"

"Well, to start with, he calls women sluts, bitches, and whores. He thinks he's a ninja and he wrote this story about killing people in the park." I told him all about Walt's creepy behavior and about the breakup with Kim on the day of the murder, how the murder happened on the path between our two houses.

Then I told him the most important point.

"Walt admitted to being on the path that evening."

He didn't seem impressed. I desperately kept talking, explaining what I found in his trash and adding more bits about his habits and history, but the detective seemed completely uninterested in Walt as a suspect. He barely scribbled any notes on the pad in front of him. The interview that I thought would be a slam-dunk was not materializing. The detective was leaning back in the chair with a smirk on his face.

Finally, he asked, "Was your girlfriend white?"

"No, she's black. Why?"

He shrugged. "Well, the victim was white."

I stared at him. Was he seriously telling me serial killers only choose victims who look like their girlfriends? Didn't I just read in one of those library books that this was bunk?

"Maybe you're misconstruing this fellow's behavior because he is black."

Now I was beginning to lose it. "I have a black husband. I have black in-laws. I have black friends. I don't think I am a panicked racist white lady who thinks all black men are killers."

He practically snickered. "Well, maybe you're just imagining things."

Now I was furious. I got up and grabbed my purse. "I am not a bored housewife with nothing better to do than spy on her neighbors and fabricate all sorts of naughty goings-on in the neighborhood. I am just a citizen who has enough brains to recognize when someone's behaviors are bizarre and there is evidence in his room that is pretty concerning!"

I stormed out of the police station in a confused state of shock. I had assumed I was doing the right thing. I had thought they would be happy that a citizen had come across information that might help solve a crime. I thought they would be gratified to have evidence in hand so quickly after such a crime occurred rather than having nothing useful for months, or years, or ever. And even if the police weren't immediately convinced that Walt was the killer, I would have thought the evidence strong enough to make him a suspect worth investigating, or at least eliminating.

What was I to do? I never envisioned driving back to the house with nothing accomplished, except maybe Walt finding out I had been in his room. I had no police to protect my family or me. I had no idea if I was totally right, or very wrong. Was I returning home to stay the night in the same house as a vicious killer, or was I just completely insane?

When I arrived home, I could hear Walt's footsteps upstairs as he moved around his room. I felt clammy as I thought about the trash bag. I should take the children and go to a hotel for the night, but what was the point of being so drastic when the police detective didn't seem to find any reason to suspect Walt? I felt numb, trapped in a surreal world. I left the kitchen, crossed the dining room, climbed the stairs to the second floor, and went to my children's room. I peeped in and they were asleep, looking peaceful under their covers, surely believing that their world was safe and secure. I went into my bedroom, closed the door, and told my husband what happened at the police station.

Tony seemed annoyed with me.

"See? You were being ridiculous. The police know their job and they would be all over Walt if they saw any reason to suspect him. By the way, I told Walt he had to go and he said he would leave in the morning." He abruptly turned away from me. "There goes June's rent money," he muttered somewhat resentfully. Then he immediately went off to sleep.

I, on the other hand, spent the night on my side of the bed with eyes wide open and a butcher knife clutched in my hands. Deep down inside, I still believed I was right.

The next day Walt put all his belongings in two Hefty bags and drove his illegal car down the driveway. He left the trash bag crowned with the pizza boxes untouched.

It would be five years before I started investigating him, and six years before the police would finally bring him in for an interview. Although my career as a profiler was beginning, I never imagined, as I watched the car disappear from sight, that this was where my life was heading.

CHAPTER 2

A LIFE CHANGED

Sometimes we all wonder, how did I end up where I am in life? I spent the first half of my childhood in Ridgewood, New Jersey, the kind of perfect town one finds in picture books. My family's colonial home with its thick pillars stood on a small walled hill and had a circular staircase at its center that was perfect for three girls to chase one another up and down until their mother got a migraine.

My father, Harry, was a civilian working with the Department of Defense. He worked with all kinds of big government projects, and I never quite knew what he did when I was growing up. But he came home every night and was a good provider and a wonderful father.

My mother, Shirley, stayed home, painted watercolor landscapes, and baked great chocolate chip cookies. We were a really traditional family—Mom, Dad, my two older sisters, and me. My parents never fought, and even we girls did little more than occasionally tattle or give one of the others the silent treatment. I never encountered drinking or drugs or violence.

SOME PEOPLE SAY to understand someone, you have to think like them. I don't know that much in my life prepared me for psychopathy; my family seemed healthy and happy. No one lied and no one cheated.

I was nine when we moved south to Virginia. I didn't much care for the area but I didn't have much to complain about either. We lived in a wealthy neighborhood and I went to an excellent school. I never heard about drugs or anybody getting pregnant. I didn't hear about any crimes being committed save the one that was committed against me.

When I was twelve years old, I was in a dark fun house, winding my way through behind my friend Sheri, when suddenly someone grabbed me from behind. I broke free, panicked, ran, slammed into a wall, ran, slammed into another wall, and then he caught me again. I felt his hands go inside my clothing and touch me on my private parts and then I broke free again. This time I made it to the exit.

"What's wrong with you?" Sheri asked me. "You look like you've seen a ghost!"

I was pale and shaky. But I told her nothing was wrong and I went home and forgot about it. Some would say that any girl would have been traumatized but I chalked the event up to being in the wrong place at the wrong time, just the girl who happened to be in front of a creep. I didn't report it because it was embarrassing to talk about, but I didn't take it personally either. I just shrugged. I come from a logical family who told me not to make mountains out of the molehills one encounters in life. I carried on as if nothing had happened.

I grew up in a land of musicals. My father loved light opera, and I became a fan of *Brigadoon*. I bought all the Broadway musical albums. I was probably the only teenager who was in love with crooner Robert Goulet. Everybody else was into the Beatles and the Monkees, and I was in love with Robert Goulet.

I wasn't terribly popular, which might explain why I wasn't aware of the darker side of being a teen. In the summers, I worked with children—some blind and some blind and deaf—at the Columbia Lighthouse for the Blind. I learned how to read Braille and to guide a blind person with my arm. One of my favorite Christmas presents was a Perkins Brailler that typed each letter with six clacking keys. I read books about Helen Keller; in the back of one was a page with the letters you can make with your fingers and I started making words with my hands under my desk as the teacher gave her lectures.

I started to read Sherlock Holmes and *The Saint* series. I loved the Robin Hood of Modern Crime. He always outwitted the bad guys . . . and the police . . . and I imagined he was a bad-boy version of Robert Goulet. These books were probably the only evidence in my childhood of any fascination with criminals and criminal behavior, and I don't think I was interested in that as much as I was in the puzzles the stories presented. I liked the challenge of trying to figure stuff out. Most of the time I did crossword puzzles, jigsaw puzzles, and cryptograms. And I read James Michener novels because I wanted to see the world.

I always said that as soon as I was old enough, I'd travel overseas. When I was five I refused to go out and play in the snow because I was warm and comfy watching Tarzan swing through the jungle. I wanted to see that jungle. At five, I was already planning my trip to Africa.

I can't speak for my sisters, because as the youngest of three girls my parents may have felt they'd seen it all by the time I became a teen, but I was largely considered the wild one. Because the same girl who loved musicals and Robert Goulet also learned Korean karate. I was one of the first students of the Jhoon Rhee Institute of Tae Kwon Do in Washington, D.C., and my first boyfriend, Howard Chung, was the owner's nephew.

I learned how to eat with chopsticks and cook some Korean food. I would take a bus into D.C. for lessons and spend all afternoon and evening there. I was invited to be in Jhoon Rhee's first film—a movie no one remembers—and I was so excited! I would be a karate star and I would get to see Korea! Then some guy, a brown belt who should have known better, kicked me in the ribs, breaking several, and I was forced to take a few months off. When I went back to class, I broke the cardinal rule of sports—I didn't warm up. I jumped right back in like I hadn't been slumming for weeks and I threw a roundhouse kick really high, way over my opponent's head, and that did it—I shredded my back thigh muscle. I lost my first and last movie role and another blonde went to Korea.

After high school, I attended Northern Virginia Community College and studied cultural anthropology. My professor, Dr. Tom

Larson, who has written a couple of books on the cultures of Botswana, was taking a group to Togo, Africa, that summer, and I jumped at the chance to join them. I worked at a garden shop and saved all my earnings to pay my way.

I eventually studied in Denmark, traveled through Europe, lived a bit in London, and then flew off to Jamaica for a little island culture.

MOST PEOPLE THINK of Jamaica as an idyllic tourist spot with turquoise water and a bit of reggae thrown in. I, however, was staying in Kingston, and that part of Jamaica is, as they say down in "De Yard," rough.

I saw my first crime scene in Jamaica. I went out on a date with a businessman, quite well to do. We drove to New Kingston, through all the red lights, without stopping. Stopping, I was told, was foolish, because you never knew what kinds of people were out on the roads at night. It was a bit disconcerting, but my faint nervousness settled as my date escorted me into a posh restaurant.

Dinner was delicious, dessert was heavenly, and one of the gentleman's friends stopped by our table and introduced himself. Then he bid us good night, walked out the door, and died. He was shot to death by his secretary's boyfriend and his wallet was taken.

I stood outside with my date, and the crowd and I stared at a man who had been alive five minutes earlier, now frozen in a crumpled position, arms outstretched, legs akimbo, eyes staring up. Blood was pooled around his head. Relatives arrived and the screaming began. The screaming is the memory I keep of that day. The screaming and screaming and more screaming.

My date and I said little as we drove back to my lodging. He escorted me up the stairs with his gun drawn and then, like a gentleman, left me there unarmed.

The sight of the dead man that night has never left me, but it certainly didn't inspire me into a life of crime analysis or police work. I think I preferred a prettier side of life.

I really wanted to be a cultural anthropologist, but I wasn't great at staying in school because I often felt unchallenged by my studies. I went to the University of New Mexico in Albuquerque and realized I hated living in the desert, so I left. I spent a brief time at some community college in California I can't remember the name of (it must not have been a very inspiring place), a fall semester at American University in Washington, D.C., and a spring semester in Denmark. I liked cultural anthropology, but I didn't see a future in it. I couldn't quite decide what I wanted to major in, so instead I got married at twenty-three.

I majored in that.

I MARRIED TONY, a Jamaican immigrant who came to America when he was fifteen years old. I became pregnant the first year we were married, had a child, and I absolutely loved being a mother.

In Africa, women carried their babies on their backs and slept with their children, so that seemed perfectly natural to me, although no one else I knew did it. It never crossed my mind to use a bottle or put my child in a crib. I nursed my daughter when she was born and she never got anything but breast milk. She didn't get water, or juice, or even a pacifier. I wouldn't even know how to make formula. And I never understood the concept of putting little infants far away from their mothers in a pen in a separate room. I slept with my babies because that seemed normal to me. I cuddled up with them and nursed them through the night.

I gave birth to my second child at home because I didn't like my first hospital experience. I decided to have an unattended birth. My son was born in my bedroom right upstairs with the help of a friend who was almost a midwife; it was "unattended" because she wasn't yet technically qualified for the job. But, I thought, if my grandmother-in-law could have fourteen children by herself, I could handle it with a friend. It was great. Well, it hurt like hell, but it was great.

I loved being a mom, an experience I never dreamed would be such a great thing. I was just madly in love with my daughter the minute I laid eyes on her and fell in love all over again when my sons, David and Jeremy, arrived. I became kind of an earth mother. My life revolved around my children, my husband, and my home.

It may have been the 1980s, but I lived a very traditional home-maker's life.

When it came time to send my children to school, I checked out the local school system. What I saw absolutely appalled me. I sat in a class for three hours. At the end of my observation period, as we left, I grabbed my five-year-old daughter by the hand and said, "They'll never get *you*." I found the children uniformly rude and disrespect-ful. I didn't like all the yelling and lack of discipline, and I found the atmosphere unpleasant and uninspiring.

I decided to homeschool, and I became part of the homeschool community in our small town, teaching my children until they went to college.

We didn't have much money, because we had only one income, and my husband, who was a mechanic at the time, wasn't making a lot, so private school wasn't an option.

People we knew thought that homeschooling was brave because it wasn't a popular choice back then, and the school authorities could hound you over such a decision and make life difficult. But I made the decision and I stuck with it.

I was already a homebody—I wanted to be Amish when I was fifteen. I found us this big, 250-year-old farmhouse in a regular neigh-borhood, and I felt I could raise lots of children here. I sponsored playgroups in our house and the kids joined the Boys and Girls Club. Sometimes we had twenty kids running around from all over the neighborhood, and my house became a big meeting place for children. We played baseball games in the front yard and water games in the back. It was a busy place, and I enjoyed every moment of rais-ing my kids here. We had lots of pets: cats, gerbils, hamsters, frogs, and iguanas. My daughter had a rat named Millie and our potbelly pig, Gwendolyn, was the talk of the neighborhood.

After my second child, I had a tubal pregnancy and couldn't get pregnant again, so we adopted a third child, Jeremy, who was six years old at the time. We were warned that he had learning disabili-ties, which I always thought was bunk. I said, "The only disability he has is the fact that the adults around him don't want to be responsi-ble. How can a child pay attention at school if he must live in foster care and doesn't know where his home is?" I realized school wouldn't be good for him, either, so I homeschooled him as well, and he's done just fine.

We read a lot of books together and because of my weakness, we went to see many, many musicals. Usually, it was at the local high school because that was all I could afford.

We attended a small community Christian church where most of the kids were homeschooled. The area homeschooling group with which we were involved included people of many different religions, or nonreligions as my atheist friend, Jack, might say, or changed religions, such as Zelda, the Jew turned Buddhist.

Today David is on his way to a master's program in economics after studying in Mexico, Hawaii, and India. Jeremy is a federal officer who runs a SWAT team as part of his work in security for NASA. And Jennifer, my oldest, is a detective working for a local police department. Homeschooling did okay by them, and I didn't ever have to go to the state prison on visiting days or pick up my kid from rehab.

AS THE KIDS matured, I thought I should have some kind of a career, because what would happen to me when they all went to college? By now I had a bachelor's degree in liberal arts, but I wasn't sure what to do with it.

I remembered how much I loved working with deaf children, so I took sign language classes in the evenings and brushed up on my rusty skills.

I did well enough that I was asked to take in a thirteen-year-old, deaf, pregnant foster child. That was one of my first life experiences dealing with someone who was struggling in a difficult situation.

Meanwhile, my husband and I were struggling in a different way. I was home full-time, raising the kids, and he went off to work to pay the bills. We started renting rooms in our big house in order to survive.

Even there, however, we were selective, preferring foreign students above other boarders. Our first was from Iran; he stayed with us for three years. Over the years we hosted quite a few from China, so there was often Chinese food cooking in the kitchen, and my children learned a lot about Asian lifestyles. I thought these relationships added color to my children's experience. Our boarders were all graduate students and most of the time studied engineering or mathematics or something else quiet and peaceful. Nobody drank; we had strict rules. They couldn't have overnight guests, so nobody brought home ladies or guys from bars. Everything fit with the lifestyle we lived.

I did read the paper, but while our county had crime like anywhere else, my neighborhood didn't. It was a peaceful little town with one thousand single-family homes, no apartments, and no businesses except on the outer limits. We have always had our own police force, our own mayor, and our own town council. The weekly town bulletin would report that there was a loud party, or maybe somebody's teenager did some silly thing, but we hardly paid any attention to the police report.

I eventually became a certified medical sign language interpreter, working with deaf people who were brought into area hospitals. That was when I started learning more about crime, because I dealt with emergency room admissions, and there were usually people there who were victims of crime.

I SPENT TEN years working in the emergency rooms at DC General, Washington Hospital Center, and Howard University. I learned a lot about forensics when my clients rolled in on stretchers.

Washington Hospital Center has one of the finest trauma units in the area and anyone who has a choice will tell the ambulance driver to bring him there. DC General—which closed in 2001—was located in the most violent ward of the city, a city with a gunshot victim a day. There was a big book that sat on the admitting desk in which they wrote the names of everybody who died each night, and some nights the list seemed to go on forever. It was a true community hospital where all the homicide, assault, and rape victims went, so when you worked at DC General, you saw just about everything.

Whenever I was called in, it was usually for something pretty vicious. I would walk in and see guys with holes in their bodies and blood pouring out of them from gunshot wounds. I saw people with stab wounds, people who had been beaten. I saw a lot of domestic abuse. I interpreted for dozens of rape cases, and because I was an interpreter, I was in the room with the doctor the entire time. If the patient went into surgery, I often went with them until they went to sleep. If they didn't go to sleep, I stayed throughout the operation and watched the doctors work.

Many times, I was called back within the next few days if the patient had a follow-up appointment with the doctor. I got to know a lot of the regulars. I spent time on the psych wards, too, learning a good deal about psychology, and I began to recognize the "frequent flyers." If they were psychopaths, I got to watch them over a decade's time; I watched their ongoing manipulations and how they behaved in the hospitals when they were trying to mislead the doctors, telling outright lies and seeking drugs they didn't need. I could see the psychological progression.

I studied forensic medical books while my patients slept, and all around me in the hospital I saw what I was reading about—what a stab wound, an abrasion, and a laceration looked like, even what happened when somebody took a hammer to the head. I looked at x-rays with the technicians and the doctors. I saw cases come to life. It was a tremendous learning experience.

People who came into these ERs weren't terribly wealthy. They lived in bad neighborhoods, suffered a lot of injuries, and were often victims of crimes.

An interpreter is considered a machine in a hospital. An interpreter is not allowed to interfere with the process between the medical staff and the patient; they are only there to interpret what the medical staff says and what the patient says. The deaf patients understood this very well, so they knew whatever they told me before or in between the doctors coming in and out of the room I was not allowed to express to the staff. So some of them, the psychopathic ones, would behave one way with me, and they would act in a different way with the doctor. It was absolutely amazing to watch.

Eric, for example, liked to get Percocet. He claimed to have sickle cell anemia. He had a friend named Desmond who *did* have sickle cell anemia and for whom I also interpreted and from whom Eric learned all his tricks. Desmond had legitimate sickle cell attacks that would put him in the hospital because he was in such severe pain. I interpreted during many of Desmond's sickle cell crises, so I knew what they looked like and how he often needed Percocet to take home with him. I saw how agonizing it was for him. He sometimes had problems getting the drugs he needed because a lot of medical personnel don't understand sickle cell and they thought he came in to get drugs to sell to other people. I can't honestly say that Desmond wouldn't do this on the side. He was poor and sick and he needed money. His buddy Eric, however, learned how to copy Desmond's behavior quite convincingly.

Eric would lie on a stretcher, clutching his chest, signing, "Oh, the pain is so bad! Oh, pain, pain, pain!"

"Where is the pain?" the doctor would ask, and I'd sign for Eric.

"Pain in the chest, pain in the back, it's really bad, bad," Eric would sign back.

"On a scale of one to ten, how bad is it?"

Eric would sign, "Ten, ten, ten," putting his thumb up in the air and shaking it back and forth for "ten."

"What do you need?" The doctor would always ask this, as each sickle cell patient had a regimen that worked specifically for him.

"Intravenous Demerol and Percocet" was always Eric's reply.

The doctor would say, "Okay," and leave the room to order the medication.

Sometimes Eric would clutch my hand to his chest or his face in front of the doctor as if I were providing him comfort. Once the doctor would walk out of the room, Eric would open up one eye and a big grin would hit his face. He'd sit up and sign, "Hey, what's up?" and chat on perfectly calmly.

Then he'd see the doctor coming in his direction and would throw himself back down and groan, the pain having returned again.

I was not allowed by the code of ethics of interpreters to tell the doctor that the guy was a lying dog, that he did not have any pain at all. I just watched the doctor write out the prescription and hand it to

Eric, and then he'd be happy. He got what he wanted and he'd saunter out the door. I think it took five years for one of the doctors to say, "I don't think that guy has sickle cell!"

THESE WERE THE kinds of things I watched at the hospital as an interpreter. I was an observer more than I was ever a participant in a lot of this, and I was never allowed to speak for myself.

But one day I had to speak up. I broke the code of ethics, because I couldn't stand it anymore.

A young man came into the hospital. He was a really strong-looking fellow who played football at Gallaudet, the university for the deaf in Washington, D.C. Students from all over the world came to Gallaudet to get the college education not available to them in their home countries. This young man was from Africa and he came in with kidney failure. Nobody knew why he was in kidney failure. He did not use drugs, he did not drink, and nobody the medical staff interviewed knew anything about this young man's lifestyle that would have led to such an illness. He was a sports and health nut.

His mother was in Chicago and they notified her that her son was in critical condition with kidney failure.

"Oh, do you think I should come?" she asked.

The nurses said, "What the heck's wrong with this woman? She doesn't want to come?"

Three days later she arrived via Greyhound Bus.

When she came into her son's hospital room, she didn't say hello to him, give him a hug, or ask him how he was feeling. She didn't even bother to look in his direction. Instead, she started chatting up the nurses: "Thank you, thank you, you are such wonderful people. I so appreciate what you've done. You're helping my son. That's so marvelous. What's this piece of equipment? Oh, what does this do? How does that flush out the kidney?"

I looked at the boy's mother, thinking, *She's paying no attention to her son whatsoever!* I got graveyard chills from this woman. I began to wonder if she had Munchausen syndrome by proxy, a disorder in which a person, usually a woman, harms her children for attention. These women love to visit hospitals and interact with doctors and nurses, being in the spotlight and the center of a drama. It is a type of psychopathy.

Women who hurt, smother, or kill their own babies are the most common presentation of Munchausen syndrome. These psychopaths murder their babies one after the other and hope the doctors think it's sudden infant death syndrome, or SIDS. And most of the time they do—that is, until someone realizes it has happened nine times. Many of these women are interested in the nursing profession in some manner or form. They like to be involved in medical procedures, because it gives them the thrill of controlling life and death. They like pulling plugs and causing emergencies so they can be heroes when they save the patients. Or they like to watch everyone else scurry about trying to save the person they just sent into cardiac arrest. They also love a good funeral.

When this mother eventually sat down next to her son, he looked at her like she was a big cockroach and he moved away from her. I thought, *That's an odd response to your mother.* For the rest of the day the mother ignored him and spent almost no time tending to her poor, miserable son, but she said to the nurses, "I can't leave his side. No, I can't go down to eat now, I must stay with him." Yet she never looked at him. The woman enjoyed talking with me about herself. She bragged about this and that and most of what she said was not all that believable. She never talked about her son, about how he was doing in college or about his deafness, nor did she express any worry over his possible future demise. She was narcissistic and grandiose and lacked empathy for her own flesh and blood, all traits of a psychopath.

I wondered if this woman could be the Munchausen type who liked working in the medical field.

I said to her, "Are you a nurse?"

"Yes, I am," she said, beaming at me.

"Do you work in a nursing home?"

"Yes."

"Midnight shift?"

She nodded, looking at me suspiciously, wondering how I knew that.

I thought, *I wonder if they have any suspicious deaths at that nursing home?*

I asked the nurses if they knew where the son had been recently. They said he had just gotten back from visiting his mother in Chicago when his kidneys failed.

I thought about whether the mother administered something from the nursing home to her son, some kind of drug that caused kidney failure. I asked whether they had tested him for drugs or any kind of medications that could be available in a medical setting, and they said no, because they had no reason to test for that. Yet none of the tests they had done offered any clue as to why this boy's kidneys had suddenly gone into failure.

When I couldn't stand being alone with my suspicions another minute, I went to the hospital authorities. "Look," I said, "I'm breaking the code of ethics but I cannot stand by and watch this. I'm not saying I know that this woman did anything to her son. I'm saying you need to test for medications that she could have gotten from her place of work."

I explained Munchausen syndrome by proxy, and they all looked at me like I had horns growing out of my head. They didn't know a thing about it. That's not surprising; most medical staff never learns of this form of psychopathy and that's why so often women get away with it.

The blank looks told me they just weren't getting it. I said, as I was leaving the room, "If he ever ends up dead in the future, you better check that mom out." The young man survived, and I hope he was smart enough to never get near her again.

ONE NIGHT I received a phone call from Washington Hospital Center—they needed an interpreter on a rape case.

I went in and the victim was Rochelle, a deaf woman I knew from many previous visits.

"Rochelle—you were raped?"

"Yeah."

She was smiling at me when she signed it. I thought, *You don't look too bent out of shape for a rape victim.*

She went through the whole process.

Medical technicians papered the floor, removed her clothes and put them on the paper, and the doctor performed the rape kit. Afterward, the police came in and talked with her through me.

She claimed that she got off a bus and was attacked and raped by a man in an alley. But after the doctor and the police detective left the room, she brightened up and started digging around in her purse for her photo book.

"Hey, wanna see my pictures from the Christmas party?" she asked cheerfully.

I oohed and aahed over her various poses with friends and then she asked me how my kids were doing and I told her some funny stories and she laughed. But when the doctor returned, she "got sad again" very quickly.

The very next night, my pager went off again at midnight, this time from DC General, and there was another rape victim waiting for an interpreter.

Sure enough, it was Rochelle.

"Rochelle, did you get raped again?"

"Yes!" She looked at me with an amazed, innocent expression.

Apparently she got off another bus and got raped for the second time in two days. Of course, the doctors did their job, she got the rape kit done again, and Rochelle got a great deal of attention. She was mad they didn't have any crackers available that night.

I SAW WHAT a lot of people would never see, because they see only what a person presents to them. When a doctor encounters a patient, the patient is ready for the doctor, and the doctor observes only what happens in the ten minutes that he or she is in the room with the patient.

As an interpreter, I sat in rooms with patients sometimes for up to twenty-four hours straight, so I learned a lot about those patients. Many told me stories about their entire lives. Some would ask me for food; some for other favors. I would get all the lowdown on them, and when they switched hospitals to play the game on the next well-meaning but oblivious medical professional, I was often the interpreter there, too. Most of my clients were nice people, but there were those who were not. These were the users and abusers and the criminals, and among them there were a number of psychopaths. There are a lot more psychopaths in society than people realize, and deaf people can be psychopaths, too. They murder, they rape, and sometimes they rape deaf girls because they know they won't hear them coming. This kind—the deaf psychopaths—lied in front of me all the time to the doctors. They knew I knew, but they didn't care that I knew because I couldn't say anything.

I saw behind the charade that psychopaths use to fool people. Psychopaths, whenever they encounter a particular person they want something from, put on their game face—they lie and manipulate—and I was in the unusual situation of watching them ply their trade.

AND SO THAT was my life. I taught my kids and I worked at the hospitals. When the kids were a little bit older, I worked at night a lot more. When my husband was home, I could go down to the emergency room and work all night, and I managed to live that life for ten years.

That would have been the totality of my life if, along the way, Walt Williams hadn't moved into our spare room as a boarder.

MY HUSBAND WORKED hard.

He was an engineer for Siemens Medical Systems, where he still works today, fixing x-ray equipment. He was a very, very good father to the kids. We had a family bed when the children were babies. He slept with our daughter on his chest, put her to sleep when she wasn't nursing, and, as the children got older, he was always involved with their activities.

When they were of school age, he was the soccer coach in town.

Everybody loved him. He was involved with the Boys and Girls Clubs. He was a great dad.

Our life as husband and wife, however, had its problems. None stemmed from being of two different cultures or races. I had his support for homeschooling the children and being a sign language interpreter. The years of investigating Walt after that fateful day at the police station was another matter.

When the Walt incident occurred, he did not support me in going to the police because, he said, "Why cause yourself this trouble?" which really meant, "Why cause me this trouble?" "Just forget about it," he told me. On the other hand, oddly enough, he did nothing to stop me from pursuing more information about Walt after the police took no action. On rare occasions, he would be curious and ask, "Did you find out anything about Walt today?" When I started investigating Walt, even he found it fascinating—not my work, but the stories I told about him.

Tony did not really believe that Walt was a killer. He did not believe it was necessary for me to do what I did. He did not believe I would be able to do anything. He saw me as a homemaker. This is the man who saw me pregnant. This is the man who saw me birth our children. This is the man who saw me nursing twenty-four hours a day for more than two years with one child, then two years with another, babies always with me, the absolutely devoted mother. This is the man who saw me kneading bread on the table and playing games on the floor with my children and holding them on my hip while I tried to get things done in the house.

He always said two things about me: "You're honest" and "You're intelligent." Those were the two things he respected about me, but he didn't think I could take what intelligence and schooling I had and apply it practically. He didn't see me as being able to understand psychology and getting into profiling and detective work. To him, that was something completely foreign. He thought I was being grandiose in my goals.

When I later wanted to pursue criminal profiling as a career, he said he couldn't see the point, I was already a successful sign language interpreter, and he didn't seem to understand I wanted to achieve something different at this point in life. He was a man who didn't like change and wasn't interested in risk taking; he thought I should just give up my mission.

So when I came home at the end of a day of being insulted by local law enforcement, he didn't say, "Don't worry, honey. I believe in you." He went about his business and I went about mine.

I wish I had been a criminal profiler before I got married; then maybe I could have seen the writing on the wall before I stepped up to the altar. After twenty-five years of marriage, I ended up divorced, my family torn apart. If I feel even one hundredth of the pain a family destroyed by the murder of their child experiences, I can't begin to imagine how they endure. I at least still have all my children. They don't.

CHAPTER 3

WALT
THE SUSPECT

In 1990, the police did nothing with the evidence I brought to them following the murder of Anne Kelley. But in spite of my nerve-racking, dead-end experience at the police station, I still assumed the detectives would be knocking on my front door within an hour to interview Walt Williams. If they had, they might have gotten the evidence they needed to make him a person of interest. The day after the murder, Walt went off on a hike. He put on long pants and a long shirt to leave the house, and I thought, *God, that looks uncomfortable*. It was a hot, muggy day in June, and while I knew he was headed to a wooded area where it made sense to cover your legs for mosquito and tick protection, he'd never done it before. Why all of a sudden, when he always wore shorts and a short-sleeved shirt, was he suddenly covering himself from head to toe? Was he covering scratches on his body?

If the police had interviewed him right away, as I begged them to, they could've said, "Roll up your sleeves," and they might have seen scratches.

Anne Kelley was murdered on Saturday and the evidence was in their hands on Monday, less than forty-eight hours later. *They're gonna come. They're gonna do what they have to do,* I thought. We'd all breathe a sigh of relief, and that would be it. I didn't want to be a hero. I just wanted the case to be handled, my life to return to normal, and Walt to go away.

TONY TOLD WALT—on my insistence—that he had to leave our home. The day after I went to the police, Walt walked out my door and kept right on going, without ever being considered a suspect.

I was left in a complete void, not understanding what the heck had happened. It was like being in Rod Serling's *The Twilight Zone.* It shook my sense of reality. Was I making connections where there were none? The police were not impressed by anything I told them, making me feel that I was a delusional housewife and just making stuff up.

But I never said I *knew* Walt Williams was the killer of Anne Kelley. What I said was that his behaviors were in line with a person who could have committed her murder, that if one put together his admission of being on the path that night with the evidence I found in his trash and his bizarre behavior, an investigator should want to learn more about this guy. That's what my brain told me. My information should have led the police immediately to consider him a suspect in this crime, yet it didn't. That meant either the police were incorrect in their perceptions or I was a pitifully amateur armchair detective.

I COULDN'T GET what had happened out of my mind. I got the newspaper every day expecting I would open it and read, *Walt Williams has been arrested for the murder,* and I would go back to my normal routine. But time moved on and there was not another word in the paper about the crime. I waited and waited, and finally, confused, I stopped expecting to see a newspaper story with any developments in the investigation.

I went back to homeschooling my children and working nights as a hospital sign language interpreter. As for the police, they never called.

A rumor went around town that the killer of Anne Kelley was another young man, Michael Potter, age eighteen, who lived with his parents in a house that stood right where the path intersected with the road. Michael was known to have hung out with other teenagers in the area where Anne Kelley's body was found. It was a woodsy area where they would party and smoke pot. The word was that this young man shot himself five days after the crime and that he was the one who murdered Anne.

I was stunned. That was why the police never contacted me. *I guess it wasn't Walt. I must be wrong.*

It seemed that it was simply coincidental that Walt exhibited such strange behavior, had circumstantial connections to the crime scene, and junk tossed in his trash; maybe this other young man was equally as disturbed but the one who had actually committed the crime.

I tried to put it out of my head. I was wrong. Michael Potter was the guilty party.

Michael was said to have broken up with his girlfriend the same week Anne was killed. He called his girlfriend in the days following the homicide to tell her he was not happy about something he had done in his life. The thing he was "not happy about" was alleged to be the murder. Yet he never confessed to murdering anyone and no one seemed to know exactly what he was feeling despondent about.

I heard through the police grapevine that there was also supposed to be some blond hair at the scene. The boy had blond hair. And, more important, his DNA was there, and he had scratches in his genital area from the briar bushes.

I thought, *Well, that's pretty good. I don't know if I could argue that one. There's DNA, and there's hair, and scratches.* DNA is solid proof. His hair on her, if there was a root still attached, could provide mtDNA for analysis, not as absolute as DNA, but pretty useful as supportive evidence if the mtDNA matched his. *And how would he get scratches in the genital area unless he had his pants off and he was raping somebody? If the rumors were true and the evidence existed, he* must *be the guy.*

* * * *

MEANWHILE, KIM TOLD me that Walt was let go from his job.

Right after he left, the company received a series of unusual bomb threats. Kim said that the man sounded just like Walt.

But as suddenly as the calls started, they stopped, and Walt dropped from sight. Kim never saw him again.

I WOULD HAVE left this whole miserable episode behind me if something hadn't kept nagging at me. The police never actually stated that Michael Potter killed Anne Kelley, and nothing was ever written up in the newspaper about the case being closed. In theory, it could have been administratively closed because the suspect was dead, but with all that supposed evidence I would think they would let the community know that there was no longer a killer out there. This lack of clarification on the part of law enforcement irked me. Was the case closed or wasn't it? Did they have positive proof that Potter was the killer or were they only guessing it could be him and no one was challenging their assumption?

I decided to talk to the Potter family. When I told Michael's parents that I thought their son might be innocent of the murder of Anne Kelley, they welcomed me into their home.

The story they told me was really sad. They were grieving over their son's suicide, and then five months later the police showed up and insinuated that he killed Anne Kelley. The family was stunned. Why would they accuse their son of doing that? It's bad enough that a child committed suicide, but then to be told that he sexually assaulted and murdered a woman was another thing altogether.

They said he was always a sweet kid, that they didn't see any violence in him. Michael wasn't perfect; he had dropped out of school, and he did have a problem with his girlfriend. He was depressed. He felt like a failure. They believed that was why he killed himself. They couldn't believe he had anything to do with Anne's death.

I asked if I could see the autopsy report, and they gave it to me.

There was nothing in the autopsy about any briar marks or scratches anywhere on that boy's body. The medical examiner should have noted such abrasions if he saw that trauma, however minor. Instead, outside of the damage caused by the actual shotgun blast, the rest of the body was "unremarkable."

Then I wondered about the rest of what I had heard—whether there was actually blond hair and DNA found that matched Michael.

It turned out that neither existed. That's why the police couldn't announce that Michael Potter murdered Anne Kelley. They didn't have any physical evidence connecting him to the crime, only that he conveniently committed suicide five days later.

I called Anne Kelley's father, and he said that the police told him that Michael Potter killed his daughter and he was told about the scratches and the matching DNA and hair.

He chose to believe the police, and in his mind, there was nothing more to discuss. He didn't want to hear anything about it from me or anyone else. He said his wife was satisfied hearing that Michael Potter killed their daughter. She accepted it because believing it gave her closure.

"I don't want you to ever contact my family again, and if you do, I'll sue you," he told me.

And that was the last time I spoke to the Kelley family.

I understood if the police couldn't develop evidence that Walt was the killer. They had to have evidence; without that, they couldn't charge him with a crime. Although I thought that the police mishandled the case, I wouldn't want them to arrest someone without probable cause. That would be another miscarriage of justice.

I could even live with the fact that they thought Michael Potter had something to do with it, if enough of the evidence supported such a conclusion.

But when they pinned the crime on him and told the grieving families of both Michael Potter and Anne Kelley, that crossed the line for me. That, to me, was inexcusable.

Why wouldn't they do their job? Why didn't they just bring Walt in and interview him? Why didn't they take a DNA sample from him? And if they still couldn't bring a case and an alleged perpetrator to court, then at least they would have tried.

In my opinion, if anyone stopped to compare the evidence supporting Walt Williams's possible involvement in the murder and the evidence supporting Michael Potter's, they would have a few short lines on Potter's side of the paper and a whole lot of lines on Williams's side. But for some reason—for some yet unclear reason—I believed the police department simply ignored the better suspect.

People ask, is there a perfect crime? I say, no, there isn't, but there are plenty of "good enough" crimes. They're good enough because nobody saw anything, they're good enough because the body was in water and the evidence got washed away, or they're good enough because the body wasn't found for three or four weeks until the dog walker tripped over it and there it was. They're good enough if the police had a "damn good" suspect but still looked the other way.

Because there are so many good enough crimes, a substantial portion of crimes will never be prosecuted because the evidence won't be there.

Citizens should have cared more about an innocent girl being slaughtered in their town; they should have protested when they never got an answer as to who killed her. But no one spoke up except me. And when I did, I was told to forget about it. If a woman is murdered in the woods and nobody speaks up, does this mean the victim and the homicide don't really matter? The system did not function properly. We should all care more about our fellow man and about doing what's right. That's what spurred me on the path of becoming a professional criminal profiler.

I DECIDED TO educate myself about psychopaths, serial killers, and serial homicide investigation. I spent the next four years at the "Pat Brown School of Criminal Profiling," which held study sessions in patients' hospital rooms, doctors' waiting rooms, and emergency rooms.

I wanted to know more about the field of profiling and serial homicide investigation. I wanted to learn about forensics and psychopathy. I wanted to learn how to analyze, dissect, and reconstruct a crime.

The first thing I did was look for a college-level program. I had a liberal arts degree, which was heavy in anthropology, sociology, and psychology. Those fields were surprisingly useful because I had studied how people behave in society—in the United States and in other countries. I studied how people behave in subcultures, how men and women deal with each other, and their roles within their communities. I learned about deviant behavior and why people commit criminal acts.

But I didn't have any formal education in criminal profiling or in criminal behavior, crime reconstruction, and forensics, the three fields that are the foundation of criminal profiling. The University of Maryland, near where I lived, offered a criminal justice program, but nothing really useful for profiling. In fact, there was nothing in the entire United States for those not in law enforcement that was focused on criminal profiling. I found a forensics program at George Washington University, but it was pretty much a lab program. The course really wasn't geared toward criminal profiling, and I wasn't interested in getting a job as a technician.

There were many programs in psychology—which people often think is what criminal profiling is based on. A profiler is supposed to understand the behavior and the mind-set of the killer, but little of psychology is ever about aberrant behavior and psychopathy. Most of what was taught was general psychology, which didn't apply to murderers and psychopaths. The few courses I found that focused on deviant psychology and mental disorders were all about treatment, and I couldn't have cared less about curing rapists and murderers. I figured that by the time you were a bona fide serial killer, you were a hopeless case and a nasty piece of work. I am not one of those who believe that psychologists can rehabilitate a guy who has killed ten women. And even if he could be rehabilitated, he doesn't deserve the chance. I always say, when you bring the dead woman back to life, then you can give the killer treatment.

So how was I going to learn criminal profiling?

The only straight-line methodology I found was joining the FBI.

First of all, I was too old; they wouldn't even let me try. Second, when you join the FBI, you don't just become a criminal profiler. You can't say, "Now that I have joined, this is what I want to do." You become an agent, and twenty years later, you might still be sitting in Iowa doing whatever FBI agents do in Iowa. Maybe someday, if you were really, really lucky, you'd become a criminal profiler; but then again maybe you wouldn't. So for me, the FBI was out. I had to find some other way. What was left? That's what I wanted to know.

There was nothing out there, apparently, so I concluded the only solution was to create my own criminal profiling program, study it on my own, and take advantage of anything complementary that I could find.

I found courses offered online by Brent Turvey, who has a master's degree in forensic science. Turvey was one of the first independent profilers in the country and he strongly encouraged the Sherlock Holmes scientific method of deduction that he called "Deductive Profiling." He may have a master's in forensics but he clearly studied much on his own to learn all the other skills necessary to profiling. These weren't accredited college courses, but they were informative and I was gathering my education from every existing source that I could find.

I took all the classes that Turvey offered, purchased the recommended textbooks, and learned a great deal. That opened the door to attending a serial homicide conference in Ann Arbor, Michigan, and a death investigation conference in Florida. These experiences exposed me to the skills and tools I needed, acquired at the feet of some of the world's most accomplished detectives and crime analysts.

On my own, I read and studied some four hundred books related to profiling, crime analysis, serial homicide, and forensics over the next four years. There is nothing better for studying than hours and hours of quiet time at the hospital waiting for the doctor to come in, the surgery to end, and the patient to wake up.

Later on, I earned a master's degree in criminal justice because I wanted to learn more about police operations and procedures and the challenges of the criminal justice system in general. It wasn't criminal profiling, but it was an issue with which I was concerned.

The fact is that people are stuck on the concept that you must attend a particular program that certifies you as a criminal profiler. But to date, there are no specific requirements for participation in the field. Any way that you learn, as long as you gain the skills and you understand the field, is an education. A college program is a wonderful opportunity if such a program exists (and today there is a college-level criminal profiling certificate program available that I developed for Excelsior College) but, even with a college program under one's belt, learning is an ongoing process and one should always seek new information and skills.

During that time, I began to develop my own idea of what was wrong with the present practice of criminal profiling. I disagreed with a lot of what I read. Much of it didn't even make sense. Some of the methodologies I was reading about seemed like hocus-pocus to me. I couldn't fathom anything scientific behind certain theories that added up to nothing more than picking something out of a hat.

There was sleight-of-hand being sold by a few profilers who had been practicing for a long time. I'm not saying they didn't do a good job when they worked their cases; I'm not saying they weren't good profilers. But by the time they shared their techniques in books, everything became a show of "How brilliant I am" and "How every profile I did matched the suspect perfectly!"

Oh, please! There's no way you could have gotten those things right, because the methodology didn't make any sense. You couldn't have known the things you claimed. Profiles are science, not magic.

I watched a television show about famed FBI profiler John Douglas and a case he worked on in Alaska. On the show, Douglas theorized that when they found the perpetrator, he would have a stutter, and he did! Now how in the world would anybody—I don't care how much training you've got—figure out that a guy who committed a particular crime stutters? From where do you get *that*? Well, Hollywood twisted the story around like they so often do.

It turned out that the police already had a suspect in mind, and they asked Douglas if he thought that the man they had in custody could be the serial killer, this man who owned a small plane and stuttered. Douglas profiled the crime and, since the profile matched the police suspect, he said the killer would be a stutterer. He already *knew* that the guy stuttered, but the television show didn't make that clear. In his book *Mindhunter,* Douglas points out that he knew the suspect stuttered, but Hollywood made him seem like he could pick this trait out because of his brilliance.

While the Hollywood spin on profilers makes for exciting reading, students of profiling are often mystified and discouraged because they can't understand how they could ever possibly figure the same things out—what color car the suspect drives, that he likes to watch the news, that he is a sports lover. I have news for them. I can't figure those things out, either.

SOMETIMES, A PROFILER applies inductive profiling to a case.

A sexual homicide is almost always committed by males. How often do you see a woman convicted of sexual assault? Almost never. It's an extremely unusual crime. A profiler could take statistical information and say, "If you have a girl who's been raped, then I'm going to say it was by a man." Anyone can guess that. And most males who commit crimes are between twenty-two and thirty-two. We can start creating a profile by staying with the safe bets: "The sexual assaults were committed by a man between the ages of twenty-two and thirty-two." Then if a guy committed a number of poorly planned crimes, all locally, I could say what he's not doing well in his life: he's probably unable to maintain a job or a relationship. And he's not very clever. I bet I will still be batting close to a thousand with this profile.

But unusual guesses, like a stutter, could not possibly be known logically or statistically.

As I learned about profiling, I discovered that there was a great deal of mythology about the field—promoted by profilers themselves—to make profilers seem like some kind of gods. They want the police and general public believing there are only so many people in the world who could ever do this, because they're so brilliant and gifted. They can simply look at a scene and—voilà!—they know all the answers. It's ridiculous.

Brent Turvey pushed for establishing an increasingly scientific practice of criminal profiling. I support his efforts and have continued to promote the deductive method of criminal profiling—one based on evidence, the scientific method, and solid explanations for profile determinations.

A profiler has to spend a long time studying autopsy reports and crime scene photos, doing crime role plays, crime reconstructing, and crime analysis. It is hard work. Deductive profiling isn't as "sexy" and "mystical" as profiling that makes amazing conclusions through inside information or luck, but it is a much better tool for homicide investigators, and that is the only thing that really matters.

IN 1995, FIVE years after the Anne Kelley murder, I still believed Walt Williams should be a suspect.

Now having greater knowledge and training, I went back into Walt's history to question once more whether I was right about him, and if he could be connected to any other homicides in the area.

Starting anew with the Anne Kelley homicide, I found it hard to believe that a crime of this nature would be a perpetrator's first and only crime. Kelley was bludgeoned and strangled. She was sexually assaulted and brutalized. The description of what happened to Anne was one of the reasons I never believed that Michael Potter, just turning eighteen, could have committed a crime this brutal.

I started building a background of Williams by interviewing the people with whom he had worked. The past is the first place to look for psychopathic tendencies. Many times on television, an interviewer says to me of a crime suspect, "Well, everybody says he's a great guy." I say, "No, no, they're saying that *now, before they have had a chance to reflect,* but look back into his past—really look—and you'll uncover all his psychopathic behaviors. They were there for years and years, ever since he was a kid."

The prospects of interviewing people made me nervous, because I had never conducted an investigation before. I had never knocked on strangers' doors and I didn't know how people would respond to me. I felt kind of silly, actually, like a new salesperson making cold calls to advertise some product. Even when I was a Girl Scout, I didn't like selling cookies.

I had now completed all of my studies and had reached a point where I considered myself a criminal profiler, whether anybody else wanted to consider me one or not. I designed my first business card and off I went to test the response.

I decided to start with Walt's former employers, and the response I received was incredible.

I went to a law office in D.C. where he worked as a clerk just before he moved into my house. When I got there, I said, "I'm a private investigator," and I handed my P.I. license to the receptionist. "I would like to talk to somebody who Walt Williams would have worked under. I'm looking into some of his past work history."

The receptionist went away and a fellow came running from the back room and actually leaped over the counter. No kidding, leaped.

"Walt Williams?" he cried. "Oh, my God, *that* guy?"

He hauled me back to his office, and he couldn't stop ranting and raving. "That guy was trouble. He would come to work wearing a black fishnet shirt. I'm like, 'Walt, it's a law office. What are you doing in a black fishnet shirt?' Or he'd be dressed like a comic book character. He was obsessed with comic books, Spider-Man and other juvenilia like that. He was a twenty-three-year-old guy enamored with this kid stuff."

According to this attorney, Walt behaved inappropriately with women in the office. They were uniformly uncomfortable around him. And he was always coming up with excuses for not getting things done.

"Why did you hire him?" I asked.

"Have you ever tried to hire somebody for a job as a mail clerk? You get pond scum," he said. "But Walt came in, he was dressed in a suit, and he had a great résumé—"

"Which was a pack of lies," I said.

He looked embarrassed. "I know that now."

He handed me Walt's résumé—it was quite amusing to read, and I was also amazed that this man still had the paper in his files so many years later; Walt must really have gotten his goat. I said, "How

come, when his next employer called you up to get a recommenda-
tion, they were told he was a great worker?"

He shrugged.

"I just wanted to get rid of him."

As we all know, many people lie about their ex-employees these
days. They don't want to get sued for telling the truth, which is why
recommendations have become rather useless. When I told my friend
Kim, who hired and dated Walt, she was furious. She said, "Oh,
that's just great. They sicced him on us knowing darn well he was a
terrible employee."

Reading Walt's résumé for the first time I learned some fascinating tidbits. He wrote that he did "secret work" for an air force colonel. *Really?* I actually located the "colonel." He laughed when I
called. "Walt worked as a mail clerk in my office in Virginia," he said.
"I've been in the military, but I've never been a colonel." That was a
gross exaggeration.

Walt worked for a department store, as a security guard, so I
went there.

"Oh, *that* guy?" his supervisor said. "Geez, he was so creepy. He
was the only person who worked for me to whom I wouldn't give my
pager number. I didn't want to be contacted by him. Walt told me once
that he was going to snipe me on the way into work, 'joking' about
gunning me down. Once he said that he had gloves that had stun guns
in them so he could knock people out. Another day, Walt told me that
he got a girl pregnant, and I said, 'Is she going to get an abortion?' He
said, 'Yeah, I'm going to do it myself.' That totally freaked me out."

I drove two hours south to meet with his father. I honestly didn't
expect him to speak with me. I rang the doorbell and when he answered, I explained who I was.

"I'm a criminal profiler, and I'm trying to learn a little bit more
about your son, because he's either committed a serious crime, or
he's gotten himself into trouble by making himself look like he committed the crime."

Walt's father looked at me and rolled his eyes.

"Come on in," he said.

We spent the next two hours talking and he told me all kinds of things about Walt from way back when he was a child. "He's *always* been a problem," he said. "I had a difficult time with him. I've had problems with him constantly lying, and one time he stole a bunch of quarters from me, I think it was a jar."

He told me Walt couldn't keep a job, had no ambition, and all he wanted to do was play Dungeons & Dragons with his loser friends. He was a disappointment as a son.

His dad said that Walt served in the air force, but that he was discharged because the military said he was schizoid. He used the word "schizoid." Walt later told me himself that he was let go because they also said he had a personality disorder. I thought that was interesting, because I believed he had a personality disorder and not a mental illness. How long did it take the air force to discover and make this evaluation? Four months.

When our interview ended, Walt's father said, "If you need any more help, you let me know." He could have slammed the door in my face, but he didn't. In fact, he gave me new insight into his son.

My confidence was building with regard to my ability to run a background interview, and my suspicions about Walt were growing. Next I tracked down his sister.

She also invited me into her home and I sat down with her for two hours. At one point her husband and kids joined the conversation, and everybody had something to say about Walt.

She cried and said, "I've never understood what was wrong with him. All my life, I've had problems with him."

Her husband said, "He creeps me out completely."

And the kids added, "Uncle Walt creeps us out, too."

They described incident after incident in which Walt struggled with the people around him and displayed peculiar behaviors.

Everyone I asked for an interview agreed. The family did not seem shocked or shaken that I was investigating him in connection with a sexual homicide. How many families would not object to a stranger sitting in their living room and questioning them as to whether their son, brother, brother-in-law, or uncle might be a murderer? Walt's family members weren't upset at all. Not one of them.

* * * *

I TOOK THE information gained from my interviews and turned it over to the police department that had jurisdiction over the crime. In the beginning there had been a dispute over who should work the case; the park police, because Anne Kelley was murdered in the park, or the county police, because the park was within county jurisdiction. It would have been better for the county police to handle the case, because they had a lot of experience with murder investigations and the park police had very little. I never knew why the park police won out, but it was clearly their case. I had to go back to them with my new information and I got another tepid response, but I handed over the information anyway and went away again. I had compiled a substantial history on Walt, including all the places I knew he had worked, and a list of his old girlfriends. Whether he murdered Anne Kelley or not, I did not know, because that must be proved with evidence, but based on my investigation, there was no doubt in my mind that he should be a suspect or at least a person of interest. Information about him now came not just from one "bored housewife" but also from employers, family, and friends. Now there were even more reasons for the police to take a look at Walt Williams. I could only hope they would.

IN THE SPRING of 1996 I got the phone call that I had been waiting for for the last six years. Walt Williams finally became the number one suspect in the murder of Anne Kelley.

A new investigator had taken over the case, and he said, "Can you come in? I want to interview you about Walt Williams."

I said, "Thank God."

We talked the next day at police headquarters. I was back in the same building I had first walked into carrying my cardboard box of evidence all those years before. The investigator looked at me, motioned toward the evidence—my evidence—sitting on the table in between us, and shook his head. "I don't know why they missed this the first time around. This is crazy. This is crazy."

The police picked Walt up, brought him in for an interview, and polygraphed him. The police told me afterward that they laughed about his interview because it was full of bogus information. They were most amused that he had been given the "option" to leave the air force as part of a "Manpower Reduction Program." They said that he now had an alibi for the night that Anne Kelley was murdered, that he had been playing softball at the time. That was an alibi we could strike down, because he told me that he left Kim's and came back to the house. He never mentioned a softball game to me.

The polygraph showed that he was being deceptive. "He's our guy. We know it's him. We got his DNA and we're waiting on the test to come back." I don't know if Williams gave consent for the tests willingly or if he was pressured into it or if there was a court order, but I was happy to hear that they were going after physical evidence.

Then the investigator looked at me and said, "You should watch your back. Walt's really angry now."

I said, "Can I get a Maryland gun permit? A carry permit?"

The police said no. In Maryland, you can get a carry permit only if your life is being threatened, and since Walt hadn't threatened me, I couldn't get one.

So that was that. I went home, relieved it was almost over, exhilarated that all my hard work had paid off, and thankful my analysis of Walt Williams hadn't been so wrong after all. Then I waited, and I waited, and I waited.

People think DNA tests come back quickly, but this one took five months. While intellectually I never thought he'd come after me, and he didn't, emotionally it was unnerving to know that he was out there and angry. He knew who turned him in and he heard that I had visited his relatives asking questions, so there was no doubt in his mind that he ended up being interviewed by the police six years after the murder because of me.

I kept calling and calling the police station. "What's going on, what's going on?" Finally the investigators received the test results.

"Walt has been excluded by the DNA," the detective told me.

"*WHAT?*" I shrieked.

He said, "Yeah, the DNA excluded him. He's no longer a suspect."

I went berserk. I was just blown away. I could not understand it. "What are you talking about?"

"He's been excluded."

"I don't believe this," I said. "I can believe that it's inconclusive—*that* I can buy. 'It's inconclusive'—we don't have enough DNA to prove he did or didn't do it. I can accept that and it's okay with me if you can't take it to court. You can tell me that and I'm not going to hound you over it. But please don't lie to me."

"Mrs. Brown," he said, "you need to get a life."

I DID GET a life, and I decided something needed to be done about the police investigative system, because I no longer believed that catching killers was being handled properly. The system was failing and innocent people, mostly women, were going to be killed because of it.

Some people said, "You just can't accept defeat. You totally believe this guy killed this girl, and that's all there is to it. No matter what evidence there is, you're going to believe he did it, and you won't admit you were wrong. You've got some kind of issue that you've just got to prove yourself. You're just obsessed."

But my problem wasn't that. The investigator's justification didn't make sense to me. I'd grown distrustful of how the system worked, and I wanted proof. Six years ago I was told Michael Potter killed Anne Kelley, but that was never proven. Now I was being told Walt didn't do it and they were looking for someone else. If Walt's DNA didn't match the DNA at the crime, then he was innocent. But I wanted proof. Prove to me he didn't commit the crime.

For a year, I called and called, pushing for the right to see the DNA report. I was always refused. One day, for some reason, I got hold of another investigator and he read the DNA report to me! Go figure. But what a bonanza, because that officer said, "There were no PCR products obtainable from the sperm factions." In other words, *There was no DNA.* A later statement by the Maryland State's

Attorney's Office confirmed what the detective had told me: "There is no DNA evidence to take anyone to trial."

One of the reasons they could not confirm that Anne's killer was Walt was that there simply wasn't any DNA found in or on Anne Kelley that could link him to the murder. The results were inconclusive. He had *not* been excluded.

I was furious, because the investigator *did* lie to me.

Now I knew that the DNA was inconclusive and that Walt should *still* be a suspect. And I wondered whether they ever tested the condom I found in his trash. It didn't seem that they had, but if he were the killer, the victim's DNA might have been found on that. I guess they didn't think killers ever used them.

SOMETIMES I LOOK back at the Anne Kelley case and I realize the first investigator wasn't especially skilled at solving cases. The park police had never had a murder in their jurisdiction before, so this guy probably had little or no experience in homicide or criminal profiling or psychopathology. And in comes a housewife with a box, she tells him a great story, and he shrugs it off.

And then there were the politics involved in the particular case, which no one could have predicted and I didn't learn about until almost a decade after the crime.

Anne Kelley's family was friends with George W. Bush, the future president and, in 1990, son of the then-president of the United States. The family reportedly asked W. to help them. W. reportedly called Bush Sr., and he called the state's attorney, who was told to take good care of this case.

I was told that the state's attorney was pursuing a federal judgeship, and he did not want his career going down the toilet because of a police department that had never handled a murder. So when Michael Potter, an eighteen-year-old boy who lived near the wooded path where Anne was murdered, blew his brains out five days later, the police said, "Eureka, he's the guy who did it! Case closed." Everybody went home happy. Except me.

It took nearly ten years and a volatile town meeting to find out that information. The park police showed up to defend their handling of the case and bragged about how hard they worked on it because Anne Kelley's family knew the Bushes.

Then, behind closed doors, they told me Walt Williams was still the one and only suspect.

THERE WAS NOT much more I could accomplish on the Anne Kelley case. All I could do was keep an eye on Walt's whereabouts.

Then he got married. Married! Walt had problems dating. Girls refused to go out with him; girls dumped him. Kim lasted a month and she still wonders why she gave him a chance. Now Walt was married. To a "smart" woman, with a master's degree, who worked for a college. She was also a religious woman and she didn't tolerate drinking or drugs. Her mother told me that she had reported her first husband to the police when she found marijuana in their home. But here she was with Walt. And they had a child.

I felt bad about suspecting a family man, but I couldn't let that sway me. I went to see Walt's wife's mother. She gave me a nice two-hour interview. "Yes, Walt is a bit odd and I know he has some problems, but what man doesn't?"

"Did he tell you what he did for a living?"

"I believe he was a police officer with the MPD at the time. He left the job to have more time with his wife."

The interview proved that Walt was still lying. I knew he couldn't qualify for a job with any police department. I sent Walt's wife an e-mail and attached all the information about Walt on it. I told her his background and that he had been a suspect in a sexual homicide.

She got mad. She e-mailed me back and told me to "be a woman" and talk straight to Walt about my suspicions. Okay; I called.

"Hey, Walt!"

"Hey, Pat, how are you doing?"

Walt was mighty jovial that day. I could hear his wife telling him to find out what my problem was. I told Walt that he needed to clear up a decade of lies if he wanted me to think he wasn't involved in the Kelley crime.

Walt admitted to what I already knew and could prove and denied anything he thought I was unsure of or couldn't prove. I asked him questions over the phone while his wife listened in. I couldn't tape the conversation without his consent because I lived in a state where this was illegal, but I am a fast typist and I transcribed the questions and answers.

WALT WILLIAMS: "I NEVER walked that path home. I don't like the path. That night I broke up with Kim, she told me she didn't want to see me anymore. It was starting to get dark on the way home and I said, 'Hell, no way, I'm not walking down this path.'"

(This was the first time I had any idea as to the exact time he walked down that path. Originally when he told me the story, he simply said he was on the path; he gave no time frame. Now that he stated it was getting dark, this put him even closer to the time of the murder. If he was telling the truth here—about it becoming dark when he "decided to cross the stream"—then if he did NOT do what he said, he would have ended up at the site of the murder approximately the same time as Anne Kelley.)

WILLIAMS: "I decided to jump from this side of the stream bank to the other. I lowered myself and I ended up landing in the water. It was waist deep to my surprise and I pulled myself up, dirty, muddy, and wet."

(He also mentioned it was too far to go back to the road on the path and too far to the next road to continue. I have looked at the location. It would have been approximately a five-minute walk to the intersection of the next road.)

WILLIAMS: "I threw my clothes away. I don't like wet jeans and threw them away—after they get wet, they get hard as a rock. After shoes dry out they don't feel right. Yeah, I washed them before I threw them out. I wiped the mud off my shoes with the plastic because I didn't want to track it into the house.

"The condom was just curiosity. I had never used one before. I didn't ejaculate in it."

(That was likely a lie because the condom was stuck together and stiff.)

"It was just taken out of the pack and put back. I threw them away because I didn't need them because I wasn't with Kim anymore."

(I asked him about his paranoia of AIDS and his time in the military.)

"Yes, I had sex but AIDS was not a fear back then; I just picked girls that looked healthy.

"The letter opener was really a throwing knife I bought at Beltway Plaza when they had a store with martial arts stuff."

(When I had seen this in the trash after the murder, I didn't recognize what it was. It looked like a filed-down letter opener. Having looked at martial arts equipment since then, it did indeed look like a throwing knife and this was more consistent with what Walt would have owned. It is still interesting that he tossed a perfectly good knife.)

WILLIAMS: "The next day I covered my arms and legs because it was cool in the mountains. I always did that.

"The night of the murder, Kim and I broke up and she came over and stayed in the [Brown] house. She was on the bed and I was on the floor on a mattress. I had called her on the phone and talked with her—I was hurt. I did everything I could to get her to come over and she did."

(I questioned Walt on this and he then admitted maybe it wasn't that night—I had no recollection of Kim EVER staying overnight in our home, especially in his room.)

WILLIAMS: "The park police left a message on my voice mail. They called three times. I called them back. They said maybe I could help in this investigation and they picked me up.

"They told me to write down where I was living. [The detective] told me to write down the names of the girls I dated. Then he read me my rights.

"He told me he had been looking for me for a year. I was in the next county over, so I don't see why he would have any trouble finding me. I moved there about six months after I was put out of your house.

"In February, I was incensed. I told the detective, 'When you see I had nothing to do with anything, I want an apology.'

"He showed me an artist's rendition . . . from somewhere and asked if it didn't look like me and I said no."

WILLIAMS: "I didn't get the name of the girl that was murdered. I started getting irritated. He said, 'Why don't you take a lie detector test?' and I said, 'Fine.' I fell asleep during the time they were setting it up."

WILLIAMS: "I asked 'Why am I here?' but they never gave me any answers. They kept me six hours and I missed my work. Then he said, 'What about a blood test?' I said fine and we went to the hospital.

"They didn't tell me anything about why they brought me in.

"I volunteered for both tests.

"I called the police department every day. Nobody would tell me anything.

"Finally, I got the detective and he told me I was excluded by the DNA and he was sorry he had been so hard on me.

"I should sue them for the way they treated me."

(We also discussed Walt's work and dating history; he disputed the veracity of much of my information.)

WILLIAMS: "I did NOT call in bomb threats. I went to pick up my check. I came back to visit and someone said, 'Walt did it.'

"I quit—they didn't fire me.

"I didn't get fired from that security job, either . . .

"I worked for that man but he wasn't a colonel.

"All of my life, I have kept my family at arm's length.

"I lived with my aunt—yes, I was suicidal.

"Tiffany Byrd was the girl decapitated on prom night. No, she was not my girlfriend. I made that up."

(Byrd did die on prom night in an accident. She did not get decapitated. She was not from Walt's school and he apparently borrowed the story from either the paper or friends.)

WILLIAMS: "I know I have done some extremely stupid things. I just wanted to be accepted. I wanted sympathy.

"I never stole anything except some quarters from my father's piggy bank during high school."

(He knew I had talked to his dad.)

WILLIAMS: "I got depressed in the air force. Didn't like my job classification. They sent me to another base for evaluation. Said I had a personality disorder.

"I was upset when my father remarried. He changed completely. The woman was a friend of the family and I didn't like her and I wondered if she was around before my mother died."

WILLIAMS: "No, my mother didn't die in my arms.

"I am very close to my sister. I talk to her every day. No, she hasn't seen my son yet. I will get over that way one day. I sent her pictures."

(His sister says he does tend to call her every day for weird abbreviated conversations but she had seen him only once after he got married.)

WILLIAMS: "I tried for the MPD, but that one dropped charge on my record for supposedly carrying a machete on a college campus screwed me up.

"My wife and I knew each other one week before we got married. Met through the phone dating line. I fell in love instantly. We knew we were for each other. I put the message on in August. I said, 'I am Walt. I work as an SPO [special police officer]. These are my interests.'"

WILLIAMS: "No, I didn't have any college. I said that because I was ashamed when I got married."

(Walt put down that he attended college for three years on their marriage certificate.)

WILLIAMS: "I have never felt I was good enough for anybody. I wanted so much to be useful to someone; I tried too hard.

"If I didn't know the person, it wouldn't concern me."

(This was in response to my question of why he was so blasé about the murder of Anne Kelley.)

Walt said that he spoke in such detail with me after all these years because he wanted to set everything straight. He said that my investigation and suspicion of him changed his life for the better and he no longer tells lies and foolish stories. He now tells *only* the truth. He practically thanked me for getting him in this situation and making him face his foolish behaviors.

It was interesting to note that Walt wanted to set things straight only after I contacted his wife and she wanted me to talk to him. Until then, although he had my phone number and knew where I lived, he never attempted to contact me and discuss anything. He never called me to tell me to knock it off. It was my conclusion that he simply wanted to impress his wife with his "honesty" so she would think *I* was the crazy one.

What struck me as odd in this conversation was that Walt talked to me as though I were a close friend, although he knew me for only four weeks in 1990 as his landlord. Why the strong connection? Why no hostility? Perhaps Walt was telling the truth and he was just one great guy, but more likely it was one major snow job. His wife stayed on for a few more years and then divorced him.

I was happy to find out that Walt was on the path exactly at the time Anne Kelley was murdered. In 2009, a detective from a town nearby told me that Walt Williams remained the only suspect in the murder of Anne Kelley.

WHEN I LOOK back on twenty years of dealing with the murder of Anne Kelley and the walking anachronism that is Walt Williams, I still wish more than anything that this case could be resolved.

I have the private satisfaction that the police still consider him a top suspect, that they agree the circumstantial evidence is convincing enough to believe Williams might have committed the murder. Sure, there is always a possibility that Williams is a nutjob who lies and says and does stupid things and on the same night that he waded across the stream, another killer popped out of the bushes and murdered Anne. Anything is possible, and that's why you have to have enough evidence to convince a jury that a suspect is truly guilty.

Although I know that I was justified in gathering evidence and pushing for the police to pay serious attention to Williams, everyone just got the story secondhand from me. If I had to go to a court of law to prove Williams should be the number one suspect, I could do it; I have enough statements, written and oral, to back my claim. I couldn't prove he did it, but I could prove the police should have investigated him thoroughly.

But nobody else—and I mean *nobody*—saw what I saw and experienced what I experienced.

I didn't go looking for this case. It came to me. I never thought the world of Sherlock Holmes I enjoyed as a child would become my reality three decades later. Sometimes fate takes a very strange turn. Here I was, a homemaker and sign language interpreter no more.

I was a criminal profiler.

CHAPTER 4

A NEW CAREER

I'll never say that I know what a family who has lost a loved one through violence goes through. I don't have a family member who was the victim of a horrible crime. No one wants to be that person. I don't ever want the knock at the door that tells me my child has been murdered.

I have observed the agony families go through and how they never get over it. I have talked with many families of murder or suicide victims and have heard them express their despair over feeling separate from all others, and of being alone. Friends don't want to hear about it after a while. They get sick of you. *Oh, there you go again.* They have normal lives. They don't have killers in their past. They just want to talk about what happened at their son's baseball game or how their daughter has a new costume for Halloween. They don't want to think about evil monsters. They don't understand what you're talking about or why you're so obsessed. You become a pariah, a strange being with knowledge that nobody else has and a situation of which nobody else wants to be a part.

Once upon a time, people who were grieving, people who were ill with a terminal disease, people who were struggling with alcohol or drug problems, also felt quite alone. They had to rely on their small circle of family and friends and whatever religious faith they might have. Sometimes they had no one with whom to talk. Now there are support groups for just about every problem, including wonderful groups to help victims of crime and families of murder victims.

I was in a weird, lonely spot of my own, because I was chasing a killer but nobody had killed my child. I went to some support groups for families of murder victims, hoping to find a form of kinship, but I was not really a person who fit the criteria. When I started to speak, I immediately felt my problem was trivial in comparison to what the others in the group were going through. We were all frustrated with the criminal justice system, but when I expressed my feelings about my struggle, I felt like some whiner complaining about heartburn to a group of heart transplant patients. I realized my faux pas, apologized, and never went back.

There are no support groups for people who think someone killed somebody. No support groups for people chasing serial killers or for those who want to become criminal profilers and change the system. I was a victim of sorts, but there was no support group listed in the newspaper that served someone with my "problem."

I shared many of the same emotional difficulties that families of victims of unsolved murder suffer from: anger, frustration, rage, fear, and desperation. Thoughts about the crime take over one's life and, worst of all, the thought that one must continually do something about it. One mother of a murder victim told me she hadn't swum in her backyard pool since her daughter had been killed because the first time she jumped in, guilt overwhelmed her.

"My daughter will never get to swim again," she told me. "How could I dare enjoy myself while her killer was still out there?"

I thoroughly understood where she was coming from. Police had done nothing to shake my belief that Walt Williams might have killed Anne Kelley. It was hard for me to do things like go to the movies or read the latest best seller—selfish, frivolous stuff; someone might die because I was wasting time in a theater eating popcorn.

I know this sounds a bit egotistical, like I thought I was the only one who could save the world, but what if I *was* the only one who really did know who killed Anne Kelley? What if it *was* Walt and he continued to be a free man? That knowledge dumped a load of responsibility on me and I couldn't just walk away from it.

So there I was. I felt my time should be dedicated almost exclusively toward solving this mystery, developing evidence, doing *something*. It was stressful, and there was nobody who understood that.

Then there were the people who started telling me that I was nuts, which didn't help. And the folks who didn't say anything, but I could see they didn't get it because they had that look that says, "We must tolerate those who are a bit out there."

I would be plagued with doubt. I started questioning myself, thinking, "Gee, maybe I am wrong." Then I would reread my notes and the evidence would get me back on track.

I became obsessed with working this case night and day, and that was a strain on daily life. I still taught my children, of course, and I still went to all the Boys and Girls Clubs games. I still went to the hospital and did sign language interpreting. The minute I walked into the treatment area I changed my expression completely and everybody would say, "What a Pollyanna! You're always cheerful and always happy." They had no idea what I was going through, none.

At a certain point, I was exhausted and realized that I didn't know how to balance my life. Several people suggested I should get some therapy and counseling, which I eventually concluded was a good idea. It might help me get things in place. I went to a counselor and she immediately thought I was nuts. She suggested medication. I tried to explain the situation as carefully as I could, but the therapist was already pulling out the prescription pad. I didn't get angry; I just left. I understood exactly what the therapist was thinking upon hearing my crazy-sounding story. I get a lot of those phone calls and e-mails myself, from a lot of people who *are* nuts, who *are* psychopaths and attention-seekers.

But once in a while, there is somebody who is telling the truth. I am familiar with the way people communicate and I can usually separate the attention-seekers from those I think are being honest. The ones who are telling the truth I do contact, and I talk with them and work with them. They can't believe someone professional is willing to give them the time of day instead of telling them to "seek psychiatric help."

I tried counseling three different times, and then I gave up. That first therapist wanted to put me on antipsychotic drugs of some sort.

The second one wanted to hear the cool story and *then* put me on medication. And the third one told me that she was going to have to take calls *during* my appointment. "During my appointment?" I objected in disbelief, since I was paying for the damn thing.

The psychotherapist looked at me blankly, apparently failing to see the problem. "Well, some of these people could be suicidal."

"And some of these people sitting in your office could be homicidal," I muttered to myself, wishing I could have carried a weapon. Then I just shook my head, walked out, and laughed all the way home. At least the absurdity of it all was good medicine.

A few days later, I called a hotline myself, the one my health care provider offers for online advice, mostly to complain that the whole mental health system sucked along with the criminal justice system; I was in a bit of a foul mood. I told the nurse who answered, "I am so frustrated with the system because I see I can't get anywhere with it!"

She actually listened to an abbreviated version of my story and didn't tell me I was nuts. She said, "You're fighting to do the right thing, what any good citizen should do. Don't even bother with any mental health therapist. They will only give you drugs. I think your biggest problem is that you are overfocused on one case. You keep picking at that same gnarled knot and if you don't see any progress with it you have no other easier knot to work with or distract your mind. Why don't you develop *more* cases?"

People talk about the "Aha!" or lightbulb moment in their lives when a truth becomes self-apparent, that point when they go, "Of course! That's what I should do!" And I probably owe the rest of my career in part to the advice of that hotline nurse. Wherever you are, I thank you.

DURING THE YEARS I waited for the police to act, I became a regular reader of my local newspaper, *The Washington Post*, and I learned that Anne Kelley's death was not unusual at all.

My original view that this was an anomaly or some freaky circumstance proved to be the height of naïveté. There were dead women turning up all over the Washington, D.C., and Maryland metro area.

In Washington, D.C., alone there were 123 unsolved murders of black females between 1986 and 1996; add in women of other races and female victims killed over the borders of the city in the neighboring states and God knows how many women have been murdered in the area over recent years. If we add in sexual homicides of men and children, the number grows even larger.

Who killed Nia Owens, Dana Chisholm, and Ann Bourghesani? Who murdered Chandra Levy, Joyce Chang, and Christine Mirzayan? Could criminal profiling link any of these cases? Were these murders the work of a serial killer?

How many killers were really out there, living in our neighborhoods, blending in among us, and committing heinous crimes with little fear of being apprehended?

Why had all of these cases remained unsolved?

Dead women were turning up everywhere. It's like when you're pregnant and suddenly you notice how many other women are pregnant.

What freaked me out was that not only were there so many dead women, there were no arrests made on a good many of these cases, particularly on the homicides that were clearly serial murders. A woman doesn't usually end up strangled and naked in the bushes because she had a bad boyfriend. And even if one woman had a boyfriend who raped and murdered her, it's hard to believe each one of these dead women had a separate rapist for a boyfriend. I didn't think so. All indicators pointed to serial killers.

I realized that the Anne Kelley case wasn't an island unto itself. But it was the only knot I was picking on, trying to loosen up a lead, make a bit of progress, and it was driving me nuts. *Why don't you get some more knots?* I asked myself.

That advice was brilliant. Without knowing it, it was precisely what I needed to hear. Many victims of crime find that if they can put their knowledge to use and help someone, maybe the unfortunate event that fate brought them wasn't all for naught. That's when I first got the inkling that while I may never solve the Kelley case, there are plenty of unsolved murders out there. Who committed those?

I printed out what pictures I could find of female victims of unsolved homicides in my county, and I rented a booth at an outdoor festival. I laminated all the pictures and hung them up in a big circle around the table. Under each, I wrote, "Unsolved."

People would walk up and their mouths would fall open.

"These are all unsolved in Prince Georges County?"

"Yes," I'd say.

"You mean nobody was ever caught?"

They'd recognize a picture of Lisa Young, because their daughter had known her at school or because they were in town when the crime occurred.

"Didn't the police ever catch Lisa Young's murderer?"

I'd just shake my head.

Then they would point to another photo.

"They never caught that killer either?"

"Oh, my God," I heard over and over again. "I thought these murders were solved."

The pictures I selected represented just fifteen unsolved cases, less than 10 percent of female victims of homicide in my area over the last two decades. I realized that I should have been trying to get ten guys off the street, not just one. And the problem wasn't that one police department had made an error or that one political decision made by county executives was irresponsible or that one prosecutor was more concerned with his win record than public safety. There was an epidemic throughout our country of sexual homicides and we were obviously not getting these cases solved. Police departments might say, "We have an 80 percent closure rate," but in reality they had a high rate of case closure when the suspect was connected in some way to the victim; the closure rate for stranger homicides was abysmally low.

I estimated that the actual closure rate for serial homicides was 5 percent or less. If you want to get away with a crime in this country, serial homicide is your best bet.

* * * *

MY EFFORTS AT more knots began with Citizens for Case Closure (CCC), an organization I started with the concept of bringing all victims' organizations together to fight for increased case closure, with citizens having rights within their communities to hold police and prosecutors accountable for unsolved cases. But it didn't work. I couldn't drum up enough interest. It was a frustrating beginning in the field of criminal justice.

I realized my message wasn't getting through after an article about me appeared in the local newspaper, in which I stated my belief that law enforcement hadn't done its job in the Anne Kelley case.

I wanted the story to be about police and citizen accountability and how cases like that of Anne Kelley were being swept under the rug, the police refusing to allow the public to know what really had happened and the public apparently not caring to know. A newspaper reporter came to my house and interviewed me. But when the story came out, almost nothing was mentioned about the police and prosecutorial problems in the Kelley case and how there needed to be more accountability. The headline read "Local Homemaker Starts Victims' Rights Organization," and it was a sappy human interest story about a nice lady who wanted to help families who had loved ones with unsolved cases and wasn't I dedicated and caring?

The story made it sound like a very personal campaign, but that wasn't what I was trying to say. I didn't want the story or CCC to be about Pat Brown. I wanted it to be about political issues and criminal justice. But the newspaper didn't see it that way and subsequently, neither did the community where I lived. The reporter wanted to tell a nice story about a local homemaker, but it undermined the serious work I was attempting.

I gave up on CCC and decided to try another approach.

By that time, I had met many victims of crimes, and I started applying my growing knowledge to their cases. That provided a tremendous release. If I couldn't get Walt put away, maybe I could make a difference in the long run. I could help identify other likely killers, or maybe I could change the system so that this didn't continually happen.

WHILE I WAS trying to figure out how to make an impact in cold case closure, I ran a short seminar aimed at teaching women that self-defense doesn't work for us.

There had been a rape in the area, and a number of frightened women rushed to get training at the University of Maryland. I attended one of the classes and was appalled by what I saw. There were guys dressed up in big, fat, red insulated suits. The men in these suits were supposed to come at the women and go *"Arrrrr!"* and the women were supposed to defend themselves. The instructors taught women how to punch and kick and break out of basic holds.

I had practiced martial arts—tae kwon do—and I was pretty good at it. I watched these women throw punches, and I thought, "Oh, my God, they're going to break their wrists!" They always had their wrists cocked downward in a horrible girly position.

"Let me see if I've got this right," I said to the teacher and class. "You are out on a bike path, and a guy the size of Mike Tyson pops up from behind the bushes. You go, *'Yeahhhh!'* and attack him with a little punch you learned in your self-defense class, with your little crooked hand?"

It sounded truly ridiculous just saying it out loud.

First of all, you will break your wrist. Then he will kill you. You'll be dead and the police will wonder how you broke your wrist along the way. Maybe you'll try a kick. Kicks are hard to execute well. Say you want to do a snap-front kick and nail your attacker in the groin. They teach this kind of kick in self-defense classes and you will practice it a few times. To do the kick correctly, you have to get in the proper position, raise your front knee, get your hip behind the kick for power, and then apply your foot to the target with a fast strike. If your attacker is kind enough to stand in front of you until you get your kick in action, you will still probably miss his vital points and softly scuff his thigh. Then he will crush you.

It gets even more amusing if you are in heels.

I went home that night and I said to Tony, "Grab my right arm as hard as you can." He grabbed it and I was immediately kneeling on the floor in agony. I couldn't move my hand. I couldn't get out of that grip if I tried. And he was just doing what I asked. He hadn't snuck up on me from out of the shadows.

Classes like those give women a false sense of confidence. They feel it's safe to walk down a dark street or alley or into a deserted parking garage because they think they actually can beat people up after three hours of "training." They can't. So I started my own program and taught courses on how you *couldn't* survive one of these things.

"You're walking along and suddenly you're hit on the top of the head. What are you going to do for self-defense?"

One of the women inevitably said, "Well, I'm kind of unconscious."

"That is a problem, isn't it?"

My first objective of the class was to knock down self-defense misconceptions. There is no sense signing up for a fight with a heavyweight when you are only a lightweight. I also advised women that if they really wanted to learn how to fight off an attacker they would have to study martial arts or boxing for years. They still will lose against most attackers, the ones who jump out and nail you before you can react, or the ones who are simply too big for you to do anything about. But it is possible that one truly good punch or kick might give you a chance to run like hell.

Once I got through to the women that fighting off an attacker was not likely to have a good ending, I taught them how to think smart and keep from becoming a victim in the first place.

A local television station did a news segment on my program. It was one of my first television appearances and I quickly discovered the power of TV. People paid attention to what I had to say because they saw me on television.

It also framed the real challenge before me: I was a forty-plus housewife with a liberal arts degree trying to tackle crime investigation and justice issues, a totally unorthodox, self-trained crime analyst who hadn't worked her way up in the field coming out of college.

Who was going to listen to Pat Brown, homemaker, sign language interpreter, female, self-made profiler? How could I possibly accomplish the changes that I wanted to make in a male-dominated profession if I persisted in being the lady the media presented as simply a volunteer do-gooder? Women still struggle for respect outside the traditional roles for females and I was stepping into that daunting, mostly male arena. The wall seemed impossibly high to climb.

I realized that since I was over forty, I wasn't going to get in on the ground floor and work my way up through the FBI. And I wasn't going to get in on the ground floor with some other law enforcement organization either. So I made my own way. I didn't have the luxury of time. And I already knew what I wanted to do: profile.

How could I get to the point where somebody would start listening to me and I could start affecting how profiling is used and how serial homicide investigations are conducted? What could I do to communicate with law enforcement and be taken as a serious professional and not as a bored housewife?

I consciously decided that I could achieve my goals if the media liked me and viewed me as a credible resource; then I could use the media to promote the advantages and art of criminal profiling. I set out to become a recognized name in the profiling field, not just locally but across the United States.

I also promised myself that when I was on television, I would always tell the truth. I would speak my mind, even when doing so was risky and might put me at odds with certain individuals or groups. Occasionally, I have been criticized, but it hasn't stifled my beliefs or my voice.

I was still rather insecure, however, and received no outside support. I started with no idea of how to do these things. Not a clue. Could I actually work with police departments in far-flung areas of the country? Could I actually appear on television and speak my mind convincingly?

These were not activities in my comfort zone. I was familiar with my home. I was comfortable with curling up on the sofa with one of my babies. I was at ease doing sign language and interpreting for strangers in their time of need. I needed to convince myself anything was possible, and that I could do the impossible.

I also discovered that I had to become a businesswoman. But I had never run anything in my life. I didn't run any clubs in school; I never even joined any. I wasn't the cheerleader type. This was like shooting myself into space and having no idea how powerful the rocket strapped to my back would be, where I would land, or how I would ever get back to earth. But I learned what I needed to know to get where I wanted to go.

I am still a pretty terrible businesswoman, though, when it comes to victims and casework; I speak to victims for hours sometimes. I give them information and advice and don't charge them. I would make a lousy lawyer. I also still do pro bono work and pay for all the expenses out of my own pocket. I learn a lot and I provide a good service, but I have been told that no one works for free, so why am I doing that? I don't know. I guess it's because I think the work needs to be done.

LIFE AFTER MURDER becomes a life possessed. Victims of violent crime can't think of anything else. They want to learn who killed their loved one. That's *all* they want to do. They don't want to go to the movies, they don't want to go to a birthday party, and they don't want to read a stupid book. They just want to know who killed their daughter.

Unfortunately, their other children suffer. "Why don't you care about *me*, Mommy?" And it isn't that she doesn't, but Mom just can't think about anything else. Senseless murder weighs on one's mind.

I've developed a methodology for those victims. I say to them, "In order to fight another day, you have to be mentally and physically healthy, or you are going to fail in your job to find your daughter's killer. Get a box, a figurative box, put a bow around it, and imagine your daughter is in there. Your memories of her, the whole murder and everything else, are safe in that box. When you get up in the morning, take that box down from the shelf, and talk to your daughter.

Say, 'I'm going to be working on your case this afternoon at three.'
Then put the box back on the shelf, and do what you have to do.
When you're feeling unhealthy, take the box down, and say, 'Honey,
I'm going to go to the movies and laugh for a while. I need a little pres-
sure off me so I can go find your killer.'"

I learned to do this myself. Finally.

THERE WAS A six-year gap from the day I turned in my information on Williams until the day he was finally considered a suspect.
During that time I developed my skills to do criminal profiling. I
trained myself, which has always been a major issue for a lot of people who say, "How dare you?" and "What makes you qualified?"

I hung up a shingle and called myself a profiler, and I've received
a tremendous amount of flak for doing so. In the beginning it wasn't
even the purpose of my studies, but now that I had learned so much,
profiling became my focus. I started a new organization, the Sexual
Homicide Exchange (SHE), and this one would leave behind the political fight to push accountability and instead offer profiling services
and police training and work to transform serial homicide investigations. This organization worked.

FOR A WOMAN who needed to become well known so she could
make solid changes in cold cases throughout the nation, there was
nothing like the one-two knockout punch of the Internet and cable
television.

When the D.C. sniper case exploded in October 2002, it was
the first of its kind, a killer or killers driving around the Washington, D.C., area, shooting people at random. Someone was shot at a
bus stop, another at a gas station, a third while walking down the
street. People throughout our area were afraid to go out in public to
do everyday tasks such as pumping gasoline into their cars and trucks.
The TV news media went into a frenzy seeking out experts for comments and opinions.

We got our first computer when my son, David, wanted to use one for schoolwork. It's hard to remember when the Internet was so new, but David told me I ought to get an e-mail address and I actually asked him why. It seems laughable now. I wouldn't be here today without the Internet. When I incorporated SHE as a nonprofit in 1996, I hired a Web designer and put together my first business Web site. When the D.C. sniper started shooting up the area, producers from cable television tossed "criminal profiler" into the search engine and they found me. I got my big break in television. During this random assault on Washington, I turned up on television for as many as eighteen hours a day. It was a crazy time, and I could be seen on every imaginable local broadcast and national cable news network, talking about who the sniper or snipers might be and what motivated their horrific rampage.

On one show, I appeared with a female ex-FBI profiler who said the sniper would be white. Why? "Because there are no black serial killers!" My mouth dropped open, aghast. I certainly couldn't agree with that view; the perpetrator could be of any race. He—or they—was shooting from a distance. How would I know if they were white, black, Hispanic, male, or even female?

I appeared on a tremendous number of television news and talk programs in a short span of time and, by the time the D.C. snipers—there were two, both African American—were caught, my presence and expertise were established. I received a call from Montel Williams and soon appeared on his show. Then the phone started ringing off the hook. Desperate families contacted me as word got out that I worked pro bono; suddenly I was profiling for families and police departments.

My caseload increased more dramatically and rapidly than it ever would have if I hadn't gone on television and if I charged a lot of money and nobody knew who I was.

In the old days, the only way to be a profiler was to be in the FBI. Police departments didn't hire profilers. They didn't have any money for that. Local law enforcement brought FBI profilers in to work on only the most extraordinary, perplexing cases. But, because of my presence on television and the Internet, I was approached by law enforcement from across the United States as well as families who saw me on television and hoped I could revitalize a cold case stuffed in a drawer in the file room of a local police department.

Television instantly awarded me more clout with detectives because they could hear for themselves what I had to say about cases and how I analyzed them.

My husband was wrong. I was becoming exactly the professional I swore that I would be—although, I have to admit, for all the declaring I did that I would succeed, I can't quite believe things worked out as well as they have.

PART 2

PROFILING
CASES

CHAPTER 5

SARAH

MURDER BEHIND THE BAR

The Crime: Torture, rape, homicide
The Victim: Sarah Andrews, an army private stationed at a military base in the Western United States
Location: Nightclub parking lot
Original Theory: A drug deal gone bad, involving a local gang

Overlooking crucial evidence often throws an investigation off course, and my first case as a criminal profiler proved how true this could be. It was 1996, the year the Sexual Homicide Exchange became a reality.

The 1987 unsolved homicide of army private Sarah Andrews, found brutally murdered behind a bar, was brought to me courtesy of Manny, a bounty hunter–private investigator I met during a class in bail enforcement. Manny insisted the murder was drug-related, and had spent many, many investigative hours funded by the family. He wanted a criminal profiler to support his theory and credibility.

This was the first time since investigating the Anne Kelley murder that I talked to the family of a homicide victim. I heard in detail what the mother and father of a murder victim go through as

Sarah Andrews's parents recounted the years of agony they'd suffered from the time they heard that their daughter was brutally murdered.

Sarah's crime scene was ugly—horrifying—because she was not only raped and left in a parking lot nearly naked, but two coat hangers had been wound around her neck and mouth like the halter of a horse—that's how she was killed. The coat hangers cut back into her mouth and pulled on both sides of her face, and the other part was around her throat. The murderer twisted it together, strangling Sarah to death. She was brutalized, internally as well as externally. The ending of this girl's life was torture.

For parents to think of their child being abused like this, being killed in such a horrific manner, was heart wrenching. And then they had to endure years of agony hoping the murderer would be caught, listening to theory after theory, willing to jump at any little bit of hope, begging the police department for news only to keep hearing those famous words, "We're working on it," when, quite frankly, they may not have been working on it at all.

Listening to the grueling details that made up the last nine years of the Andrewses' lives humbled me. Like that moment of realization at the victims' meeting, I knew that I didn't have it so bad. I may have my frustrations and struggles but I spent every day with all three of my children, happy and healthy. I didn't exhaust my nights being tormented by nightmares of my daughter being murdered only to wake up and realize it wasn't a dream.

Years had gone by and the police were willing to buy into Manny the bounty hunter's scenario. That's where my involvement in the story begins.

CASES THAT INVOLVE American military personnel, especially females, are particularly disturbing to us all. How wrong it seems that men and women who volunteer their lives to serve their country and defend our freedoms are then killed by their fellow citizens within their own country's borders.

The violent criminal, of course, being a psychopath, couldn't care less that his victim was doing him a favor, protecting the very system that allows him so much freedom and providing him a criminal justice system that treats defendants and the guilty better than do most countries in the world.

Sometimes, we see strife between couples within the military, boyfriend-girlfriend disputes. Military life can be a difficult adjustment, stressful at times, and relationships can be difficult to maintain. In the case of Sarah Andrews, there was no evidence of domestic disturbance between her and anyone else, so the detectives did not think she had a boyfriend who went nuts on her.

THIS WHOLE CASE was peculiar from the start. Sarah was murdered in 1987, and I was brought into it nine years later; it was the first case I officially took as a profiler. I can still look at the profile I did on this case and be satisfied with it, which I'm thankful for, because sometimes you look back on your early cases and think, "Oh, my God, did I not know what I was doing?"

It's a good thing they didn't know how new I was to profiling back then. One always feels a bit of guilt in the beginning of such a career because someone has to be the first "victim" and you can only cross your fingers and hope your work doesn't suck too badly. Of course, the same is true for other professions—there is always a first patient, a first client, a first group of students. Someone gets to be practiced on for anyone to actually become a professional.

I opened the Sexual Homicide Exchange in 1996 and was starting to hear from interested people, even while continuing my studies. I met a few questionable characters at a class called "How to Become a Bail Enforcement Agent," and when I finished, I got a cool bail enforcement badge and a jacket with the words "Bail Enforcement Agent" across the back. Manny the bounty hunter–private detective was lecturing at this course. When he found out that I was a criminal profiler, he glommed on to me. He figured he could manipulate me and get me to do his bidding. Families, when crimes go unsolved—and the Andrews case had been on file for an eternity by the time I came into it—will try anything. They become desperate, which is why most of them will try psychics at some point. They want answers for their deep misery; they want closure.

Unfortunately, their emotions are raw and they aren't always thinking clearly, making them great marks for people who will try to make money from their pain and suffering. One of the reasons I always give my service pro bono is to eliminate the notion that I am using these people to make money. Most private detectives don't apply this same standard. And while there are plenty of qualified, smart PIs who do good work, there are even more charging $50 to $100 an hour when the likelihood of solving a murder is slim to none. They accept retainers on cases for which the police don't have any evidence to effect a prosecution and never will, but bleed the family dry nonetheless.

In a stranger homicide, where there is no clue who committed the crime, the PI could interview the entire city and still produce nothing. I've seen families lose as much as $40,000 hiring private investigators and rarely getting answers from them.

Manny convinced the Andrews family that he was working hard on investigating their daughter's murder. He shared his suspicions about drugs being involved and how Sarah was likely taken and executed by a gang.

Even the police believed that was possible in the beginning, providing Manny a credible theory on which to base his investigative forays. There were a lot of drugs floating around the area; it was a major drug hub. Sarah had quite a few friends and relatives who were said to be involved in drugs, and some said Sarah herself could be caught up in something illegal. So the police immediately labeled the homicide a drug-related crime, stating, "We think that she was taken someplace and tortured, and then dumped in the parking lot. It had something to do with the drug trade."

Manny took off running with this concept. There were lots of people involved in drugs around the area where Sarah was murdered, so he could theoretically do lots and lots of investigating and collect lots and lots of checks. Somewhere along the way, he decided— and I still don't understand his decision-making here except to think that it was simply arrogance—that having a profiler agree with him would add fuel to his farce and keep the checks coming. He thought I would replicate his own profile of the crime, a notion that had nothing to do with the evidence but included a large cast of characters for him to track down.

He gave me information about drugs and gangs in the area, thinking I would jump on board with him and inspire the family into thinking he was headed down the right trail. But Manny was a lousy profiler.

I told the family that the murder was a sexual homicide committed by a lone serial killer, not a revenge killing by drug dealers. Manny was not a happy man.

THERE HAD BEEN multiple theories over the years in Sarah's case. There was the drug dealer approach, and then there was the idea that it was a lesbian crime. I thought that was a most interesting one—not correct, but curious.

This theory suggested that it was a lesbian-on-lesbian killing because women don't use their hands to strangle and men do. But this is not true. Men use their hands and other methods as well. Apparently, some folks have never heard of a male killing a woman by ligature strangulation, which I thought was amusing, because one of the most common ways that men kill women is exactly that way. The man sneaks up behind the woman and throws a phone cord, a belt, or the cord of a window blind around her neck. Ligature strangulation can be useful in preventing the woman from clawing at your hands, leaving scratch marks on you and getting your DNA under her nails. Women use ligature strangulation for this reason also and because it's easier than strangling someone with your bare hands, especially more delicate female hands. But in Sarah's case, it made no sense whatsoever. First, she wasn't a lesbian. Second, the woman would have had to be one heck of a big, tough broad to do what the killer did to Sarah.

One of the things I always tell the police and families is that while everything is possible, not all things are *probable*. You can't waste a lot of investigative effort on an extremely unlikely scenario; you have to stay with what makes sense. If we do get some odd information that proves it might be of interest, yes, of course it should be taken into consideration because you shouldn't eliminate anything, either. But truly, every possibility is not really worth looking at.

The Andrews case showed me where criminal profiling and crime reconstruction are useful and that police departments often jump over this part of dealing with a homicide. Sometimes it is a matter of lack of training or funds to hire profilers, but a good portion of the time the investigator just doesn't have hours and hours to spend analyzing one crime when they have new ones showing up daily. He goes with his gut—hopefully, a good one based on years of experience—and, if all goes well, it pans out and the case moves in the right direction.

Police are used to run-of-the-mill homicides, which include most of the homicides many investigators see. One guy pisses off another guy in a bar and gets stabbed. A drug dealer rips off another drug dealer and gets shot. Big deal. They don't feel sorry for the victim and they don't have to do much analysis to figure out the crime.

But Sarah Andrews was different. When the police showed up to view the body lying desolately in the empty parking lot behind the nightclub on that cold March morning, their blood ran cold from more than the winter weather. It was a chilling case that likely still lurks in the recesses of the detectives' memories.

Sarah was found lying on her back, a little bit to her left side— "posed," according to the police. At a distance, she looked almost artistic, like a Botticelli painting, the way she was lying there, her arms out and her legs bent. Her skin looked like marble against the gray pavement, her hair framing her face, a few dark strands across her eyes. Clumps of white snow seemed to accent the landscape. One could almost see a model lounging for the artist as he put brush to canvas, creating his masterpiece. Unfortunately, instead of being viewed in a portrait gallery, Sarah became part of a crime file, the police photographer snapping his picture methodically.

She was naked except for a shoe on her left foot and the leggings hanging off of it. The double coat hanger was at her mouth and around her neck, and that's what was used to strangle her. There were bite marks on her breast and hand. She had been sodomized with an object. Her right nipple was missing. It was a gruesome crime.

Sarah's Maryland driver's license—which had expired—was lying under her body. I will never know for sure whether the murderer tossed it to the ground along with her to say, "Ha, ha, here's who this is," or whether he was sending a message to somebody that he killed Sarah, or maybe he was just being funny, saying, "Look, she's expired just like her license."

One of the things you never know with an offender is what's going through his mind, exactly. Sadly, serial killers and sex offenders are sometimes quite amused by designing their artistic projects. Others couldn't care less and will simply rape, kill, and drive off. So one of the interesting behaviors in this crime is that the killer left Sarah's license with her. We will never know why, but we do know that he had access to her license and he left it at the scene.

When you've worked in the field a long enough time, there's little you can see that would make you say, "This is the worst thing I've ever seen in my life," because in homicide investigations, you see so many awful things. It almost becomes a joke, like, "Well, she's still in one piece. That's fabulous!" Or "She's been stabbed sixty times, but her head's still attached. I think that's a plus." This is the way some investigators actually think and talk after being on the job for a while. It's sad but true. At a mechanic shop where body parts are found scattered about, you might hear if you snuck onto such a scene:

"Do you need a hand over there?"

"I'm not sure we can piece this one together."

"This guy really doesn't have a head for business."

Sometimes the puns just bubble up amid the horror. But, in Sarah's case, there was likely more workmanlike quiet as the police handled the scene.

As a criminal profiler, I am not looking at the fresh crime scene but at photos, which dulls the incoming sensory stuff quite a bit, so I have a great deal of empathy for the detectives who stood there at the scene and saw this horrific sight firsthand. If a crime involves a drug dealer who was shot, that may not be the worst thing they've ever seen. In fact, they might say, "That's messy, but he deserved it."

Then they walk away and forget it. But if the same investigator sees a child who has been murdered, he might completely lose it, because that, to him, might truly be the worst thing he has ever seen.

Sarah was a beautiful young military recruit, brutally killed and tossed like garbage in a parking lot. It took a great toll on the detectives. They wanted to get the perpetrator, that son of a bitch. They asked questions, did the legwork. They pounded the pavement, just like in the movies, hearing stories, compiling leads. Drug dealing was mentioned and it was implied that maybe Private Sarah Andrews wasn't the perfect soldier. Theories flew. Maybe Sarah was in the middle of something dirty; maybe a drug dealer retaliated against her for something she said or did—or didn't do.

Big-city detectives rarely have the time to stop everything they're working on and spend even a day or two exclusively considering the evidence of a single case, analyzing all the photos and reports. And most police departments don't have a dedicated criminal profiler on staff to assist their analysis. The detective, under pressure to get all kinds of other cases closed, may have had no choice but to look at Sarah Andrews and quickly reach some conclusions.

Once he says, "It looks like a retaliation crime," conflicting evidence can be overlooked, because it's incidental to the accepted theory of the homicide at hand.

In this instance, the quick theory was that Sarah was abducted, taken someplace, and tortured—the crime somehow related to the local drug trade—and then brought back and tossed aside in the parking lot. A lot of people were looking askance at army personnel, the kinds of people with whom she was involved, her friends, and anybody she dealt with on a regular basis.

Although there were clearly sexual aspects to the crime, oddly enough, the idea that the crime was a sexual homicide was not given much thought. A serial killer was on the loose, but nobody was looking for him.

IN 1997, WHEN I came in and studied this case, I found some interesting elements that were overlooked, much of which had to do with physical evidence. For an unsolved homicide, this was a case with a tremendous amount of information that could be gleaned from the body and the crime scene. Some crimes have almost nothing useful to help you with an analysis. You have a dead girl in a field, she's been horrifically raped and strangled, and that's all you see. Dead girl, naked, nail marks on her neck, semen in her vagina. That's it. You can't imagine what happened, before, during, or after, except you know she was raped and strangled.

In Sarah's case, the evidence created the threads of a mental video of the entire crime, that's how good it was. I could tell what happened first, second, third, fourth, and fifth in this crime. Very unusual. You don't get this too often. By analyzing the autopsy and crime scene photos, you could tell certain things occurred.

For example, Manny the bounty hunter's original theory conveniently matched the police theory that Sarah was taken someplace and tortured. However, it's not usually the MO of a drug gang to strip a girl because they are angry with her, nor do they leave their victims naked and strangled as a message to anyone. More significant, what ruled out Sarah being carted off to some room to be tortured was that her leggings were left hanging off her one remaining shoe. Otherwise she was completely naked; her right foot was completely clear, but that legging was still hanging off the shoe on her left one.

Everybody knows certain things about specific behaviors because they're male or female or because of the culture or times in which they grew up. As a female, I could tell you exactly why that girl had leggings hanging off her left leg. That's because women who have sex in the backs of cars end up with leggings hanging off one leg. If a man takes a girl home, he has the luxury of time and space. He can lay the girl on his bed, grab both shoes, and pull them off. He can then grab the leggings and, pulling them directly toward himself, peel them off both her legs, and, voilà, he has a nice naked girl to enjoy the rest of the night with.

But a car scenario presents a few problems. It is cramped and usually the sex act is a bit rushed. The man would remove the shoe closest to him, the left shoe if the lady is in the passenger seat of a small to mid-size vehicle and either shoe if the woman is in a larger van with a large space between the front seats or if he has gotten her into the back. He would pull the leggings down until he can free up one foot. He doesn't need to bother with getting the shoe and leggings off the other foot. He has the access he needs to continue with either vaginal or anal intercourse.

This is my hypothesis. She was sitting in the front passenger seat of the offender's vehicle when the attack began. Her killer then pulled her into the back of a vehicle to fully assault her, and this is when he pulled off her bottom clothing just as much as was necessary for him to do what he wanted to. The fact that Sarah was still wearing her left shoe with her leggings attached proved that Sarah never left that vehicle. She never went to any other location. She wasn't thrown into a shed and attacked. She was attacked in the vehicle where the guy did the minimal possible to accomplish what he wanted. The entire crime went down in a vehicle.

That immediately eliminated this crime as a kidnapping for drug retaliation purposes.

NOW WE HAVE a girl in a vehicle. Let's rewind that evidence "videotape" of the scene. Sarah somehow got into that vehicle. Did she get in consensually? Was she forced?

There was an interesting piece of evidence on her body that I believe showed she got into the car without being forced, that she had been sitting peacefully in the passenger seat when the crime began.

Sarah appeared to have known and felt comfortable to some extent with the offender. Having consumed some amount of alcohol and eaten relatively little over the course of the evening, she may have been less wary than usual. She may have been willing to take slightly higher risks or she may have accepted a ride home from someone she felt relatively safe with as an alternative to the possibly riskier situation of walking home alone or accepting a ride with a stranger. I believe that Sarah knew the offender well enough to feel safe, but the offender was not a personal friend or family member.

It seemed to me that it started out with the two of them getting into a van. It would have been a van because she was assaulted in the back of a vehicle with a large, flat cargo area, and I will prove that shortly. But she started out sitting in the front seat—the passenger seat—with the fellow on the left side. There was an attempt at some type of sexual act in the front seat of the van; we don't know how far she wanted to or did go. She had been drinking. She might have thought he was going to take her home. She might have thought they were just going to talk for a bit. They might have gone out to smoke some herb. Who knows what they were doing when they started out in the vehicle, but at some point he attempted to kiss her. And whether she kissed him back consensually I don't know, but at some point she said no.

It is also possible that she simply said no from the beginning and he kept pushing himself on her. With a good amount of alcohol consumed, Sarah might have been slow to resist, maybe even allowing the man to remove her upper clothing. Inebriated women may allow men to go a lot further sexually than they would if they were sober. Sarah may have realized too late, perhaps when he started biting her, that she wanted out of the vehicle. She might have tried to fight him; she had quite strong arms, but she was not that big a woman and she had been drinking. Her killer clearly got control of her.

Sarah didn't like where this was going, and this is when it became violent. At this point, the offender may have attempted to kiss her, then bit forcefully on Sarah's lips. Tearing off the clothes is common with this type of offender and he may at this point have ripped off her clothing without her consent. The offender became more aggressive and violent, biting at the nipple of Sarah's left breast.

He did, in fact, sink his teeth into her left breast because there are bite marks around the nipple. Sarah attempted to protect herself by putting her right hand over her left breast, and so he bit her right hand as well. That is in the evidence. Her left hand wasn't bitten, which makes sense because it is more natural to try to cover one's breast with the opposite hand. Furthermore, her left arm was probably trapped along the seat next to her body. The right hand, according to the physical evidence, bore a bit of grime ground into her palm, proof that she was pushing against the floor. She was fighting. She was trying to get this guy off her, and then she tried to protect her left breast. This was the evidence that proved she was sitting in the front seat, that she hadn't been abducted at gunpoint, dragged off, and attacked.

The offender then most likely grabbed Sarah by the throat with his left hand, choking her and at the same time punching her abdominal area a number of times. She may have passed out at this point.

Sarah was then dragged into the back of the vehicle, onto the floor, and there he pulled off her leggings. He then grabbed two uncoiled coat hangers and twisted them into ligatures about her neck and mouth. He may have slapped her on the buttocks with a belt to wake her up, or the injury to that area may have occurred during the ensuing anal assault.

It would appear Sarah attempted to get off the floor, pushing sideways with her right leg. She may have abraded her left arm and received numerous abrasions and damage to the left side of her face as she struggled and possibly struck the bottom of one of the front seats or other objects inside the vehicle.

Her chipped tooth and the multiple bruises on her chin may have occurred as she resisted the ligatures and her head was slammed downward onto the vehicle floor and onto any object at that location. At this point, the ligatures would have strangled Sarah, whether intentionally or by accident.

(The autopsy report is not sufficiently detailed to determine the amount of pressure the offender used in the attack.)

At the end, he flipped her over, and for his coup de grâce, he bit or cut off her right nipple. At least Sarah didn't feel the pain of this last act as she was already dead in the back of the vehicle.

SARAH WAS NOT dumped out of the van right after she was killed; she lay on the floor for a good long time. This is important evidence as it could help establish a time line and also suggest certain offender behaviors. One of the reasons I know Sarah remained in that van for a period of time after death was that there were two round circles on her butt. The copies of the photos I had of the autopsy were pretty awful and the lighting made it difficult to clearly analyze certain impressions and bloodstain patterns, but I still could make out two odd circles from something that had pressed against Sarah's skin at some point before she was tossed out of the vehicle into the lot. I knew she couldn't have gotten those circles on her butt after she was dumped because there were no objects of that shape under her body where she was found lying.

Each of the circles had almost the same look. They were round and each one left a double outline. But the peculiar aspect to these circles was that one part of the circle appeared a bit flattened. If you looked at the circle like a clock, the area from twelve to three flattened a bit, and the other circle had the one to three area flattened a bit.

"What the heck caused these?" I asked the investigators.

"We don't know what those are," they said.

Nobody ever tried to figure out what made the circles. They just said there were some weird circles on her. Crop circles in Iowa might be inexplicable, but not these. These just required more thought and research. This is the problem when people don't do a crime reconstruction, because that piece of information might well be the missing link. Unfortunately, no one on the case may have time to think and think and think about what some odd piece of evidence might be.

There were guesses, though. Some thought they were caused by a can of chewing tobacco. Others suggested they were imprints of crushed soda cans. They had ideas, but nobody ever actually took the time to find out exactly what they were.

I took the exact measurements recorded in the autopsy, and I recreated those circles precisely. I concluded that I was looking at some kind of a lid, but I didn't understand why it was flat on one side.

I started by going to the local Walmart store. I didn't want to go broke buying every circular item in town, so the only way I could find out what caused the impressions was to walk into stores and press whatever I could find that was circular against my body. I'm sure I made quite a spectacle.

"What is that blonde doing in the hardware section, picking up item after item, pressing the tool onto her arm, saying, 'No, that's not it,' throwing it back, and then repeating it with another one?"

I started running out of room on my arm, so I pressed items against my thigh. Then I went through the neighborhood drugstore, continuing with press tests. This was where I located a one-ounce can of Skoal snuff, which several people thought might be the matching product. When I pressed it against my body, it made two rings, measuring .5 cm apart. But the circles on Sarah's body were 1 cm apart. The soda can concept didn't even make sense. It had only one outside edge.

Eventually, I wandered into a hardware store, went to the paint and enamel section, and picked up a can of Minwax.

"That looks like the right top," I said aloud, to no one in particular.

By that time, I was pretty aware of what kind of impressions various lids would make just by holding them. The Minwax can's lid is embedded into the top of the can, making an airtight seal, so I couldn't pull it off in the store. But boy, it sure looked right. I turned the can over and pressed it against myself, and I said, again out loud, "This has got to be it."

I took out my tape measure and measured the lid area, and it had identical measurements to what I was seeking, the extra thin lines, and the little rim part with two double lines.

I bought the Minwax—to the relief of a befuddled clerk and several customers—and brought it home to my "lab." In order to properly do the lid press test, I had to pry the lid off the can. As the top is forced up and off the can, one side flattens out a little. I took the lid and placed it next to the photos. It looked exactly like the circles in the pictures. I double-checked the measurements of the lid, and the measurements were exactly the same. The flattened edge of the lid top fit into the twelve-to-three spot of the clock face. I determined a couple of Minwax can lids were indeed what left the mysterious rings on Sarah Andrews's bottom.

Could there be something else out in the universe that could make the same marks? Absolutely. But at a certain point, one of the things any detective or profiler has to ask is, "When do I stop looking?" The universe is a big place. I could look for every possible similar lid in all of creation, and I could spend thousands and thousands of hours doing it. But at some point, you have to stop. I stopped here because after looking through dozens and dozens of commercially available products, this one made sense to me, because we were talking about the victim being in the back of a van. What would be on the floor of a van? A lot of guys use various paint and enamel products in their work and hobbies. If they are in the painting business, if they have motorcycles, if they do carpentry, they might have a few cans of Minwax paint or enamel in their vehicle. They might have jimmied off the lid tops and tossed them onto the floor in the back of a van.

My theory was that Sarah lay on top of a couple of Minwax can lids or something very similar to them until she was dumped out of the vehicle.

SOLVING THAT MYSTERY led back to another: Why was she lying in the back of the vehicle?

There were a couple possibilities. One is that the guy killed her while he was on a break and then went back to work. If he was a bouncer at the nightclub, he might have been on a break (sometimes bouncers just vanish for a while), but then continued working until the club closed and the crowd dispersed. He could have been hanging out until four in the morning. (Officially, closing time at the nightclub was two a.m. No one was ever sure if it actually closed at that time, however.)

One of the possible suspects I suggested to the police worked at the nightclub. He was a bouncer, an ex-con with a history as a violent offender and a burglar, and he had been in and out of prison. A big guy, he fit the profile.

So it's possible that Sarah went out to the van to smoke a joint with the bouncer and during that time, he took a fancy to her and wanted to have his way with her. She fought him off, which made him angry. He lost his composure, threw her in the back, and raped and strangled her. All of that takes a lot less time than people ever imagine, ten minutes, fifteen minutes max, because we are talking about someone who acted in a rage—and who was likely on the clock. He was what profilers call a power rapist. He wants what he wants and he wants it his way on his timetable. He gets angry when he doesn't get it, and then he follows through in a forceful, violent way. That's a power offender. He wants to prove his masculinity. *"How dare you turn me down?"* That kind of guy doesn't take long to rape and murder somebody. If he could have controlled her, he might have done less damage to her, but Sarah was known to be a fighter, not someone who would give up without a struggle.

People who don't know better imagine he must have been at this for a couple of hours. But no, he needed to be gone for only fifteen or twenty minutes, and then she's dead in the back of his vehicle. He throws a blanket over her so nobody can see her if they peep in his van windows. He goes right back into the club, cleans up, finishes out the night, and by early morning, with the club closed and everyone gone home, he can go back to his van, now the only vehicle left in the lot.

At that point he could have picked her up by an arm and a leg, flipped her out of the van, and she would have dropped onto the ground. The police thought she looked posed. I didn't think so. If a fairly strong fellow shoved the body to the edge of the car, he could pick her up, swing her body out from the van, and she would have landed just as Sarah did.

Then he would drive away and toss the rest of her clothes—and maybe some of his own—when he realized he still had incriminating evidence in his van.

The bouncer is just one possible suspect and the story above just one possible scenario. Sarah could have left with someone else who was at the club, she could have left and been on the way back to the club with someone. I couldn't say exactly who the killer was but I could tell you he had some connection to the area around the nightclub, wasn't a total stranger to Sarah, did some kind of work painting or fixing stuff, and was relatively strong. And we were looking at only one killer, not two or three, or a gang. Just one sick monster.

We were looking at somebody who likely *did* know Sarah, but not necessarily well. It could have been a casual acquaintance, but the behavior suggested an experienced sex offender. This had nothing to do with drugs.

If an investigator or profiler deduced this originally, the police could have run away from all those other silly theories and focused on sexual psychopaths who were in the vicinity of the nightclub that night.

WAS THE MURDERER someone from the same base as Sarah Andrews? Was it an army guy?

Sarah had bite marks on her breast and hand, and who, on the base, if they had killed Sarah, would want to display her body so it would be found within two hours?

Any army guy knows that the investigators would be all over him in a heartbeat, getting his blood, demanding dental records or impressions of his teeth. He would be at the top of the list.

If the killer was a member of the military, my guess is that Sarah would have been driven back into the mountains that were nearby, her body thrown down a ravine by the side of the road. She would have been discovered weeks later. But because the killer didn't care, or even wanted her body found right away, I doubt her killer had anything to do with the army base.

I believe it was someone who was an arrogant sex offender who didn't think anybody would even consider him. As a matter of fact, one of the reasons he left her where he did was because it amused him. When the police showed up in the morning, he could make an appearance and say, "You found what? A dead girl in the parking lot?"

I think he watched and enjoyed the police spectacle. Or it could be possible he simply dumped her and left town, a smile on his face as the miles added up between him and the body. He could see the police action at the scene in his mind and be nowhere around for them to even interview.

IT IS MOST likely that the offender was employed in a blue-collar profession that did not require high levels of training. He was probably a high school graduate with no college education or a short period of education at a local community college. He would have considered Sarah pretty much his equal, someone who should think of him the same way. In fact, it is possible that Sarah looked down on him a speck, that she thought her army career put her on a bit higher level. She may not have been interested in any romantic liaison with him, at least not when she was stone sober.

He was in possession of a work van that had some objects strewn about the floor. He may have used the van for his work or it may have been primarily for transportation. The presence of coat hangers in the vehicle and possible other tools, such as a wire cutter or pliers, may indicate employment in auto mechanics or welding. He also may have used those tools for personal reasons. The wire coat hangers may have been used to help people who locked their keys in their cars or they may have been used to break into vehicles for the purpose of theft.

The perpetrator may have been employed as a waiter, bartender, or bouncer in one of the clubs the victim frequented. He may have been employed at one of the locations in the same strip mall as the nightclub as a clerk or a security guard. He may have done service work for a local business that used panel trucks for service and delivery. Serial killers tend to kill near their homes or employment, as they spend much of the day trolling for future victims, fantasizing about their conquests-in-waiting, until one lucky day—well, lucky for him, not her—he gets his opportunity.

It is likely that the offender was not in a permanent relationship with a female, due to his lack of security with his masculinity. However, it has been my experience that even men who fail in relationships in general can eventually find a woman willing to enter into a relationship with a weirdo. In this case, it was at least likely that Sarah didn't think the guy was in a serious relationship. He was probably single and a little bit older than Sarah, just enough to make him feel he was more experienced than she was, that he could control her. He was probably somewhere between twenty-five and thirty. The race of the offender was most likely that of the victim. It is, however, not true that this kind of offender kills only within his own race.

The likelihood that the offender was Caucasian has a basis in demography and cultural issues. The makeup of the community was predominantly Caucasian. The victim was Caucasian and socialized with predominantly Caucasian people. These facts make the chances of the offender being white statistically pretty high. But this doesn't mean Sarah didn't have some male friends who were black or wasn't attracted to black men or maybe just went off to smoke a joint—as she had been known to do—with a black male at the club. Statistically, probably white. But, possibly, black.

The perpetrator was probably well muscled, as it appeared he picked up the body of the victim from the floor of the van, swung her by an arm and a leg away from the vehicle, and dropped her to the ground. I know she wasn't pushed from the van or dragged out of it because there was snow next to her that wasn't touched by tire marks or footprints. The van had to have been a few feet from where her body was tossed in an area where the snow had melted. The killer also was able to twist coat hangers, either by hand or with a tool such as pliers, indicating a reasonable amount of hand strength. This would lead one to speculate the offender may have been involved in a blue-collar activity such as auto mechanics or construction. He may also have been involved in weightlifting or other sports promoting general body strength.

SOMETHING ELSE I noted about the Sarah Andrews case: there were so *many* creepy dudes around her.

It was one of those cases in which sex offenders and weird guys were coming out of every hole and from under every rock. One of those fellows suggested by the FBI's ViCAP (Violent Criminal Apprehension Program) crime linkage data base was a guy by the name of Jeffrey Todd Newsome.

This convicted murderer supposedly served in the army at the same base at some point in his career. He was not known to have been in the area at the time of this murder. On the other hand, it was not proven that he was *not* in the area at the time. He was African American; he was not a soldier when Sarah was there, but he might have known the area, been visiting it, and taken off after the crime. However, we have no evidence Sarah ever knew this man, nor did anyone at the nightclub know of him.

At the time that I profiled this case, Newsome was jailed in Alabama for the sexual homicide of a young Alabama woman. He also committed a similar crime in Germany and he was a suspect in a number of other sexual homicides in the state of Alabama.

Newsome fit this profile in a number of ways. He would also appear to be a power-assertive-style rapist, although one could view him as an anger-retaliatory serial killer, the type who kills to get revenge on society and those he considers to have wronged him, usually women. Actually, these two types tend to overlap and much of the time it is the profiler who decides what issues the killer had and what his motive would likely have been. While I sometimes label a killer the power type, the anger type, or the sadistic type, I tend to categorize serial killers in two groups: quick and slow. The slow types are the sadists, the perverts who like to lock a woman up in a dungeon under their house and torture her for days. The quick type just wants to prove that he is powerful, that he can rape and kill and get away with it. Sarah's killer was the quick type. So was Newsome. However, it would appear that Newsome had a very specific MO that consisted of taking the body as far away as possible so that it could not be found. He was adamant about that habit when he spoke with law enforcement. He had previously always used a car, not a van. He tended to blab a lot about his murders. He had been married more than once. The relationships apparently did not last.

There is no evidence linking Newsome to the area on the date Sarah was killed nor is there evidence that he owned a van at that time. A coat hanger *was* hanging from a tree near one of the bodies of his victims. But again, there is no evidence that Sarah Andrews ever had any contact with Newsome. Newsome was definitely a serial killer; he also strangled a girl in North Carolina with a coat hanger. In considering him, we look at what people call "signature."

Everybody who has ever read a murder mystery or watched a movie of this genre knows the term MO, which stands for modus operandi, or method of operation. It means, simply, what you have to do to do the crime. Abducting a girl, that's an MO. The fact that he raped her is an MO. If he tied her up in order to rape her because she was struggling, that would be an MO.

But "signature" is something that the FBI profilers are very fond of and they've gotten a little carried away with declaring it. The signature is what the serial killer does that makes a murder his own piece of artwork. It's an act that he had no reason to do except that he thought it was really cool, and driven by his own psychological needs, he just had to do it.

I think signature elements are not about something they *had* to do. It's something they wanted to do, yes, something that amused them at the time of that particular crime.

In the attack on Sarah, I found a few possible signature elements:

- The killer used the coat hanger contraption that resembled a horse bridle when he strangled her.
- He threw her body into the parking lot.
- He left her body faceup: But was that a signature, or was it just the way the body landed?

It would have been to his advantage to simply drive away and dump her in a ditch. So to me, the fact that he left her in that public location to be found immediately was indeed a signature element that he wanted the fun of her being found.

- Leaving the ID with her was definitely a signature move.
- The fact that he repeatedly bit her showed his style. He didn't have to do that—you don't have to rape anybody, either—but

he obviously liked doing that, and the fact that he excised the right nipple also suggested to me that this was something that gave him an extra cheap thrill.

These signature elements showed us what kind of offender he was. It showed us how he got his thrills. But it didn't necessarily mean that every other crime in which an ID was left with a body or there's a bite mark meant that it was the same guy, and it didn't mean this person would do the same things the next time around. Some guys are repetitive just because they get used to doing something and like doing it. But there are other guys who get bored with what they're doing and don't bother with that particular act next time. We have to be cautious saying that every time there is something unusual in the crime that it's going to be a trademark that he's going to sign every one of his crimes with. That would imply that any crime without that trademark isn't him, and every crime with it is him. That's nonsense. There will be crimes he's committed where none of the elements are the same, and the crime is still his, and there are other crimes that look just like his and aren't his.

Back to convicted rapist and strangler and murderer Jeffrey Todd Newsome.

In Alabama and North Carolina, he strangled girls with coat hangers, but there was something different about Jeffrey Newsome's crimes. He always used a car; he never used a van. He transported the bodies to distant locations. He was proud of the fact that nobody would ever find them, and that's what he told people. So it didn't seem likely to me that he would kill Sarah Andrews and dump her where she was sure to be found the next day.

As a matter of fact, that reliable trait is what did Newsome in. He abducted his last victim in a car and drove her way out into the woods so he could rape and strangle her, which he did. But then his car got stuck in the mud and he found himself in a bit of a bind.

Newsome did what every guy would. He called a buddy.

"Hey, can you come down and help me? My car is stuck in the mud."

Of course, he had a dead, strangled girl out there just yards from his car and when the authorities found the dead girl, they were able to pin it on Newsome. He erred when he went off-road with his sedan to dump the body.

WE KNOW THAT Sarah was involved with several guys, including Suspect #1, a married man, who supposedly made some passes at Sarah. This did not end their relationship, as they were close friends. They were both stationed with the army at the same place.

Suspect #1 was away at military training the night of the murder. He reportedly said to his wife, who was out of town, that he left training to fix a military vehicle, but then he denied that he left training when interviewed by the police. It is odd that his superiors would have no record of his leaving. He would have been driving a military vehicle, not a van. He did not own a van.

Suspect #1 supposedly had some scratches on the left side of his neck. This is the only piece of information that interested me when considering #1 as a suspect. I would have been interested in knowing more about those scratches.

SUSPECT #2 WAS an extremely violent cross-dresser who was imprisoned in another state at the time I profiled Sarah Andrews's murder. He was serving time for the abduction and aggravated assault of his wife and three children.

His brother was also on the same base as Sarah at the same time she was there, and it was possible that Suspect #2 visited or ran drugs there. He supposedly worked the bars in that area—yet another bouncer enters the picture. He may have been introduced to the victim or had access to a van through his work.

His possible connection to a construction company might be important as I believed the two ringlike indentations on Sarah's body were consistent with the lids of Minwax sixteen-ounce cans of wax, polyurethane, or enamel.

Suspect #2 was a strong suspect due to his violent nature and his connection to the murder location. Although he was married, that relationship was bizarre. It was clear from his behavior that he felt entitled to do what he wanted with women. A number of people were frightened of him and hinted at a possible connection to the crime. That Suspect #2 was not in jail for life and had a violent reputation may have deterred people from ratting on him. It was possible he spoke of committing the crime, alluded to it, or people knew he was there at the time of the murder but were afraid to speak up for fear of retaliation.

The only two reasons he was questionable as a suspect were that the comfort level Sarah would have felt getting into a vehicle with this person wasn't there, and the lack of purpose the dump site would serve for this particular suspect.

The police never quite proved Suspect #2 was in the area at the time of Sarah's murder. One of the reasons that some people thought it might be him was because he worked with horses, and Sarah had two hangers wrapped around her head. But if you look at any kind of pornography or bondage, you find lots of women with bridles around their heads. That's the way brutal men control women.

Sarah was bitten, bludgeoned, punched, strangled, and brutalized. This was not done by what you would call a sadistic serial killer. It wasn't that at all. This wasn't a guy who took her someplace and tied her up in his basement and tortured her for days on end. Remember, we're talking about a guy who committed a crime probably in fifteen minutes flat. This was extreme rage, anger, and power that he threw at her all at once. She surely fought back while he was striking out at her.

While she certainly suffered a torturous experience, the perpetrator wasn't someone who set out to torture her. The contraption he put around her head, neck, and mouth was probably more to control her in a moment of anger than anything else.

A danger of the investigator's or profiler's job is that sometimes we glamorize things beyond what they truly are. On the other hand, if the guy was a horse rider, maybe he did know bridles, and it occurred to him this was a nice way to bend up old coat hangers. We can't eliminate that, but we have to be careful not to overstate it, either. So this cross-dressing weirdo was a decent suspect.

I GOT SOME more information about the ex-con bouncer—Suspect #3—who worked at the nightclub. And while the facts were a bit sketchy, what I learned put him near the top of my suspect list. His father owned a repair service. There was no information as to whether Suspect #3 owned a van or his father's business used vans in the course of their work, but it was likely.

It was reported that Suspect #3 suggested to police that Sarah got into a van with two black males the week before her death. He also stated that she danced with a black male the evening of her murder. It was interesting that Suspect #3 found it necessary to implicate black males. Was it an attempt to focus the investigation away from Caucasians or to focus the investigation on soldiers, as most black men in the area were connected with the military at that time? Was it an inadequacy issue? Was it a method of inferring the victim was "loose" because she would hang with black men? Was it a way of saying she deserved to be killed? Or was he just being helpful?

Members of Sarah's family told me that she had mentioned to them that she dated a bouncer from a nearby town, the location of another murder victim. I don't know if this bouncer she reportedly dated was the same one who worked at the nightclub. As a bouncer at the nightclub, Suspect #3 would have excellent knowledge of the movements of the locals and the police in the early hours of the morning. He would have been well acquainted with the back lot of the nightclub. He would have lived in the vicinity and have had no reason to travel out of the area with the body of the victim. It would serve a purpose to leave the body behind the club where he could participate in the next day's activities and have a legitimate reason to be there.

Bouncers at clubs get to know regular customers, are familiar faces to them, and are knowledgeable of their comings and goings and observant of their behavior. It was also possible a bouncer might keep coat hangers available to help customers who locked their keys in their cars. They also might be available to give a ride home to someone.

A bouncer can often leave his job and not be missed for a period of time. It is possible that the reason the police and army CID (Criminal Investigation Division) never identified him as a suspect was because they overfocused on the military connection and ignored possible civilian candidates.

I SAW AN overdose of theories and ideas concerning Sarah's murder that served only to distract and confuse the investigative process. Many of these well-intentioned theories were a result of a lack of familiarity with sexual homicide. Even police investigators and FBI agents can lack understanding of this area of crime and psychopathology. Too many approaches and an unlimited number of suspects led to no progress at all.

One of the main purposes of bringing in a profiler on a case is to reduce the number of suspects and to prioritize investigative avenues. While *anything* is *possible*, everything is not probable. If we give equal weight to any and all theories, we accomplish next to nothing. If we wished to bring Sarah's killer to justice, we needed to focus all our attention and resources on the top suspects.

LET'S REVIEW THE elements of this case that were important and what evidence was valuable in identifying the perpetrator:

There was only one perpetrator in the murder of Sarah Andrews.

From the forensic evidence presented, the attack was not economically motivated and not one of revenge. The offender appeared to be what is called a power-assertive rapist, one of the quick types. No one neat label can exactly explain the behaviors of these kinds of offenders, but the more dominant features fit the behaviors of the offender in this crime.

The power-assertive rapist has doubts about his masculinity and his sexual adequacy. He likes to exert his power in a situation where he can win and feel satisfied. He does not necessarily plan to kill his victim, but he wants what he wants and rising anger and frustration may cause him to escalate into more violent levels of control.

Because of the level of violence exhibited in this murder, some might feel this offender would be more appropriately labeled an anger-retaliatory rapist, one who kills to take out his anger against a particular person or class of persons. It is possible that the invitation to the vehicle was just a ruse to get Sarah into his hands. He would then surprise attack her and kill her. It is also possible that some elements of this type of offender are mixed in with power-assertive elements, and all we really can be sure of purely based on the evidence is that we have a quick, violent attack by a serial killer.

From the presentation of forensic evidence in this case, it would appear that the victim entered the offender's vehicle willingly. There was no evidence of a weapon being employed in this attack. Control of the victim appeared to have been through the sheer physical advantage of the killer. Whether he planned all along to rape and kill Sarah or lost control when she refused him, we will never know. Even the killer might not really know that, as serial killers tend to twist the truth, even in their own minds, claiming, "The bitch made me do it," when, in fact, he planned to do that "bitch" in all along.

All the elements of the murder indicated a violent sexual attack, including vaginal and anal rape, biting of sexual parts, and the removal of a sexual part.

It was not a drug hit, a revenge killing, or a robbery. Therefore, it did not matter who Sarah knew and associated with prior to the murder other than to indicate that she might have crossed the path of this killer and might have known him in some manner. The elements of this homicide indicated an experienced serial murderer, not a first-time accidental killing.

The evidence for this lies in the signature aspects of the crime rather than the MO. The fact that Sarah was lured, attacked, raped, and murdered by ligature does not prove an experienced killer. This MO merely shows that the perpetrator used those methods to assault and kill her. However, the fact that the perpetrator added a second coat hanger to the ligature configuration shows he had a more advanced knowledge of bondage methodology and, perhaps, prior experience with the use of ligatures.

The boldness of leaving the body in a public place ruled out the accidental killing by a well-known acquaintance or novice killer. Also, the fact that the victim was left faceup showed that the perpetrator had no guilt about this crime; in fact, he was damned proud of himself.

The ID left with the body was another bold move. The perpetrator had little fear that he would be identified as the killer. A rule of thumb among killers is to leave the body as far away as possible or as hidden as possible, allowing for the passage of time to obliterate evidence and the memories of any possible witnesses. Killers who leave a body where it will be easily found are extremely arrogant and confident that no one will connect them to the murder. If the perpetrator was well known to Sarah or served in the army with her, I doubt he would have left the body to be so quickly found.

If the perpetrator were in the military, it is also unlikely that he would have left a body with bite-mark evidence to be found; the marks would eventually have been matched up with army dental files.

The lack of any other major physical evidence such as body fluids or fingerprints is more support for the theory of a more experienced killer.

There is a relatively high chance that the killer was watching and possibly involving himself when the police were processing the crime scene. It is my belief that the perpetrator was a local resident, not in the military, and had connections to the crime scene area. He probably has lived in the area for quite a while and committed other murders or rapes and possibly other lesser crimes. He may or may not have a criminal record.

There was no evidence of two perpetrators involved in the crime. The particular kind of behaviors evidenced in this crime led me to believe this killer acted alone. The lesbian theory that was offered by some had absolutely no credibility.

The following is my analysis of the information derived from the murder evidence:

1. One individual committed the murder.
2. The murder was typical of a power-assertive rapist type.
3. No elements of the murder were extremely unusual in the MO.
4. The signature elements of the murder are as follows:
   a. The use of an added coat hanger for the mouth.
   b. The location of the body being placed in a very public location.
   c. The leaving of the ID with the body.
   d. The bite marks on the breast.
   e. The excision of the right nipple.
5. The signature elements of the murder, while in combination point to a particular kind of personality, are not separately unusual in the history of sexual homicide.
6. The killer did not appear to have used a knife as a weapon in this homicide.
7. The vehicle used was most likely a panel van; the body of the victim was probably dumped from the right side of the van from the open sliding door of the vehicle.
8. There was no evidence of binding of the hands or feet.
9. The victim appeared to have been raped and murdered in the vehicle.
10. There was no evidence of torture.
11. There *was* evidence of extreme violence.
12. The entire event probably occurred in a relatively short time, between twenty and thirty minutes.
13. The perpetrator probably used some kind of pliers to twist the coat hangers. He may also have used an instrument to excise the nipple, perhaps a wire cutter.
14. The double-ringed circles on the buttocks of the victim provide evidence that following her death, the body was left in a supine position. It would appear that following her death by ligature, the perpetrator then rolled the victim onto her back and excised

the right nipple. The buttocks rested on two lids that left the marks.

15. The two circles were the exact dimensions of the lids of sixteen-ounce Minwax cans of polyurethane, enamel, or wax. The warp in the measurements is likely due to the removal of the can lids by prying them up with an instrument of some kind. There may have been other possible sources of these circular marks, but we should be careful not to base any investigative avenues on sources that have not been proven to be of those exact dimensions described in the autopsy report.

16. The prioritizing of the suspect list should have been based on the following:

    a. The suspect must have a power-assertive rapist personality.

    b. The suspect must have access to a panel van or similar vehicle.

    c. The suspect must be relatively strong.

    d. The suspect must have no relationship or a minimal relationship with the victim.

    e. The suspect must have some connection to activities using Minwax, pliers, and coat hangers.

    f. The suspect must be very familiar with the area where the victim's body was left.

    g. The suspect, having no guilt about the murder of Sarah, most likely has psychopathic personality traits.

The suspects that I determined deserved top priority in this investigation were as follows:

1. Suspect #3.

2. Suspect #2.

3. An unknown guy—some man described in one report as having lived in the area and who cut off a woman's clothing and bit her breasts: this behavior *was* consistent with a power-assertive rapist.

4. Any new suspect that came to light who matched the characteristics of the profile.

* * * *

THE ANDREWS FAMILY was furious.

She was not killed on army grounds, but there was an army investigation. The Andrews family thought the army did a pitiful job and failed to do what it could to locate whoever killed Sarah. There was a sense on their part that the army abandoned Sarah, one of their own.

I received a lot of notes from her parents over the course of my investigation that showed their frustration. The case eventually ended up in the hands of the local police department, where one detective worked the case and then another. Neither one solved it.

The family also became very angry at me at one point.

Families of victims, when they get frustrated, tend to take it out on the professional people around them. I did a lot of work on this case and came up with a solid profile—and I did it for free. At one point, I uploaded information about the crime to the Sexual Homicide Exchange Web site. Mrs. Andrews had told me that it was okay for me to post certain details about the case—including that Sarah's nipple was cut off—but Sarah's father went absolutely berserk.

"How dare you put that detail about my daughter up on a Web site?" he screamed.

The Andrews family stopped talking to me at that point.

I did it because we were seeking more information, and there is a tendency in certain crimes to repeat behaviors. If somebody knew of a crime where an attacker similarly brutalized a woman's breasts and nipples, it would be a valuable thing to discover. And I wasn't the first one to put it out there; the police had talked about it before, the detail had appeared in some papers, and this was nine years after the crime occurred. It wasn't something only they and the offender knew or at this point would hurt the case.

The parents were still extremely emotional, and they haven't talked to me since.

I pulled the information about Sarah off the site after that and we lost an avenue of bringing in fresh tips.

* * * *

I LEARNED A tremendous amount working on the Andrews case—both about crime reenactment and the sensitivities of long-grieving families.

I told the Andrewses what I thought about the crime and that they were wasting their money having Manny chase useless leads all over the United States. Manny, in turn, telephoned me in a rage, furious that I killed his cash cow.

A month later, Manny dropped out of sight, and I was working on my second case.

CHAPTER 6

VICKI

A KNOCK IN THE NIGHT

The Crimes: Two homicides and one attempted homicide
The Victims: Lisa Young and Deborah Joshi (homicides); Vicki
Davis (attempted homicide)
Location: Maryland and Delaware
Original Theory: Bad friend, bad husband, bad luck

Sometimes crimes don't go as the criminal planned—which makes it harder for the profiler to figure them out.

Anyone working in the profiling profession, as a consultant or as a homicide detective profiling his own cases, soon becomes aware of the incredible intersection of victims, suspects, crimes, and coincidences.

In the second case of my career, I profiled the horrific 1995 near-murder of Vicki Davis, age thirty. Vicki, in spite of being beaten, sexually assaulted, stabbed dozens of times, and having her throat cut, survived the brutal assault and wanted justice.

Harold Painter, the top suspect in the crime, was a mechanic. He was also investigated in the murder of seventeen-year-old Lisa Young, who was murdered six months before Vicki was attacked. Painter lived about four miles from where Young's body was found. Lisa was abducted, stabbed, beaten, and her throat was cut. Her body was found lying on the side of a small, winding road. Not only had Painter admitted to being at the shopping center where Lisa was waiting for a ride home at around the same time, but he once lived with his wife and her best friend on the road where Lisa's body was dumped.

It was the first time I ever heard a case first-person, with the *victim* describing the attempted homicide—Vicki didn't die, but as hard as that guy tried to kill her, she should've been dead.

I'll never forget when she said, "He grabbed me by the hair, pulled my head back, and he took the knife and drove it into the right side of my neck, and there was this horrible crunching sound. And then he said, 'Oh shit, I broke my knife,' and he dropped my head and left the room to look for another one in my kitchen."

If Vicki had died and the killer had taken the knives away with him, I might have thought there were two killers involved because most attackers don't carry a set of knives with them.

The attacker came back from Vicki's kitchen with a new knife and continued cutting her throat until he thought she was dead. Then he pushed her off the bed, tossed a blanket over her, and left.

Vicki, barely breathing, managed to stand up, her chin touching her chest because her throat was cut so badly, and she somehow staggered, still tied up, to the next room and tried to call 911. That's when her thirteen-year-old son came out from hiding, found his mom dying on the floor, and ran to the neighbor to get help.

And she lived to tell her story.

AFTER SENDING MY profile off to the detective on the Sarah Andrews case, I got the call from Vicki Davis.

She wanted me to find out more about Painter.

Vicki was a single mother living in a trailer park. She was furious and frustrated because Painter, the man she identified as her attacker, had been arrested, kept in jail for almost a year, and just before the trial date, the case was dropped. The DNA on a cigarette at the scene not only didn't match Vicki or anyone else connected with her home, but didn't match Painter either. No other evidence was left by the attacker; there were no fibers, not enough semen for DNA tests, no blood—nothing. At least that was the claim made by the state prosecutor's office, and Painter was released.

Vicki was at home asleep on the morning of September 19, 1995, when she says a thin white man, about five four to five six, with shoulder-length dirty brown hair, a beard, and a mustache, knocked on the door of her trailer at 1:52 a.m. and said, "My car broke down, can I come in and use the phone?"

She said no, because she was home alone with her young son.

He said his name was Jack Wilson and she offered to call someone for him. He gave her a local number and she called it, but the man who answered did not know anyone by the name of Jack Wilson. She told Jack what happened and he left.

But the man's appearance at her door in the middle of the night unnerved her enough that she called the police. And she was right to do so—even if the police never did show up—because fifty minutes later there was a loud bang at her front door and she got out of bed to find Jack Wilson in her kitchen. The lights were on and Vicki got a good look at the man as he grabbed her and held her at knifepoint in the living room.

"You made me have to break into my car, bitch. I locked my keys in it and you wouldn't let me call anyone for help," he hissed at her.

The attacker blamed her, justifying why he was going to teach her a lesson. Then he pushed Vicki past her son's room, toward her bedroom. She grabbed the doorframe to stop him from taking her to the back and raping her.

"Stop fighting me, bitch," he growled, grabbing at her hands. She pushed him against the wall and actually pinned him to it but she couldn't hold him there for long. As he pushed her away, she made a desperate lunge for the knife and they grappled over the weapon. He won. He had had enough of Vicki refusing to give in.

"If you don't stop fighting me, we will kill him," he told her, breathing hard. Vicki thought the "we" her attacker was referring to might mean someone else was outside the house.

"Just let me tie you up and I won't hurt your son." His eyes were cold like a snake's and he held her against the wall with one hand, his other hand waving the knife at her face.

Vicki was terrified and exhausted. She knew she couldn't fight him much longer. *To save my son,* she thought, *I have to cooperate.*

She let him tie her up—with a Nintendo game cord—and she immediately knew it was the biggest mistake she had ever made, as he cut her undershirt and panties off with the kitchen knife and gagged her with them. He began kissing her, sucking her breasts, and rubbing her legs. He didn't technically rape her, but he did roll her onto her stomach, putting something under her belly to elevate her buttocks. He then masturbated and ejaculated on her buttocks and back.

How stupid is this? she thought. *The guy comes all the way up here to rape a woman but doesn't bother—or can't?* Instead, he masturbated, and when he finished, he took out a knife and started cutting Vicki's throat.

He cut her throat on one side, then the other.

Oh, my God, Vicki thought, *he's going to kill me.*

The attack continued.

When he tried something different, stabbing her in the neck, his thrust literally snapped the blade.

"Look!" he said conversationally, as if he and his victim were sharing an evening meal. "I broke my knife!"

He went to the kitchen, rifled around for another one, came back, then stabbed her over and over until her throat was cut on both sides and he had stabbed her repeatedly in the back and neck.

She should have been dead.

But she wasn't.

"Aren't you dead yet, bitch?" he said a number of times, and eventually he thought she *was* dead because she stopped twitching. He pushed her off the bed.

Vicki later remembered that her head hit the nightstand by the bed when she went down. She didn't think it much mattered that she hit her head, because if this wasn't death, it wouldn't be long.

The perpetrator threw a blanket over her and walked out, taking with him a few items of little value.

Vicki lay there until she was certain he was gone. Then this remarkable woman, bleeding to death, throat cut, stabbed many times, managed to get up despite the fact that her feet and hands were tied, and she staggered to a telephone. She knocked the receiver off the hook trying to call 911.

Just then, her son—who was pretending to be asleep during the attack—came out and found her. Seeing that her son was safe, Vicki muttered with her last conscious breath, "Go get help!" and passed out. Her terrified boy ran next door, banged and screamed until the residents came to the door and called 911. Emergency medical technicians came and Vicki miraculously survived.

It's just mind-boggling. The damage that was done was seemingly beyond repair. It still amazes me, and Vicki, that she survived one of the most horrific attacks imaginable.

It seemed like one victim was going to see justice. She lived to be able to identify her attacker.

One month after the crime, Painter was arrested. On October 1, 1995, a neighbor called to report a suspicious person in Vicki's yard. He was sitting in a red pickup truck near Vicki's home. The arresting officer noted that not only did the driver match the description of the suspect but the composite drawing the police sketch artist did was actually taped to the windshield of his truck! Painter told the officer that he had been visiting his daughter, who lived in the same trailer park, and had just left Vicki's trailer, where he had said a prayer for her. He was photographed, interviewed, and released.

The next day, Vicki picked Painter out of a lineup of six photos and said the man in the picture was the man who broke into her home, sexually assaulted her, and stabbed her.

He was arrested again four days later when Vicki's son independently identified Painter from the six photographs he was shown.

"He seems to have some kind of thing going on in his brain that he thinks he is God," Vicki later said of Painter. "He told the police that he felt strange vibes that told him to go to my house and burn a candle and pray for me right after the attack. When the police finally arrested him, they told me that during the entire ride to the courthouse, he was chanting."

Painter said he was in the area at the time of the attack on Vicki, visiting a former wife and stepdaughter who lived in the same mobile home park.

That should have been the end of the investigation.

But in reality, the victim survived and the case died in the hands of the criminal justice system. Vicki knew something was wrong early in the investigation when the police seemed determined to keep the crime out of the headlines.

"They did such a good job of keeping quiet that it really pissed me off," she wrote to me in an e-mail. "I didn't realize what they were doing until it was too late. The detective actually pretended to cry because he knew I was a caring person [and] he led me out through the back of the courthouse to be sure that I didn't talk to reporters. He also told me not to talk to any of the TV stations that were calling me. *Stupid!!* I was so caught up in making sure that everything was done right and that *I* would not mess up anything that I believed all the crap they fed me along with it. I wish I could have done things a whole lot different. I would have walked out of the court and screamed at the top of my lungs to all the reporters that the system is shit.

"I had seen on TV that the victim is allowed to help with her own case. When I asked the detectives about that, they said, 'No way.' I'm sure that they are so busy that they are either overlooking and missing a lot of good info, or they just don't want me to know the real story about how much they have misplaced. I gave them everything, I made sure that I was writing notes while I was in ICU, giving them all the details. They were very accurate. How could they not be able to use it?"

The Delaware grand jury decided that the state had enough evidence against Painter and handed down an indictment charging him with first-degree attempted murder, burglary, kidnapping, first-degree unlawful sexual contact, and possession of a deadly weapon during the commission of a felony.

Painter pleaded not guilty.

The case was continued several times as prosecutors waited for the FBI to complete its DNA tests on evidence. Meanwhile, Painter underwent a psychiatric exam in which he said he did not know where he was or what he was doing on September 18 or 19, 1995. A doctor diagnosed Painter with "undifferentiated schizophrenia" but declared him competent to stand trial.

"I find no reason to believe that he would not have been responsible at the time of the crimes," she wrote.

Two days before the attempted murder trial was scheduled to finally begin in Delaware, Vicki Davis was notified that Painter would be released and would not be going to trial for attempting to kill her.

"I called in and I demanded that the detectives explain how he could have done this to me and not left any hair or fibers," Vicki wrote to me. "I was so confused. . . . I wish I had thought to say at the time, 'Did you guys just screw up?' But I was protecting the detective that had told me confidentially that the evidence was lost."

PAINTER ALSO BECAME a suspect in the 1995 murder of Lisa Young.

Lisa was a seventeen-year-old living in a state near the nation's capital. A junior in high school, she left her after-school job at closing time and sat outside on a brick flower box with two bags of clothes she had purchased earlier and a soft drink, waiting for friends to pick her up. Then she just vanished. There were reports that she possibly got into a maroon or burgundy car, leaving her belongings on the sidewalk.

The next day at 5:30 a.m., a passing motorist found her fully clothed body about a mile down the road. She had been strangled, her head scored with knife wounds, and her throat cut. Her jewelry was stolen.

Painter became a suspect in the homicide investigation because he had a car that was similar to the one that allegedly took Lisa away, and he was in the area at the time. He was in jail awaiting trial in a nearby state, and this homicide looked awfully similar to the assault six months earlier of Lisa Young (though that case was ultimately dropped). The detective working the Young case decided to pay Painter a visit in jail.

The detective interviewed Painter and found that just prior to his arrest, Painter had disposed of his late model, burgundy car—had it crushed, actually—because, he said, "It had a bad smell in it."

There was white dog hair from a boxer found on Lisa's body. According to neighbors, Painter got rid of his dogs right before a detective showed up to question him.

It seemed like another easy case to close. "This is the guy," the detective said.

Lisa's mother, Jessie Young, called me in January 2000. She wanted my help investigating her daughter's 1995 murder, but asked that we keep it quiet for four months, until after the fifth anniversary of the crime passed. She said she had not seen the autopsy report—nor did she care to—and she didn't want me to see it, either. She wanted to keep the details of her daughter's death private.

PAINTER, EVEN IF he wasn't responsible for the attacks on Vicki and Lisa, certainly seems to have anger-retaliatory issues with women.

My take on him is that he views women as the cause of his problems and may have sought to regain his lost power through assaults on females. Painter certainly exhibited anger and violence five years earlier when he assaulted a girlfriend who told him she was leaving him. He was arrested but got only one hundred days of community service working in a food bank.

So the attacks on Young and Davis could have been perpetrated by him, too. They reflect similar, though escalating, anger and violence. Both the Lisa Young murder and the assault on Vicki Davis showed premeditation, some level of skill controlling the victim, and a violent rage against women. Although I could say there were elements of sadism present, the purpose of the assaults appeared to stem more from anger.

The offender in the Young and Davis crimes brought a knife with him but used materials present at the scene for the binding of the women. He planned part of the crimes but not all of them. However, it should be noted that the offender exuded a good amount of confidence and may have felt no need to bring items he knew would be readily available and less traceable.

Both crimes showed evidence of overkill. Much more violence was done to the women than was necessary to kill them. Vicki by all rights should have been dead, and the assault on her showed an uneven temper. The offender was calm when he was in control and became enraged when he lost control.

An experienced offender committed the crime against Vicki. The man who killed Lisa also showed some level of experience, but not quite as much as in Vicki's assault. Were these two different offenders or did the same man commit both crimes, Lisa's and then Vicki's, showing more capability in the later crime once he acquired more experience? The calm manner in which he assaulted Davis without being terribly hurried showed practice. He took care to not leave evidence and he even commented to Davis that he had "seen it all before." He put effort into restraining her and controlling the crime scene. Therefore, I thought it was of the utmost importance to look for unsolved rapes and homicides that occurred prior to 1995.

My investigation revealed that Painter was a homebody, and it seems more than coincidental that both the Young and Davis crimes were committed within a couple miles of his residence or the residence of someone he was visiting. I also looked at other crimes that occurred near his previous addresses and places of employment.

I concluded that earlier murders in these areas that did not include binding and knife wounds should not be ruled out as possibly being connected to Painter. Often, earlier crimes of the perpetrator are less complicated and take less time. The perpetrator's choice of weapons can change due to acquired preferences or availability.

While we may think that the place where a body has been dumped is significant, in fact, most offenders dump a body where it is convenient rather than for some emotional reason. Some pick places where they feel the evidence will be eliminated. For example, a stream could be chosen because it will wash away DNA and fibers or simply because it was available. Perhaps the offender prefers dumping the body in a stream, but there are none nearby, so he instead chooses a field. Most of the time, the dumping of the body is done in the most expedient way. *If,* however, closer locations are ignored, then there may be a specific reason for a particular dumping location. Sometimes the offender remembers a place nearby where he had a picnic and thinks, "Hey, that place had some nice woods!"

My profile of the perpetrator is someone who liked to be in control. He seemed to savor the moment. It was my feeling that any crime committed by this individual would take a reasonable amount of time. He would not be the sort of anger-retaliatory killer who was in and out of the scene in a matter of minutes. He had some aspect of a power rapist in that he spent time talking to his victim. A power rapist likes to ask his victims about their sexual experiences or how well he is performing. Sometimes he will verbally threaten the victim—he enjoys humiliating her and watching her squirm. He would have liked to see the fear in the face of the woman and he would enjoy the act of killing. However, he would not exhibit the length of time used by a sexual sadist who meticulously planned the killing and torturing of a female for an extended length of time. He would not need to bring the woman to a fixed location nor would he need to bring much more than a knife along for the job—if anything at all.

I believed the perpetrator picked victims he could easily control. He would be unlikely to choose victims from a level of society above him; women who were highly educated or wealthy, for example, would make him feel inferior. He would operate where he felt comfortable. Although neither Young nor Davis was involved in prostitution, I would not discount the possibility that the perpetrator might choose victims who were. Even if he was not the type to use such services, availability is often the reason certain victims are chosen.

Certainly the case against Painter should have gone forward. The grand jury indicted him, and it is a travesty of the criminal justice system that the case was dismissed. Last I heard he was driving a tow truck; isn't that great news for any woman who calls for help?

I DON'T KNOW if Painter was the attacker, but there was quite a bit of circumstantial evidence linking him to both Lisa's murder and Vicki's attack.

That wasn't the half of it.

When Painter was being interviewed by a detective about Lisa's murder, he suddenly blurted out, "Oh, by the way, tell Tracie Andrews I'm sorry about Sarah."

When I heard that, my jaw dropped.

The Sarah Andrews case? What the hell?

Sarah Andrews's parents lived in the same state as Painter, but Sarah Andrews had died 2,000 miles away and ten years earlier. How would Harold Painter know anything about Sarah Andrews? Why did he say, "I'm sorry about Sarah"?

It turned out that he *knew* Tracie Andrews, Sarah's mother, and he knew her very well. She was the longtime best friend of Painter's ex-wife, and the two of them had stayed in Tracie Andrews's house when she lived on the very road where Lisa Young's body was dumped. It was an incredible coincidence—if it was one. But despite all the circumstantial evidence—the car, the boxer dogs, and the bizarre-as-all-get-out connection to Sarah Andrews—Painter was never arrested for the Lisa Young murder and was never brought back in for the attempted homicide of Vicki Davis. The police were still convinced that he attacked Vicki, even though the DNA on the cigarette found at the scene in the living room didn't match him or Vicki. I agreed with them; something seemed bogus about the DNA testing because everything else pointed toward Painter, and when I called and left a message for the FBI lab technician she called back and angrily told me how great a job she had done. I thought that the fact I got a call back was strange enough in itself (because I had no official capacity in the case and I wasn't a journalist), but the technician was working overtime to say she hadn't erred. Eventually, I caught up to the original detective on the Young case in the summer of 2000 and had a nice conversation with him while he worked his part-time job guarding a liquor store.

"He killed Lisa Young and attacked [Vicki Davis]. I never doubted that."

But, unfortunately, no court ever proved he was guilty in either case.

And did Painter also go out west and kill Sarah Andrews?

I took the information and sent it to the present detective on Sarah's case, including pictures of Painter's smiling face and his dental work. If it wasn't the bouncer or the cross-dresser, the two top suspects that I came up with in that crime, could it be Harold Painter?

Sarah was sexually assaulted with an object, and it is curious that the Davis attack, with which Painter was initially charged, showed anger and rage, though not penetration by him. Perhaps in both cases the perpetrator did not commit rape because he could not perform the act to his satisfaction with his own penis.

Davis says that Painter was her attacker and that he demanded that she move her bottom around while he masturbated on her, then stabbed her over and over. So it wasn't really a surprise when Painter's ex-wife told me that he called himself a "needle-nosed bug fucker" because his member wasn't much to speak of, and he didn't think it was very useful, she said. He had a complex about it. If he was the attacker, it could follow that he would use a substitute—he didn't think his penis would be effective in that situation.

Three women, none raped in the "normal" way. But they were all sexual assaults that brought a thrill to the one who did them.

The perpetrator of the crime against Sarah Andrews could match my profile of Painter alone, but one of the things I've learned as a profiler is that there are a lot of Harold Painters out there. The bouncer at the bar may have been another, and the cross-dresser could be one, too. Did one of them do it?

On television news we often hear of reporters doing a sex offender search of a crime-ridden area and finding an incredible number of convicted offenders within one mile of some missing child. The viewer thinks, "They found what, seventy? Is every one of my neighbors a sex offender?" And the answer is . . . maybe. They intersect, and they crisscross, so you have to be careful when you arrest and convict these guys that you don't mistakenly haul in someone who didn't do it just because he may have a similar MO to the person who did.

There are only so many ways a person can commit a crime, even when the supposed signatures have been identified. And sex offenders aren't always particularly creative. They may do the exact same things as the next guy. Once in a while, we'll find one who's really inspired, but mostly we see repetitive acts. Sometimes they get their ideas from books or movies or from the newspapers (which can spawn copycats). But a good portion of the time they do something that just comes naturally to them, like spitting on the victim, leaving her in a sexually provocative position, or throwing a blanket over her body. These simple behaviors are common to many offenders, making it look like the same guy—but it's not.

The fact is, that seemingly guilty offender could have committed the crime, but then again, maybe one of nine other guys in the area could have committed the same crime. So unless we have actual evidence proving it was one individual, you don't want to say, "Boy, that sure looks like Painter, it must be him." Well, it may not be Harold Painter. It may be the bouncer or the cross-dresser. It could be someone else altogether. That's the police's job. If they analyze the crime well, then their job is to gather enough evidence to support probable cause to bring the suspect in and continue uncovering further evidence that will put him away.

WHILE I HAVE my theory, ViCAP—the computer methodology that the FBI uses to input all the information about a crime and try to match up potential suspects—matched up the Sarah Andrews homicide to Jeffrey Newsome.

I don't object to using ViCAP in that way, but I would prefer to see a suspect bank so that someone who had been connected with a crime, such as Harold Painter, might be flagged and noted. We could put a list of all the people that Sarah knew into ViCAP and boom, Painter would have shown up as a homicide suspect. We need more linked databanks.

We also need more cooperation between police departments. We need more experts to be brought in to work on the aspects of a case for which the detective is not trained or for which he lacks the time.

If, back in 1987, they had a profiler or trained crime analysts come in, and spent time reconstructing this case on that mountain of physical evidence, they might've gone down a different road a long time ago. That's one of the reasons I believe so strongly in training law enforcement officers in crime reconstruction and profiling and giving them, as individuals, fewer cases to work on.

HAROLD PAINTER WENT on with his life. The only thing on his record was that he assaulted his girlfriend. Other than that, there was nothing against him except that many people thought he was creepy.

Eight years later, I received an e-mail from someone who said, "You need to talk to Allison, Tommy Stern's ex-wife, about the Lisa Young case."

Stern knew Lisa Young at the time she was murdered. They went to the same high school and were friends, or at least acquaintances.

Stern apparently had a thing for Lisa, according to his ex-wife. Well, ex-wives. Allison sent me on to the other ex and she told me the exact same story! There is nothing like a spurned woman when it comes to getting information on a suspect. Both exes said Stern had a tattoo that said "In memory of Lisa Young" and a framed photo of Lisa next to his bed, the kind with a cute little one-stem-rose vase attached to it, which, when you are married, is not proper bedside decoration.

The ex-wives claimed Stern was dangerous and violent, had been in and out of mental hospitals, and that when they had sex, he strangled them and sang, "We are killing Lisa, we are killing Lisa."

I asked both ex-wives this question: "When Tommy was in high school and living with his family, did they have any family pets?"

I had no clue what these family pets could be, but there was that white dog hair on Lisa's clothing. One ex-wife said, "When he was in high school, his family had some white boxers."

I said, "Oh, Lord."

A new suspect had entered the Lisa Young mix. Tommy Stern was the better suspect, because when I profiled this case, I was always irked by the fact that when Lisa left work that night, she was standing on the curb waiting for a friend. She got into a car, quite willingly, it seemed. Her drink didn't fall on the ground; it was just left on the sidewalk. It didn't appear that she was abducted; it looked like she got in the car without being forced. Maybe she sat down just to chat for a second and off he went with her.

Lisa didn't know Painter. I didn't think any girl would get in a car willingly with that man. But she did know Tommy Stern, who was close to her age, so she might have had no problem jumping in his car while she waited for her ride to show up.

On top of this, just to add more to the mix, I later heard that a man was arrested for impersonating a police officer. He had handcuffs in his car. He lived on the same road where Lisa was found. Many a serial killer has carried handcuffs in his vehicle and pretended he was a cop. A suspect like this *had* to be considered.

Another crime occurred just a few months after Lisa was killed. If you drove out of the shopping center from which Lisa was abducted, passed the street where she was eventually found, and continued straight down the road two more miles, you would run into a house where another woman was murdered, the home of yet another unsolved homicide, that of Deborah Joshi.

DEBORAH JOSHI WAS stabbed seventeen times in the living room of her home. She was not raped, but her husband found her dying on their living room floor. A few pieces of jewelry and a big plastic container of quarters were stolen. Her vehicle was also missing.

I was not impressed with the way the police profiled this crime. The husband, Davis Joshi, was their chief suspect for a long time.

According to the police, Deborah came home from work in the afternoon and changed into more comfortable clothes. Her husband was not yet home and they didn't have any children.

A next-door neighbor, Ray Hammond, told the local newspaper that her SUV flew out of the driveway that day. They had two dogs, and the dogs never barked, according to Hammond. He was working in his garage on a project and he responded to the sound of a car by looking through the windows of the garage door. He saw what looked like a black man—at least a "dark" man, he said—behind the wheel.

Deborah was black, and when I went to her house, I expected that her husband might be as well. However, Joshi is an Indian name, and Davis, it turned out, was of Asian descent; he was a Trinidad Indian. It's possible that he might be mistaken for a black man if he was seen driving by very quickly. The SUV was found a mile away in a neighborhood strip mall. The plastic container that held the quarters was found in an apartment complex parking lot across from the mall but the quarters were gone. Nothing else was ever discovered.

The logistics didn't support Deborah's husband as a suspect. He would have had to leave his vehicle at the strip mall, walk home, kill his wife, then take her vehicle back to the strip mall, get in his own car, and drive back to the scene.

She was dying when the ambulance arrived. If he did it, he would have wanted to make sure she couldn't speak and would have made sure she was dead.

There was no evidence ever found in his vehicle. Also, there was no blood evidence connected to him, which one would expect if a woman was stabbed seventeen times. Davis would have committed the perfect crime in the short amount of time between Deborah's arriving home from work and when he got to the house just shortly after dark. The police looked at him right away, as they do when a married woman ends up murdered. Usually hours or days separate the time of a murder and the husband's "discovery" of the body, leaving plenty of time to get rid of evidence, wash up, vacuum the car, and so on. Yet in the Joshi murder, the police found not a shred of evidence linking Davis to Deborah's death in spite of how quickly the police were on the scene of the crime.

I went to the strip mall parking lot where Deborah's car was dumped, and I couldn't believe the coincidence: Harold Painter lived but two blocks west of that strip mall. And Walt Williams lived two blocks to the *east*.

Davis thought his dying wife muttered something about either a guy in black or a guy who was black, but she was dying, and it wasn't clear whether he was leaning on Hammond's description of the suspect or he really heard her say that.

I asked the police if they interviewed Hammond, and they said no, they didn't spend any time with him. I knocked on his door and said I was there to ask questions about the crime.

"Come on in," he said.

He had a glass of scotch in his hand, and he was smoking a Marlboro cigarette—the kind found on the ground outside a window at the crime scene and a brand that was not smoked by the Joshis. An interesting coincidence, but of course it is a popular brand.

Hammond welcomed me into his house, chitchatting about this and that, quite friendly. But he quickly turned the conversation to a sexual note, and I became uncomfortable. "So, what's a gorgeous woman like you doing in the detective business? I'm a lucky guy to have a sexy lady like you show up on my doorstep." He leered at me. *Why is this guy making sexual innuendos toward me?*

I noticed, when I came through the front door, he went behind me, let the dog out, and shut the door, making sure it was locked. That seemed innocent enough. But then he walked to another door and locked that one, too.

My skin began to crawl. *What was he doing?*

Hammond talked about the crime and walked me to the garage, where he said he would show me where he was when the murder happened. He reminded me that he hadn't heard the dogs bark when Deborah was being assaulted.

I was getting nervous about Hammond.

Did the dogs not bark because it was the husband who committed the crime? Or did the dogs not bark because the perpetrator was someone else they knew? Or maybe the dogs did bark and Hammond simply didn't hear them. Or could he be lying about it?

"I saw the car fly out of the driveway," he said, "and I saw this black man . . . well, dark, like it could have been Davis. . . ."

My mind was racing as Hammond put down the garage door to set the scene. As he did, he said something wholly inappropriate and even more anxiety inducing.

"Don't worry," Hammond said. "I'm not going to do anything to you."

Excuse me?

Why would he assume that I was thinking he was going to do something to me? Why would this cross his mind? Why was he saying this?

A sense of dread crept up on me as the door came down. I noticed that the windows were completely smeared, like they hadn't been washed in years. I found it hard to believe that that man could have seen anybody inside a vehicle from this garage.

I could feel panic just about to overtake me. I suddenly realized that I was alone with a stranger, and one who was making me feel increasingly uncomfortable. I wanted to get out of there fast. I pulled the phone out of my pocket, pretended I had dialed my office really quickly, and as he turned to face me, I said, "Oh, yeah, I'm over here at Mr. Hammond's house, next door to the Joshis. . . . Yeah . . . I should be through with the interview in about ten minutes, so I'll be back at the office by five thirty."

He suddenly looked at me coldly, and he said, "You can go now." He marched me straight to the front door and out of his house.

Hammond's behavior and the incongruity of his story made me suspicious.

Was he involved in the case? Or was he just a really weird neighbor?

I wonder to this day what would have happened if I hadn't managed to fake that phone conversation.

I STILL HAD a multitude of questions about Deborah's murder.

Why would anybody take that big plastic jar of quarters?

Did they need the money or was it more of a diversionary tactic?

Did somebody go into the Joshi residence to steal something or was it a rape gone wrong? Did Deborah fight back and a rapist ended up stabbing her before he had any fun, decided to steal a few things, and used her SUV to get home? Could the killer be Painter or Williams?

Was someone burglarizing the house when Deborah came home unexpectedly early from work? Was she killed in a panic? Was the SUV just driven to the strip mall to make it look like the killer lived farther away? Was Deborah killed because she could identify the man in her house? Could it be the neighbor, Hammond?

Or was it really Davis staging a crime to cover up offing his wife?

The only suspect was the husband, and no one has been charged.

CHAPTER 7

MARY BETH
A METHOD OF OPERATION

The Crime: Homicide, burglary
The Victim: Mary Beth Townsend, fifty-two, librarian
Location: Condominium, Virginia
Original Theory: Killed by her fiancé

When Mary Beth Townsend, a fifty-two-year-old librarian, was found dead in the closet of her condominium, the detectives had the case solved within hours. A couple days later, after grueling hours of interrogation, her fiancé confessed to accidentally killing her during an argument.

Unfortunately for the police, his forced confession didn't match the evidence when the autopsy came back.

MARY BETH OWNED a condo in Virginia that she shared with her fiancé, Sam Bilodeau. They had been together for eight years, and after seven years of living together, they were finally, happily, preparing to marry. They were also building a house together on weekends and planning a honeymoon trip to Paris.

Mary Beth and Sam got along well in their eight years together.

Her son, Art, who lived and worked in the area, knew Sam well, liked him, and had no issues with him.

On Friday, August 21, 1998, Sam left at 6:45 a.m. to arrive by 7:00 for his job at the Home Depot, where he worked on the loading dock. Mary Beth stayed behind. She took the day off from the library, where she had worked for fifteen years, planning to go down to the pool for a swim, something she did every day. Later in the day, Sam called Mary Beth but she wasn't home. He thought she must be at the pool or running errands.

When Sam finished his work shift around 6 p.m., he drove home expecting they'd do what they always did on Fridays—drive over to the property where their house was under construction and then spend the weekend doing whatever needed doing. Oddly, Mary Beth's car was not parked in the driveway out front. As he unlocked the front door of their condo, Sam noticed that only the bottom lock was locked; the top, a dead bolt, was not. He walked into the condo and noticed that Mary Beth's purse and tote bag were not there, but that made sense because she was out with the car.

I guess she'll be coming back soon, because we have plans for tonight, he thought.

He also noticed that the condo had been freshly vacuumed, which was a little odd because that was a task usually done over the weekend.

But she didn't come back, didn't call, and Sam soon grew wary. *Where is she? What's going on?*

He called friends, including Mary Beth's son, Art, around 9 p.m., but no one knew where Mary Beth was, and he wasn't getting anywhere. He called several hospitals in town, thinking maybe there had been an accident, and asked each if she was there. She wasn't. He called a friend who was battling cancer, but Mary Beth hadn't been over to visit her.

This wasn't like Mary Beth, and he grew anxious, a mixture of anger and dread. *Why doesn't she come home?* Meanwhile, he washed some clothes to pass time between 9 and 10 p.m. in the building's downstairs laundry room and chatted with neighbors.

When Sam returned to the condo, Mary Beth still wasn't there. He lay down in bed and dozed off. When he woke up, it was 1:30 a.m. He looked over at the bedroom closet, and for the first time since coming home from work, noticed that the door was closed. Mary Beth almost always kept it open, except when she vacuumed.

Sam got up and looked in the closet. There was Mary Beth, scrunched up in a fetal position, facedown on the floor of the closet, dead.

She was wearing a blouse and slip; her hair was combed as if she had just come out of the shower, which was consistent with her routine after a swim. There was no blood. Sam touched her once on the cheek and she was cold. He left the room and called 911. The police came out and took him in for several hours of questioning. He told them what happened, that he found her in the closet, and they said they didn't believe him. They asked him what really happened and he told them the same story again. They told him Mary Beth had been killed in the evening, after 6 p.m., after Sam arrived home. Nothing made sense to Sam—that his fiancée was dead and the police said he killed her. He told them again he didn't. They said he did. Then they told him to go to a hotel for the time being and they would contact him.

The police told reporters that Mary Beth Townsend's death was suspicious, but it took six months before it would officially be ruled a homicide. According to the local paper, they "insinuated" to reporters that Mary Beth was killed by someone she knew, so the public had no reason to fear that a serial killer was on the loose. The condominium unit was sealed for the next three weeks.

Meanwhile, Sam Bilodeau waited in limbo. On that Saturday, after he had been interrogated by the police and checked into a hotel, he called Art but couldn't get hold of him. Unable to just sit alone and do nothing, Sam decided to visit Mary Beth's father—his almost-father-in-law. When he was driving back, he saw Mary Beth's car, a light blue hatchback, off the side of the highway in a distressed part of Washington, D.C. The police had been looking for the car, but he was the one who found it. That made the police even more suspicious of him.

Sam called the police, who arrived on the scene with a dog that sniffed Mary Beth's car and then pulled its handler toward the woods. The police brought Sam in for more questioning and leaned on him, hard.

"We know what happened," the detective said. "You came home from work. You had an argument with Mary Beth, you pushed her, she hit her head, and she died. You panicked and put her in the closet, and you drove her car down to an area of town where you thought criminals came from, dumped the car there, and took the train back."

Sam shook his head and said, "No, that's not what happened. I didn't do this."

"She died after six p.m, sometime after six p.m. Weren't you home after six at night?"

"That's when I came home. If it happened after that, yes, I was there the whole time. There could be nobody else, because I was there."

This went on for hours.

The police said they had a new technique to bring up prints. They told him his prints were all over Mary Beth, that she was alive at six p.m., and that there was an indentation on the back of her neck that matched an indentation of his palm. They said they believed that Sam accidentally knocked her off balance and then she hit her head as she fell. Sam said he gave Mary Beth a massage that morning and that that could account for his fingerprints. (The police lied about Sam leaving fingerprints on Mary Beth's body; such misrepresentation is accepted as standard practice and is legal in interrogation techniques. Still, Sam's lawyer later told me there could be no prints and that in twenty-five years as an attorney he had never heard such a ridiculous police claim. The method for pulling fingerprints from bodies does exist now, but is not often successful, especially if the body isn't found within a couple of hours.)

The police asked Sam for a blood sample and he gave it voluntarily. They also took his shoes; he left the station in socks. (The police *still* have his shoes.) A polygraph test was administered to Sam—with his assent. From the police officers' expressions, he assumed he passed. But they went right back to telling him that he did it.

Sam eventually confessed to doing what the police said he did.

He said he didn't know how it could have happened and that he had no memory of killing Mary Beth, but that he must have panicked, hid Mary Beth's body, and tried to stage the crime to look like a burglary by driving the car to the other side of town.

Everything he said was based on what the police told him, not his own memories. He was a trusting person, he was confused, he was exhausted and grieving, and he thought the police wouldn't lie. He finally gave in. He signed a confession—and then the police let Mary Beth's alleged killer go, in his stocking feet.

On Sunday, the police brought Sam in for a couple more hours of questioning, but nothing new was brought up. By Monday morning, the medical examiner's report came in stating that Mary Beth had been strangled and that the police now had a confession that didn't match the evidence. They never called Sam—or his lawyer—again.

SAM BILODEAU MIGHT not have heard from the police again but he remained their number one suspect. In spite of the detectives' dogged belief that Sam was guilty as hell, they had no evidence with which to charge him. Worse, the more they investigated the circumstances of the crime, the less the evidence supported their theory.

The police couldn't charge Sam based on his "confession"—or anything else.

When Sam found himself in the interview room after Mary Beth's murder, there was no time of death yet determined by the medical examiner. All the police knew was that when Mary Beth was found, she was cold and stiff; she had been dead for hours, but how many, they didn't know. (They told Sam she was killed after six p.m., after he came home from work, but that was just to force him into confessing.) Sam could have killed her after he came home from work and waited a good long time to report her murder. So, Mary Beth being cold and in a good amount of rigor mortis didn't rule Sam out. The autopsy is still sealed, so we don't know what the medical examiner ruled as the time of death, but sometimes circumstantial evidence packs a wallop.

IT WAS LATER discovered that Mary Beth called a girlfriend at 9:15 a.m. on the day she died, and they planned to meet for a nice Italian lunch that day. She even sent an e-mail confirming, "See you at noon for lunch."

The police didn't know about this call or e-mail when they forced a confession from Sam.

Mary Beth never showed up for lunch, and it wasn't her style to not keep her appointments.

Why did Mary Beth stand up her friend? Why did she miss a noon appointment if nothing happened to her until six p.m.?

And that was just the beginning.

MARY BETH TOWNSEND'S death was one of eight homicides in the county that year, according to the local paper. It remains the department's only unsolved case of 1998.

The second problem for the police and their forced confession was that Sam had solid alibis and plenty of witnesses as to his whereabouts all day and night.

His time card authenticated that he was at the store where he worked, except from 12:45 p.m. to 1:45 p.m., when he left to buy lunch. But witnesses said he was gone for only five minutes and ate his lunch at the store, off the clock.

It was a thirty-minute round trip to the condo and back. He wasn't gone long enough to make the drive and kill Mary Beth. Besides, if he left at 12:45 and drove home, Mary Beth would have already been off enjoying food and wine with her girlfriend at the restaurant.

Sam also produced a receipt that showed he was pumping gas at a service station at 5:12 p.m. So we know that he was at work all day, barring the few minutes to go out, grab lunch, and bring it back, that he left work at the normal time, got some gas, and drove home. Now, it was six p.m. Once he was home, Sam was seen in the building doing his laundry and talking to neighbors at the same time that the police theorized that he was on the other side of town, disposing of Mary Beth's car.

Again, at the time of his forced confession, the police didn't know that neighbors had seen Sam doing laundry between nine and ten p.m.

THE THIRD PROBLEM was that the medical examiner came back and said that Mary Beth had been strangled. That was not in the confession, essentially because the police never told Sam that he had strangled Mary Beth. They said he hit her, so that's what he confessed to under extraordinary pressure.

The police had a false confession. People have a hard time understanding why anybody would confess falsely, but it's more common than people realize. Art Townsend's lawyer—he got one when the police started implicating him along with Sam—told me that the very detective who pressured Sam to confess claimed that 70 percent of the people he got to confess were innocent, something of which I wouldn't have been so proud, but he bragged about it.

In fact, the police department was sued because the same detective also forced a false confession out of a man accused in a woman's brutal rape and murder in 1984. He went to prison, and it wasn't until three years later that another detective in the department began to suspect that he was innocent. He was released after another two years of investigation, DNA testing, and paperwork. The real murderer, a cat burglar, was finally convicted. DNA proved he did it; the man was also a serial killer. The falsely accused man spent five years in prison convicted of a crime he didn't commit. He got $117,000 from the state for his pain and suffering.

When Mary Beth Townsend was murdered, that same detective finagled an equally false confession out of Sam Bilodeau.

At that point, the police told Sam, "Don't leave town," and he stayed. The case lay dormant for a long time. The police told the community, "There's nothing to be worried about," insinuating that Sam was responsible in spite of evidence that seemed to prove that he was not.

ART TOWNSEND, MARY Beth's son, became frustrated because nothing was happening with the case and it was going nowhere.

In September 1999, Art contacted me.

"Can you help with this case? I don't think Sam killed my mother, and I want somebody to find out the truth," he said.

I was excited to get the call. I was going to talk with the case investigator and see the crime scene photos and everything else related to the case. I was going to help them out, and this was where I got my first comeuppance.

When I dealt with the Anne Kelley case, I knew that I was not considered a friend of the police department—I lived in the community, was directly impacted by Anne's murder, and was a common housewife—but this was a totally different situation. This was not a personal case to me. This was not a case that I brought to them as a citizen. This was a case in which a family member asked me to see the police as a profiler, admittedly new in the field, so law enforcement might have an issue with that.

Now that I was working in a professional capacity, I thought that Art and I would sit down with the police detective and he would say, "We are kind of stuck. If you want to look at things, we'd like to hear your thoughts." It didn't go well. The detective in charge was not pleased that Art had the audacity to bring in an outsider to examine her case. The police were working the case and she didn't appreciate any implication that they weren't doing their job well in spite of the fact that they had made no progress on the case whatsoever. They did not want anything going public that would make the police department look bad.

She greeted me coldly and told me in no uncertain terms that I was not welcome.

"I refuse to discuss this case with you or the family," she said. "If you go public you had better be careful with what you say because I have done a lot of work on this case."

That caused a dilemma, because I obviously would have liked to see all the evidence in their possession. Should I profile a case if I can't access the case information and the case photos?

Ideally, I want the police department's cooperation and access to every shred of evidence I can possibly see, all of the reports, all of the photos. But the reality is that even a police investigator sometimes doesn't have all of this when he works a case. There are many pieces of evidence that might be missing. Maybe the elements have destroyed it. Evidence may have also been negatively impacted by first responders at the scene, by the fire department hosing down a place that was on fire. Things may have gotten lost on the way to the lab. They may have been misplaced in an evidence locker. They may have degraded. A witness may have disappeared so we can't get a statement. In a perfect world, I would have 100 percent of all possible information and evidence. But in the real world, I get what I get.

Does that mean if I don't have everything, I shouldn't try to be helpful?

The police department and the medical examiner's office refused to officially tell the family the time of death and refused to allow the family the right to see the autopsy report, even after Mary Beth's son, Art Townsend, went to court over the matter.

The family wanted to know: Why were no other suspects being considered? Was this really a death from a domestic dispute or was it a burglary-related homicide that was never investigated as such? If Mary Beth Townsend's fiancé was really involved with her death, why did the department stall on an arrest? Were they struggling to make conflicting facts fit the story? Were they wasting time focusing on the fiancé rather than pursuing other leads?

The police also successfully resisted the local newspaper in its investigation. The newspaper filed a Freedom of Information Act (FOIA) request that resulted in the release of some basic information but not the autopsy report its reporters (and Art) sought.

On the other hand, I did have information that was available through Mary Beth's son. I was also able to interview Sam Bilodeau, her fiancé, and hear his story, and determine whether I thought it was a fabrication or whether he was telling the truth.

I decided I would profile this case and help in one manner or another. Perhaps I could develop a lead that would help the police department. Perhaps I could come up with an answer that would help the family cope. Not a perfect world, not a perfect case, but if I could do anything to help, I would.

I went forward on Art's invitation because I was concerned that there might be a predator on the loose if Sam was not involved.

THE FIRST THING I did was hear the circumstances of the case from Art. He told me what had happened, and then he added some other interesting details.

After several months, the police finally released Mary Beth's car. Art attempted to drive it away but couldn't because the clutch was destroyed. He had it towed to a mechanic, who yelled at him for tearing it up so badly.

This discovery actually helped convince Art that Sam was in the clear. Art thought that if Sam had really killed his mother and was trying to dump the car on the other side of town just to make it look like the offender drove it there, he would have had to purposely destroy the clutch. Sam not only knew how to drive a car with a manual transmission, but he owned one, too. It would take clever thinking for a man who just accidentally killed his girlfriend to think, *"I'll leave the car in the ghetto and make it look like I didn't know how to drive it. If I destroy the clutch, it won't look like me."*

Art brought this detail to the investigating detective's attention and she was, admittedly, surprised. He passed along the mechanic's contact information to the police for confirmation but they never called. They were only interested in evidence that implicated Sam, not excluded him.

It's clever but unlikely that an offender in the midst of such desperation would be smart enough to cook that up. More likely, the person who actually took the vehicle did not know how to drive a stick-shift car, and that's why the clutch was destroyed. (The car was dusted for prints but the police never told Sam or Art what they found.)

That began the process of conclusively leading me away from believing Sam Bilodeau was the perpetrator.

I interviewed Sam and the people who could verify his whereabouts on the day of Mary Beth's murder. He had a pretty airtight alibi for the entire day, so if Mary Beth was missing by noon, Sam Bilodeau was not involved. He could be involved only if she was alive when he returned home from work, but the fact is she did not show up for her planned lunch, so therefore she was likely dead by noon.

I WONDERED WHY Sam had confessed.

I can learn a lot during an interview. Sam was an amiable fellow—gullible, actually. The police could have led him into saying anything if they pushed hard enough. He was a teddy bear, and he was a person under great duress, an emotional wreck who found his fiancée, the woman he planned to marry, dead. The brain does not think straight under such circumstances.

Sam had slept only a couple of hours before he woke and found Mary Beth's body. I can't believe when he got to the hotel he jumped into bed and got a blissful eight hours of sleep. By the time he was interviewed for the second time on Saturday evening, he had been up for almost forty-eight hours. Seriously exhausted and emotionally devastated, an easygoing, guileless personality is a sitting duck for manipulation by clever, seasoned detectives. He just might make a confession that he didn't really mean. He was so confused that he didn't know what he was saying anymore. He had no family present, no attorney to guide him. He wasn't a fast-talking con man, so he answered their questions as honestly as he could and he eventually gave the police what they wanted. Like many a person who has confessed after lengthy interrogation, he just wanted the questions to stop, he wanted to not talk about the horrible incident anymore, he just wanted to lie down. He simply reached a point where he was too tired to care anymore.

I was not convinced that Sam had the personality to kill. He had no violent background and no motive—there was no life insurance from which he or even Mary Beth's son could have gained, for example. There was not any great equity in the condo that she owned alone, and her death left Art responsible for an $86,000 mortgage. Mary Beth's son said that Sam and his mother got along fabulously. There was nothing there, no reason for him to kill his fiancée.

I could not envision such a docile man becoming so angry that he smacked his fiancée. I found it even harder to believe he would have strangled her. Then, for him to be so unbelievably clever and calm that he could place her body in the closet, remove items to stage a burglary, drive the car to a black area of town to throw the blame on someone else, destroy the clutch so it would look like the car had been driven by someone unable to use a stick . . . no, no, not this man.

Sam Bilodeau did not have a motive or the personality or the opportunity to commit this crime.

IN MY INVESTIGATION, I put Sam aside and looked at the crime itself.

The first thing that struck me was that the Townsend condominium was out of the way. It wasn't a location a criminal would pick purely by accident. It wasn't an isolated house that would catch one's eye, it wasn't an easily accessible end unit, it wasn't even a condo on the first floor. The killer wouldn't be someone who just happened upon Mary Beth's condo and thought, *Oh, I think I'll just slide over to that door and try the handle.* What we know happened at the crime scene was that there was a burglary; someone came into her apartment and took things that belonged to Mary Beth. He took her jewelry, he took rolled quarters that were set aside for future laundry use, and he took her vehicle.

The police said she was not raped, but neither Art nor I saw the autopsy report, so there was no way to know if that was true or not. When Sam found her in the closet, Mary Beth was not entirely dressed. It appeared she might have come back from the swimming pool or just come out of the shower, and was interrupted while she was getting dressed. Sometimes rape or sexual assault cannot be identified by an autopsy. If there is no physical damage, if the man used a condom and therefore didn't leave any semen, we just don't know if there was a sexual assault or not. He might even have had some weird sexual idea that had nothing to do with actual penetration. As the profiler, it was hard to tell whether this was a sexual assault and a burglary or just a burglary gone wrong.

Often, I find that these offenders overlap their crimes, and they don't just pick one crime to commit. They are opportunists, and if they find another temptation at the scene, they can't resist.

There was no sign of breaking and entering. Did Mary Beth open the door to somebody, or did somebody find his way in?

I was told that Mary Beth tended to leave her condo door open, or if not open, then unlocked. It was possible she went swimming and left the door open and somebody came in. Or the door was unlocked while she was taking a shower and a burglar slipped in without her realizing. Or perhaps he knocked and Mary Beth answered the door and let the person in—perhaps she knew the person. But it is not likely she would have answered the door half-dressed.

As she sometimes left the front door unlocked, it is likely someone entered the apartment believing no one was at home and surprised Mary Beth (and she surprised him). The perpetrator could have hit Mary Beth and, when she fell to the floor, strangled her to prevent identification. Upon killing her, the perpetrator grabbed what was in sight and took off. The perpetrator of this kind of crime is a relatively disorganized criminal. The planning of the crime would have been minimal and the attack a necessity for self-preservation (prevention of identification). On the other hand, maybe the guy knew she was there and planned to rape and kill her, and then stole her stuff. This would have been a little more carefully planned, but it would still be a fairly opportunistic crime, so the killer wouldn't have had to be a brilliant criminal.

Also, when he exited the condo, the perpetrator locked the bottom push-button lock from the inside, but didn't set the dead bolt.

I couldn't stop thinking about the location of the condo. You wouldn't pick Mary Beth's second-floor unit if you were just walking down the street. You wouldn't think, *There's no car in front of that condo, I'll commit a crime there.* Mary Beth's condo unit was not easily accessible to a nonresident, so a burglar or rapist would most likely pick some other unit before choosing hers.

Somebody had prior knowledge of this location. He picked it for a reason.

One of the questions I asked the son was whether he knew of anybody working on the property that day. My quick profile of the offender: a guy who was lurking around during the middle of the day, stealing money, and not doing too well at anything. Likely, he was not keeping a steady job. He arrived on foot and had to steal a vehicle to make a quick getaway. The fact that he took Mary Beth's car from in front of the building and drove it to the other side of town said to me that he was going home. He probably lived in southeast Washington, D.C., the area where the car was abandoned.

Perhaps, prior to the murder, he was in the area working with some kind of temp service. Perhaps he was going to court there because he had problems with the law. Perhaps he was doing construction work nearby.

I felt sure he was not from Mary Beth's town because he drove to Washington, D.C., and destroyed the clutch en route. I didn't think it was a joy ride. He had a place to go because he was not going to drive a car like Mary Beth's all around town when he couldn't even drive it properly.

ONE OF THE reasons I call myself an investigative criminal profiler is because I learned that you can't always sit in your office and solve a crime by just looking at photos and reading case files. Sometimes you have to visit the crime scene and ask yourself, *What kinds of buildings are here? What kind of land is it? What are the people like around here?*

I went to the Townsend condominium and looked around. I went to the site where Mary Beth's car was abandoned. Who would dump a car there? And, if they lived nearby, where did they live?

It was a poor area of town with a high incidence of drug-related crime, and it happens to be almost 100 percent African American. But I didn't want to assume that the offender was African American; maybe there was more of a racial mix than I suspected.

I wanted to make sure of that, so I started knocking on doors, and I said, "I'm looking for a fellow who dropped a car near here, what do you think?"

I asked around in the community, because those in it would know a lot more about it than I'll ever know, and every single one of them said, "Oh, no, if he dropped his car and walked from there, the guy's African American. Definitely black, because we don't have Hispanic guys around here, we don't have white guys around here. If you come in here and you are trying to do some business and you are Hispanic or white, you will find nothing but trouble. You're going to stand out. You will run into gang issues."

It was not a safe area for the people who live there, let alone those who did not.

As I talked to people in the community, I told them, "I really need your help. I've got a suspect in a murder who might live around here." Everybody jumped on board, trying to be detectives themselves. They started talking with me and giving me all kinds of information; a few even offered cookies and lemonade. Poor people don't want a killer in their community any more than middle-class or rich people do, so everybody tried to help and was pleasant.

Because of what they told me, I was convinced Mary Beth Townsend's attacker was a black man.

I believed he lived with someone or had a relative in that part of town, close to where the car was found. He worked for a day labor service of some kind, and he was in Mary Beth's community for some work- or court-related reason. He had some previous knowledge and experience with the building where Mary Beth and Sam lived, because why else would he pick it? Criminals do things that make sense to them, even if we don't fully understand their choices.

I asked Art Townsend, "Were there any temporary services working on or around the property, anybody lurking around, in the days before your mother's homicide?"

He looked into it and found that three weeks before his mother died, there was a service called Trashman at the building.

"My mother had this old computer," he recalled, "and when she saw the Trashman truck outside, she naturally thought it was a trash service. She ran downstairs and said to the guy with the truck, 'I have this old computer I want to get rid of. Can you take it?' And he said, 'Oh, no, we're not a trash service. We fix commercial mailboxes and the locks on the mailboxes. That's our job.' She said, 'Oh, darn.' But then he said, 'I've been looking for a computer to fix up.' So she brought him up to the condo, and they went into her bedroom, where she unhooked the computer and gave it to him. Then she kindly gave the man her name and phone number and said, 'If you ever have a problem with the computer, give me a ring.' "

Mary Beth was a librarian, used to helping and trusting people. The man thanked her and left with the computer.

Art tracked down the company's address and phone number and only recalled his mother describing the man to whom she gave her computer as "a young black guy."

I, of course, called Trashman. I said, "I am going to be honest with you . . ."

Honesty's an interesting policy. Sometimes, the police have asked me, "How did you get that information? Even we can't get that information without a court order."

And I inevitably answer, "I was nice."

I told the person who answered the phone, "Look, this is going to sound really strange. I'm a criminal profiler working on this case, and I have a suspicion that this woman, Mary Beth Townsend, may have been murdered by somebody who worked at a temporary service. Three weeks before the murder, a guy from your service came into her apartment and she gave a computer to him. Do you know a black guy in his twenties or thirties who worked for you at her condominium on August 21, 1998?"

The guy put the phone down for a while. When he returned, he was chortling.

"You're not going to believe this one," he said, his voice full of excitement.

"What?"

"That guy you asked me about, I have to testify against him in court."

"What for?"

"He is accused of abducting, raping, and strangling a little girl who he put in a closet."

I said, "That sounds familiar. . . ."

Bingo!

If you were looking for MO, we had a winner here. And while MO doesn't always remain the same, hey, when it's that close, a profiler can't look a gift horse in the mouth.

WHILE THIS WAS going on, I reached out to an agent I knew in the FBI to see if he could get answers for the family. I also thought he might consider getting involved in the investigation. But he talked with the detective in charge, and even though he came away feeling she was sincerely following through on Mary Beth's murder, he learned no more than the family did.

In November 1999, I wrote the following in my case notes:

The Mary Beth Townsend case made some progress. The police actually permitted a meeting with Art's lawyer and ADMITTED they were now looking at the possibility that an intruder committed the crime. This admission pretty much clears her fiancé and admits that they screwed up. HURRAH! Art is very happy.

WE COULD PLACE a stranger in Mary Beth Townsend's apartment just three weeks before she was discovered strangled and left in a closet. And he was on trial for strangling a girl and putting her in a closet.

"This is a guy we should look at," I said.

I asked my new friend at Trashman some more questions about the man. "Who is this guy, what can you tell me?"

"His name's Scotty May. He's African American, and I believe he lives in southeast Washington."

That also fit snugly into my profile.

"Do you possibly know whether he can drive a stick-shift car?"

"I actually do know that, because our vehicles are all stick-shift vehicles, and because he could not drive one, he always had to ride on the passenger side and somebody else had to drive."

I CONFIRMED WITH local law enforcement that Scotty May was indeed on his way to court, so I went back to the police department and gave the detective all the information I had gathered. She didn't seem to me to be interested in the least.

I was stunned.

"How can you not be interested in a guy that was in her apartment three weeks before she was murdered, who committed the same exact crime someplace else?" I said. "What part don't you get?"

The detective didn't know me, and maybe she didn't think profilers know what they're doing, or she didn't believe in the science of criminal profiling, but how could she deny that this guy committed the exact same crime someplace else? How could she think Scotty had nothing to do with it? That was crazy.

THE DAY OF Scotty May's trial arrived and he was charged with attempted murder, rape, and abduction with intent to defile. Art and I learned firsthand about Scotty and what kind of character this career felon was.

A high school graduate, May was five ten, weighed 185 to 195 pounds and had brown eyes. He lived in the area where Mary Beth's car was abandoned, and worked for temporary employment services, as I suspected, one in Virginia near Mary Beth's home and another in Washington, D.C. One of the last jobs he had before he went to jail was cleaning buildings that were under construction.

One of the services he worked for employed a thirteen-year-old girl with a false ID whom I'll call Shania. She was a runaway from another county in Virginia, living in a motel with an older boyfriend who was dealing drugs. Clearly, her life wasn't going terribly well. Then she met Scotty through the temp service, and things got worse.

Scotty was living with his girlfriend, Crystal Jones, and their two children in southeast Washington. One day, Shania's boyfriend was arrested and jailed for dealing drugs and she no longer had a place to stay, since he was paying for the motel room. Good Samaritan that he was, May let her stay at his house.

The girl arrived thinking she'd be safe with May, Crystal, and their kids. May said he got a call for them to go clean a building early the next morning. Shania got up, put on her clothes, and off they went in his car.

When they arrived, there was nobody else there and it was still dark outside.

"Why don't we go in the building and smoke some dope?" May said.

Shania said, "No, I don't want to."

"Oh, come on, come on," he said, pressuring her to come along.

She wasn't interested, but felt she had no choice but to go in with him. Once they were inside, Scotty started down a new path.

"Your boyfriend's in jail. You need a new boyfriend, don't you?"

He started putting the moves on her, and she said, "No, I don't need a new boyfriend, because he's getting out of jail. I don't need to be with you. I'm not interested."

But he wouldn't take no for an answer.

"I don't want to do this," she said.

"Well, you're going to," May said.

That's when he raped her.

She was terrified that he was going to hurt her, so she did not fight back. May was a big guy, and she was a little girl.

He cleverly used a condom so he wouldn't leave any evidence, and after he finished raping her, he told her to put her clothes back on, and she did. She looked sad, and she was.

"What's the problem?" he asked.

"I'm tired, I just want to go to sleep," she said.

She was emotionally shutting down from the horrible assault.

He said, "You want to go to sleep? No problem," and May put his arm around her neck in a sleeper hold, tightened his arm, and he strangled her.

When she was unconscious and wasn't moving anymore, he picked up her body and put it in a closet in the empty building, closed the door, and walked away.

It turned out there was never any temporary work at the building that day; that was just a ruse he used to get her there, and after he got what he wanted, he went on his way.

The mistake Scotty May made—besides the crimes of raping and strangling an underage girl—was that he didn't check to see how dead she was, because she was still alive. She woke up, and she got out of the closet, ran down through the building, and went to the office and told them to call the police because she had been raped and strangled.

The police came, took her in, and asked her to write down exactly what had happened to her. She wrote, "Scotty May took me to this building, and he raped me, and he strangled me." She wrote it all down, and the police went looking for May.

A year after Mary Beth Townsend's murder, Scotty May was drinking tea in his living room when he saw a police car pull up. He thought they were coming to talk to him about a fraud he committed at work, but they were actually there to ask him about the thirteen-year-old girl that they believed he raped and strangled earlier that day.

"Oh, did you hear about the fraud?" he asked.

Until then, no, they didn't know he had been ripping off the company where he worked.

"No, no," the officers said. "We're not here about a fraud. We're looking into the case of this thirteen-year-old girl that's gone missing. Shania."

"What about her?"

"Do you know her?"

"Yeah," he said, "I know her. I don't know where she is. This morning she wanted to go back to the motel on Route 1 where her boyfriend was, so I dropped her off and haven't seen her since."

"Well, Scotty, she said that you raped her," and with that the detective pushed the girl's report in front of him. "See what she's written about you?"

"That's impossible. She couldn't have written that," he said.

"Why not?" the officer asked.

"She's *dead*."

Swift move, May. Gotta love stupid criminals. May wasn't as slick as he thought. They arrested him, obviously, because he screwed that one up, making the criminally stupid mistake of saying she was dead before he was supposed to know she was dead.

THE SCOTTY MAY story could have ended there. But he decided he was bright enough that he should be his own lawyer.

To be honest, he presented himself quite well in court. On the day Scotty's trial began, Art looked around to see if he could spot him.

"Where is he?" Art asked the bailiff.

May was dressed so well that Art thought he was looking at a lawyer.

"No," the bailiff said, "that is Scotty May."

Some people can present themselves quite well in court when they dress up, so May was in a nice suit, and he thought this was enough to ensure a successful trial. He was well spoken, talkative, gentle, and respectful in his approach to the jurors. Mind you, he had spent most of his adult life in prison for committing one crime after another. He'd hardly been on the outside, but he saw himself as a pretty fine jailhouse lawyer.

Shania started crying as soon as she saw May in court. He got her on the stand, looked her in the eye, and he said to her, "You know I didn't rape you, don't you?"

She stared right back at him and said, "Yes you did, Scotty, yes you did."

All he could say to that was "Oh," which the jury didn't consider much of a defense. Maybe he thought he could intimidate Shania, but it didn't work.

He was found guilty of kidnapping, guilty of rape, and guilty of attempted murder.

Even though he looked good, he wasn't a very good lawyer. But May continued representing himself in the penalty phase. He expected to convince the jury that he was a decent guy in spite of the fact that he kidnapped, raped, and attempted to murder a thirteen-year-old girl.

What no one expected was that Scotty May was a changed man.

"I found the Lord. Yes, I found Jesus," May proclaimed. "I've been reading my Bible, I'm a Christian now, and I just want to tell you that I think you ought to give me a chance, because I'm not really that bad a guy.

"As a matter of fact, I did Shania a favor, because when I met Shania, she was a runaway. She was living with a man who was dealing drugs. She was on the streets. She wasn't in school, and after I did this to her, she returned home to her family, and she's back in school. I should get a break because I helped her out!"

That's a sign of a true psychopath, making lemonade out of lemons: "I did kidnap, rape, and strangle that girl, tried to kill her, but I did her a favor. So I think we should call it even."

Scotty May's closing argument won him a sentence of life plus thirty. He received twenty years for abduction with intent to defile, to be served concurrently; the remaining life plus ten years are to be served consecutively. May can still apply for geriatric parole when he reaches the age of sixty, which will be in the year 2028.

The court declined to hear oral arguments on the motion to set aside the jury verdict on rape. But Judge Stanley P. Klein did tell May: "Your whole defense is that you weren't there. But it was clear to this Court, based on the questions you asked the witness [Shania] on cross-examination, that you WERE there. In this Court's opinion, the jury did not make a mistake."

ART SPOKE TO a detective and told him he attended Scotty May's trial.

The detective said, "We were supposed to have somebody there, but I don't know if we did." It was the first official acknowledgment that the police were even considering Scotty May a person of interest. "We are certainly focused on him," the detective said, halfheartedly.

Later still, Art received the following phone message from the detective in charge of the case:

"Hello, Art. This is Detective B. from the police department. I had told you that I would get back with you sometime in October, and I wanted to chat with you briefly about the case. I have no new exciting news for you, except that the prosecutor and I are working toward an indictment. Unfortunately, I can't give you a time frame as yet. But I would like to talk to you. Please call me later today, or I will try you again. Thank you."

The phone call gave Art false hope that they were doing something, but nothing ever came of the indictment.

IT WAS ABOUT a year after the Mary Beth Townsend murder that Scotty May attacked the thirteen-year-old girl.

When I found out the name of the Trashman employee was Scotty May, I paid a visit to his girlfriend, Crystal Jones, to discover a little bit more of what she knew around the time of the crime. The day Mary Beth died was, not coincidentally, Crystal Jones's birthday. I believe May needed money to buy his girlfriend a present.

The day after the murder, May went to Philadelphia. Mary Beth's murderer stole her rings, and he would have had to hawk them someplace; they were worth some money. If you hawk things in Washington, D.C., you have to show a driver's license—same for Virginia—so your name will be recorded as the person selling the item. But in Philadelphia, the rules are different and it's a popular place to fence stolen goods. I figured the murderer might go there, because he wouldn't be asked for an ID. I never did find a pawn shop that could identify May, but according to police reports he sure acted peculiar while he was there. He arrived at his estranged wife's home, beat her, threatened to kill her, pulled out a gun, and, after fleeing, was chased by police to the rooftop of a nearby building. The criminal justice system didn't put him back in prison, so he moved on to raping and trying to kill Shania.

THERE WAS AN incredible amount of evidence linking Scotty May to the murder of Mary Beth Townsend, so Art and I returned once more to the police department. They still refused to look at any of the new information I brought.

Police departments are as susceptible as any business to the egos of the people who are involved and all the inherent politics. They fall prey to all kinds of issues that can be radically different from one police department to the next and from one investigator to the next.

You throw the dice when you talk about employees of any business, and, unfortunately, Mary Beth Townsend's murder drew a pair of uncooperative detectives. Getting a good detective on your case is much the same as getting lucky with a skilled surgeon.

And to my knowledge, to this day, they still refuse to look at new information. However, in the next county over, the detectives and district attorney who prosecuted Scotty May all say, "We know Scotty May killed Mary Beth Townsend." If they had had the case, charges against Scotty May would have gone forward.

I UNDERSTAND WHY the investigators immediately suspected Sam Bilodeau.

In the beginning of the investigation, they wouldn't have known what time of day Mary Beth Townsend was killed. They did not know if it had been six, eight, or even ten hours before she was discovered, and they hadn't known about the lunch date she missed, so they did not have their time frame down yet. They didn't have the full autopsy saying that she had been strangled. The police had a dead woman in a closet, apparently with a blow to the head, and there was no sign of breaking and entering.

Her fiancé said, "I came home, she wasn't there, I didn't know what happened to her, and I fell asleep. When I got up, I found her in the closet."

Uh-huh, really?

I do not put down the police department for its original views. I would have that same thought. Nothing wrong with that. When you're talking about a crime that just occurred, you have to go with the most likely theory. Women are most often killed by boyfriends or

husbands, not by strangers, serial killers, or burglars. Domestic homicide tops the list of likely places to start. The police detective will
obviously go there first. He's got the guy in the chair. He's going to
take his chance to talk to him. However, he shouldn't put words into
his mouth. And he certainly shouldn't pursue the domestic angle just
because the truth is less convenient.

The police had a reason to suspect Sam. Maybe he moved Mary
Beth's car to the other side of town and took the train back; the
couple's condominium was close enough to transportation for that
to be plausible. I have another case where that's exactly what happened. A white man committed a murder, moved the car to a poor
black neighborhood, and tried to make it look like the perpetrator
was a black man. Why? Because the white killer lived four doors
down from the neighbor he murdered and he wanted the police to
look elsewhere. It's not necessarily racist; it's just smart for a criminal to point law enforcement to an area where nobody looks like him
and the location is poor enough or has a high enough crime rate to
make it feasible that a criminal lived there.

For an innocent man, Sam did all the right things. He came
home. He made phone calls to find his fiancée. That seems like normal behavior, but a lot of people ask, "With his fiancée missing, if he
was really worried about her, why did he just go to sleep? How could
he do that?"

This is a gender issue. If it was a woman and her boyfriend was
missing, that woman would not sleep. That woman would have been
pacing the floor all night long, cussing and saying, "He better be
dead, because if he's not dead, then he's going to be dead when he
gets home." She would be standing there at six a.m., still fuming,
when that man walked in. And if he was fine, *she'd* kill him. That's
the way a woman thinks. A guy will go, "I don't know where she
is . . . Zzzzzzzz." And he'll fall right to sleep. It's amazing. Men will
snooze under even the most stressful circumstances.

Sam's going to sleep did not surprise me. He was annoyed, he was
aggravated, but he didn't know what else to do, so he did what a guy
does, he slept. When he did wake up, somewhat rested and thinking
clearly, he finally noticed that the closet door was closed.

To the police, who didn't know Sam Bilodeau at that point, it sounded like a strange story. And then, of course, *he* found the car, which made things worse for him, but because he was driving home from Mary Beth's father's and the highway ran close to Scotty May's house, that just happened to be where the car was dumped.

But ultimately, there was too much evidence to the contrary to continue being suspicious of Sam.

At a certain point, the police should have said, "The evidence shows that it's not Sam Bilodeau." He lost his fiancée. He pays taxes. He deserved to be treated like a man grieving a horrible loss, not a common felon.

The detectives never talked to Sam again after his "confession." He waited around a year for the police, and nobody ever came back to him. He didn't know what to do. That indicated to me that they weren't thinking it was him, but they didn't know where to turn next.

This is a huge problem that I hope to help more police departments solve in the future. Cases are solved by everybody working together. The medical examiner helps us understand how the person died. The crime photographer gets good photos that we can examine for clues. A ballistics expert on a case can tell us about the caliber of bullets when appropriate. There might be forensic evidence. The community might give us tips on who it thinks could have committed the crime—if we ask for the help and then listen to the answers. When all these people get together, the profiler is just a part of a larger team. Even in this case, I had the help of the family and the community to unravel the case. The police need to stop looking at it as "our" case and start looking at it as the victim's case. That's a big problem.

Criminal profiling is still a relatively new concept, and since there's been so much mythology about criminal profiling and some foolishness promoted about criminal profiling, profilers are sometimes considered gods—and sometimes they're considered frauds.

IS IT WORTH profiling a homicide if law enforcement doesn't care? If it isn't prosecuted, is it worth it?

Absolutely yes.

In Mary Beth Townsend's murder, her son, Art, got the answer he prayed was true: the fiancé of his mother wasn't somebody he had to hate the rest of his life.

The fiancé, Sam Bilodeau, got some relief that somebody believed he didn't kill his fiancée, that there was an answer out there.

More recently, I received a letter from Sam Bilodeau's sister, thanking me profusely for helping with the case, because it was such a horrible thing for her brother to live through with this cloud hanging over his head. When I spoke out in the media as to why Scotty May should be the top suspect in Mary Beth's death and explained how he—and not Sam Bilodeau—was most likely to have committed the crime, I provided some peace of mind to her family. It took her years to deal with it and write a letter thanking me, but it was a beautiful thing to receive, ten years after I worked on the case. We know that Scotty May is not going anyplace. He's in jail for life. I know the Townsend family would like him prosecuted for what he did to Mary Beth, but at least I could clear Sam Bilodeau's name to some extent so he could go on in his life and I could give Art some closure, too. That is indeed worth it, even if I can't say the case was prosecuted or the police ever formally exonerated Sam.

It is said that lightning doesn't strike twice in the same place, but there are folks who can tell you that this is an old wives' tale. Art Townsend can tell you that crime also can strike twice in the same place. Following his mother's death, Art put the condo up for rent. A nice young man who did government work, Vincent Poor, moved in. The very next year after Mary Beth was murdered, in 1999, the police department had another crime go unsolved.

Vincent Poor, finished with his day's work, came out of the train station and was robbed and stabbed to death on his way home to the condo.

Art didn't want to tell the next renter that the previous two residents were murdered.

He sold the unit.

CHAPTER 8

DORIS
THE UNLIKELY VICTIM

The Crime: Murder
The Victim: Doris Hoover
Location: Midwestern United States
Original Theory: Husband either did it or hired someone to commit the crime

---

I arrived twenty-six years too late in the Midwest.

I had just finished an appearance on a daytime talk show, where I met two of the daughters of Doris Hoover. The hour-long show was on cold cases and their mother's murder was featured. After the show, they stopped me in the hallway and asked if I could profile the killer. Normally, a case this cold is one that I would leave alone, but the facts were so interesting and the daughters so insistent, I told them I would give the detective a ring.

"Sure, we would welcome a profile of the case," he said.

I drove to the Midwest. In my experience, more people call from this part of the country for help with unsolved homicides than any other part.

After getting such a poor reception on the Mary Beth Townsend case and running into similar resistance with other police departments, it was a relief to have the local law enforcement welcome me.

When I got there, the detective ushered me into his office, a rather sheepish look on his face.

"Uh, I have some bad news for you," he told me.

I thought he was going to tell me that a superior wanted me to go home.

"The case files are gone."

"Gone?"

"Yeah, there was a flood at the warehouse and the Hoover case files were destroyed."

Okay. This was not good news. I would come to learn that it wasn't entirely rare news. A case I later worked in North Carolina would have the entire trunk of a car, the actual trunk that was removed for testing, disappear. How do you lose something that much larger than a breadbox?

"How about computer files?" I ventured.

The detective looked morose. "Gone as well. Someone thought the case was closed and erased all information on it." He half-grinned at me. "We have her name!"

I know he felt bad. Shit happens and police departments aren't 100 percent perfect. Things get lost, items get destroyed, evidence gets mislabeled . . . shit happens.

So there I was.

Not only had a mother of seven been dead for two decades but all the related evidence was eliminated.

Still, I was in town. I had worked the Townsend case with no police files, so I might as well see if I could do anything with this one. It was worth a try.

DORIS HOOVER, FORTY-TWO, was shot at home around 3:30 a.m., in her own bedroom, on November 3, 1975, while four of her children were asleep down the hall and her husband was at work. Since that early morning, the only suspect had been her husband. I could see why he might end up in the crosshairs of an investigation, but my profile of the crime ended up pointing away from him.

Doris, who was deaf in one ear and wore a hearing aid everywhere except to sleep, was standing beside the bed in a teddy and panties—no slippers—when she was shot. The Harlequin romance novel she was reading was still spread open on her bed. There was no evidence of sexual assault. When she fell, she collapsed on a stereo, knocking over the speaker and a phone that was on the top of it.

Doris's daughter Laurie, seventeen, the oldest girl living at home, was sleeping in a bedroom with her younger sisters, Denise and Dana, and her little brother, Deacon. In the middle of the night she woke up suddenly, although she didn't remember being startled awake by any noise, and saw someone pass by her open bedroom door, walking from her mother's room to the bathroom. She was half asleep, and what he was doing there didn't register right away. Then she saw him stop at her door and wipe off the doorknob. Wide awake now, she listened as he continued to the hall, down the stairs, and out of the house. Laurie heard the screen door at the front of the house open and close. She heard sounds by the side of the house, and then the screen door again. She heard the man come back up the stairs, enter her mother's room, and then he went back down the stairs and out of the house again. Scared, she didn't move from her bed. Minutes passed, only about seven or eight, and then she heard the police pounding on the front door. By the time she left her bed, the officers—who found the front door open when they arrived—were already inside the house and on the stairs.

The open door was a tip-off to Laurie that something was wrong; her mother compulsively locked all the doors at night.

The police told Laurie there had been a shooting at the house, but she said no, she had heard no such thing—then a horrible thought popped into her mind that her mother must have been kidnapped because her bed was empty when she went by the open door.

"He kidnapped her, he kidnapped her!" she cried out.

She showed the police to her mom's room and then she saw her mother's foot at the bottom of the bed.

The killer had put a small caliber gun in Doris's mouth and pulled the trigger, execution-style. There were burns on her tongue and the bullet locked her neck and her spine so she couldn't move. Doris drowned in her own blood because she couldn't move her head to the side.

Because a curtain was pulled to the side of an unlocked window, it appeared the killer might have accessed the house in this way. It is not known if the window was left unlocked or if the killer was in the home earlier and unlocked it for later entry. Because the reports and photos were not available to me, there were many missing facts that might have provided clues to exactly what happened. I would have to make do with what information I could gain by interviewing the family.

A diamond-and-sapphire necklace was initially reported as missing from the house following the murder, but that was in error. Doris's daughter Denise had it; her father had given it to her grandmother to give to her to hold for her wedding one day. Laurie had cash in plain view where the perpetrator could have taken it. He didn't. Doris's purse was missing, but there was nothing of value in it. Therefore, this crime was unlikely to have a monetary motive.

Even though much information was unavailable, there was enough interesting information to profile this case to a reasonable extent and offer avenues of investigation that might still lead to the case being solved and an individual serving time for the crime.

Doris was what one would classify as a low-risk victim. She was married, a mother of seven children, a homemaker, and a volunteer with the ladies' auxiliary of the fire department. She did not involve herself in any dangerous activities and did not abuse alcohol or drugs. At the time of the murder, she was at home in bed. One of her eldest daughters, Cathy, lived in an apartment across the street with her own family. Doris's husband, Mickey, forty-three, a paramedic and the local fire chief, was in the midst of a twenty-hour shift at a station less than a mile away from his residence. Although her husband was not at home, it would be obvious to anyone casing the place that Doris and her children were there, making her home not the best choice for burglary or stranger sexual assault. The motive for this homicide would likely have come in one of three categories:

1. **Revenge.** Someone Doris or her husband made angry, intentionally or unintentionally.

2. **Convenience.** A hit by someone who wanted her out of his way, most likely the husband.
3. **A crime of passion.** Someone who was emotionally connected to the victim.

The possibility of a hit by the husband was the motive that the police focused on the most, since no one knew of anyone Doris had made angry, and the killer apparently called the fire station, the location where Mickey Hoover worked. The call came in minutes after the crime was committed—from a public pay phone—so it was theorized that Mickey hired a hit man. The phone call let him know the deed was done, giving him an alibi at the time of the crime, and also allowing him to get home and prevent the children from discovering her body. If that scenario was true, it worked out well and the investigators made note of this.

Mickey was not home much. A combination of factors contributed to his long work shifts. He was said to be a flirt but there was no actual proof of extramarital affairs. His children saw him as a harsh, authoritarian figure in their lives. And not long after Doris's death, he began openly dating the woman who would become his second wife. She was only two years older than his eldest daughter.

In spite of these red flags, there were a number of reasons to question Mickey's involvement in his wife's death. One was that it was not possible for Mickey to have been the killer. He had an alibi at the fire station and his own daughter says she caught enough of a glimpse of the killer to know it was not her father. There was also a lack of a clear motive. He did not receive financial gain from her death, and although he later married a younger woman, there was no evidence he was having an affair with the woman at the time of Doris's death. Even if removing his wife from his life would allow him to get himself a much younger woman, a dead wife would leave him with the responsibility of raising the children alone. Mickey worked a heavy schedule and Doris bore the major responsibilities of the home and children. But Mickey's behaviors and gossip about him did raise some eyebrows and sometimes a desire to be rid of certain roadblocks to one's desires can be fuel for homicide. I could not eliminate Mickey purely on motive; I would need to see if the crime itself supported a hired hit on his wife.

The call to the station at 3:43 a.m. was an extremely unusual behavior, one I don't often see from murderers. While hit men have called their employers to let them know a job is finished, they usually don't call for help to save the victim as well. Since 911 did not yet exist in that county, one would have to call the police or fire station to get help. This call, made just minutes after the shooting of Doris Hoover, was to the fire station and received by whoever answered the phone—not to Mickey, personally. The killer didn't really even know if Doris was dead at that point, and if he just wanted to inform Mickey of the shooting, he certainly could have waited long enough to make sure the victim had expired. It actually seemed as if the shooter might either have been trying to get paramedics to Doris or he didn't want the kids to find her body.

One more thing: why was there no screaming, no struggle, if this was a hit man or burglar? Doris was up and awake, the light on; she was reading a book. Suddenly, a strange man appears in the door of her bedroom and Doris just stands there and lets him come up to her and put a gun in her mouth? I doubt it. Someone had to get near her, with her consent, someone she never thought would do such a thing, even if he was waving a gun right in her face. It had to be someone she knew well.

A few minutes after the call came in, the police, Mickey, and the rescue squad arrived at his home. Mickey jumped from his moving squad car in a rush to gain entrance to the house. It is unlikely, if he knew his wife had been shot and killed in a hit, he would have hurried into the home. He would have hung back and allowed someone else to deal with her body while he worked up a suitable emotional response. Instead, it is likely he was actually rushing to his wife's aid, hoping that she could be saved.

Denise later recalled her father sitting with the children that morning and saying of their dead mother, "Sometimes, things happen." He didn't break down and cry then, but Denise later found him leaning against a telephone pole, sobbing. Clearly the man had feelings for his wife.

* * * *

IN MY INTERVIEW with Mickey Hoover, he readily agreed to take a polygraph. He was excited about my involvement and said "it was about time" someone looked into the case again.

I found nothing concerning in his interview, and his actual behaviors at the time of the homicide as related to me by his daughters did not seem suspicious.

One way a profiler can narrow down the suspect list in a crime is to determine whether the person was a stranger or not and whether the person was a stranger to the residence or not. Whoever killed Doris that night seemed to know his way around the house. If Mickey had hired some professional hit man or even some guy he knew from a bar, that man wouldn't have exhibited the behaviors witnessed at the scene. Whoever was there was comfortable in the house but, on the other hand, was quite uncomfortable with having committed a homicide. He was the direct opposite of a hit man. I believe it must have been an intimate, an insider, and a person with some strong emotional connection to the family and the scene.

Following the homicide, the killer washed his hands in the bathroom. This shows, first, that he wore no gloves and I wondered, *What hit man would neglect that issue?* Second, having just committed a homicide, it would seem wise to vacate the premises immediately and not waste time in washing up. That could have been accomplished anywhere. He stopped in the bathroom to wash his hands. Either the sign of an extraordinarily nonchalant killer or a total amateur who was horrified by the sight of blood on his hands; the blood of his victim as it flew back at the hand holding the gun.

Also, the killer looked in on the children. Why? What interest, if he wasn't a rapist, would he have in checking out sleeping kids? And, since there were teenage girls in the house, a rapist would have been more than pleased to make such a find. But he peeked in and then left the house.

Doris Hoover was shot in the mouth with a small caliber handgun. Shooting women in the mouth is usually a sign of rage. The anger is directed at the woman's mouth, where the voice is coming out and telling you what you don't want to hear.

The strangest behavior of all in this crime, outside of the fact that the killer called for emergency medical help in a bizarre attempt to save Doris's life, was that he left the house but then came back.

This brought me to consider what behaviors occurred at the crime scene that could identify the motive and personality of the offender.

I believed the killer was comfortable in the Hoover home. He knew his way around it either because he had been in the home before or he lived in a nearby home of the same design.

The forced entry was likely staged, perhaps as an afterthought when the killer realized the murder would not look like a stranger homicide.

It was theorized that the perpetrator also took Doris's purse to add to the staging effect and mislead the investigation to focus on robbery as a motive. Clearly, since nothing else of value was taken, this crime was not a robbery. However, I do not believe that the motive for taking the purse was to steer the investigation off course. The killer left the house after shooting Doris and then returned and went back upstairs into her room and left the house a second time. It is unlikely that the killer would waste yet more valuable time staging a robbery, minutes spent that would increase the chance of apprehension.

The family does not remember the exact whereabouts of Doris's purse that night. Her daughters believe it was either in her bedroom or under a coat on the living room couch. If it were hidden under a coat on the couch, it is not likely the killer knew it was there and took it. More likely, it was in her bedroom. It was my belief that the purse may have contained some item of interest to the killer that was worth coming back for. It was also possible that the killer came back to check and see what condition Doris was in and took the purse upon leaving the room as a possible afterthought. At this same time, he may well have noticed that Doris was not dead but asphyxiating (because of bodily fluids running into her lungs). This may have prompted the call for medical assistance. It is also interesting to note that the killer, on the return to her room, did not take this opportunity to make sure she was dead.

The killer did not wear gloves. This indicated that he did not plan to commit murder. Perhaps he only wanted to talk with her or show her how angry he was. He may not have worried his fingerprints would be considered evidence of his involvement in the crime if he had previously spent enough time in the house.

But Laurie reported that the killer had wiped off the doorknob of the children's room after he opened the door—it was always closed—and looked in. However, there may be other explanations for the perpetrator to have applied a rag to the doorknob. Laurie heard the man go into the bathroom and then she saw him at her door wiping off the doorknob. The bathroom light was on and the hallway was illuminated. He was tall and thin and wore a winter hat, denim shirt with long sleeves, and dark pants, and his head was turned back toward Doris's bedroom. It was possible that, following the crime, he went from Doris's room straight to the children's room to look in and see if the shot had awakened them. The fact that he went into the bathroom and washed his hands indicated he had blood on them, most likely caused by back spatter from the gunshot wound. He may have left bloody fingerprints on the door to the kids' room that he then wiped clean. Considering that the man wore no gloves to begin with, I wondered why he wiped down that door alone if his only interest was eradicating fingerprints, and not bloody fingerprints, from the residence.

That the killer took time to wash his hands indicated he was not comfortable with blood on his hands. It would therefore be unlikely that this person was a hit man or a hardened criminal.

And the fact that the killer looked into the bedroom of the children and did not attempt to harm them showed he had concern for the children and no ill will toward them.

The lack of clear forced entry meant the killer was either admitted to the house, had a key to the house, or entered through an unlocked door or window, perhaps one he had left open before so he could get back in.

Laurie claimed to have heard him leave the house; she heard the screen door slam closed.

Then, terrified, she heard him come back into the house and go into Doris's room. She believed he took something from the room and went back downstairs, where she heard something fall—she later discovered it was a box of crayons. She never heard the sound of a car.

Laurie later heard the voice recording of the killer's call to her father's fire station that reported the shooting. She thought the low voice sounded like it belonged to a black man, although "it could have been somebody with a Southern twang accent." It was not a voice Laurie recognized. Either the killer was someone Laurie did not know or he disguised his voice so he would not be recognized. A Southern accent is one of the easier speech patterns to mimic—even if to a Southerner the effort might be laughable.

A person who wanted Doris dead, or didn't care if she died, and didn't care if the kids found her body, would not have made the call. The killer also knew the Hoovers' exact address, indicating he was familiar with the location—so familiar that he would have had to live nearby or be a regular visitor to the point of knowing the address. In theory, the killer *could* have walked outside to get the address or looked at mail lying about to get it, but again, it was unlikely he would do this for any reason except to attempt to save Doris's life.

THERE ARE A number of versions of the events of the evening at the Hoovers' home prior to the homicide.

The most interesting discrepancy, reported by the other sisters, involved an older sister, Debbie, who was married and did not live in the residence, and Debbie's friend Carl Barlow, who sometimes visited Doris without Debbie, and the issue of Debbie bringing a dog over to show Doris.

Her sisters say that in the early days of the investigation Debbie said she had been at the house with Carl, showing off her new dog. But when I spoke to her she said that Carl had visited separately before she had arrived that night. Debbie's sisters also say that Debbie told them that both she and Carl had witnessed Doris arguing with

Mickey over the phone. Carl, likewise, seemed to not remember exactly who was where and when. Carl told me that he couldn't remember if he and Debbie were there together or not that evening.

Also, there was the issue of the argument ensuing on the phone that evening between Mickey and Doris Hoover. Mickey did not remember such an argument that evening.

According to her sisters, Debbie was defensive at the time when questioned about Carl and seemed to be holding back.

Carl, on the other hand, was almost *too* helpful in his interviews and responses to my e-mails. Although he said he wasn't extraordinarily close to Doris and the family, he then detailed very intimate moments with them. He seemed eager to help solve the crime and appeared to be fishing for information about the status and progress of the case.

Carl also made odd statements in his interview that led me to believe there was more that he was not telling me.

CARL HAD A thing for Doris and used to take walks with her. They discussed stuff that seemed a little odd for a mother to be discussing with a boy who was close with her daughter and in his early twenties. They were a little bit too intimate.

Doris had seven children, and she had been seriously overweight until shortly before her death, when she enrolled in Weight Watchers and was steadily, purposefully, losing weight.

I think Carl was looking for a mother figure and might have confused her with his sexual needs—he became attracted to her in a none too wholesome way.

Here is what Denise Hoover told me about Carl in an interview:

"Carl Barlow was weird," she said. "Very quiet—he was my older sister's age, in his twenties. He was at the house a lot. My mom walked every day and there were times he walked with her. After Mom died we never saw him again. He called her Mom, but all of our friends did.

"A friend thought he had feelings for Mom but it was one-sided," she continued. "He was there that night. My sister Debbie was there with him, *but* she says he was already there when she got there. It was around eleven p.m. I don't know where he lived relative to the house. I think he had a car."

Laurie told me that when she described the person she saw wiping the girls' bedroom doorknob that night, Debbie told her that she had first thought of Carl.

When I began my investigation in 2001, I received an e-mail from Carl Barlow that said that he was a good friend to Doris and all of the children. He told me in the e-mail that he had gone by the house the evening that Doris was killed, but had to leave. He found out the next morning about the murder. The police asked him to come down to the station, where he said he "spent about three hours being questioned, having finger prints, palm prints, and pubic samples taken." But he said that he never heard anything else from the police about that night.

Carl went on to describe the setup of the family room in detail—he said that he understood the person came in through the window in the family room. He said, "There was a couch in front of the window and the window was about 5 to 6 feet up from ground level. The windows were wood frame and not easily opened, they also had storm windows; I don't remember them ever being open."

He ended the e-mail by offering to help my investigation in any way he could.

He gave up some interesting information without even being asked; in particular he commented that Mrs. Hoover was unable to have sex. That was kind of an odd thing for a young friend of the family to be discussing with his friend's mother.

He's one nobody suspected. He was so unlikely no one had thought of him. It just couldn't be him. But my review of the evidence raised questions about his possible role.

Now if only I could provide enough evidence to support my hypothesis.

CARL'S INTERVIEWS WITH me sent up many red flags.

"I have my own theory," Carl told me. "This is way out in left field. I really wondered about Mickey, her husband. Me and him . . .

he was intimidating to me. . . . I had peculiar feelings about him. . . . She couldn't have sex; maybe it hurt too much.

"It also could be something she just said to me. Like we were a lot like mother and son but a lot more than that. But there was never anything physical between us. . . .

"I didn't care a whole lot for Debbie's husband at the time," Carl added. "Something about him I didn't care for. He was in the military. . . .

"The windows were always closed and locked. Wood frame windows with a swing lock on the top. And no ladder . . . would be impossible without a ladder.

"[There was a] double window in the family room and the couch was against the wall under the window. No footprints that I know of. I think one of the younger girls said he left and came back. I don't know if the girls know if it was the same person. . . . Maybe someone else came to the house and left. That was always something Doris [did] that meant they were in bed. If she was in bed I don't think the door was open and if someone knocked, she probably wouldn't hear it. In my younger days, if I was driving by and the lights were off, I wouldn't stop.

"I couldn't tell you a whole lot about Mickey.

"At the time I didn't have a gun, not even an air gun.

"I only know that Doris had a gun. I just took her word that she had one. I know she told me she had one under her pillow or mattress. She always had it there in case she needed it.

"I think back then there was a three-day wait to pick up a pistol.

"I don't remember the police questioning anyone. I just think it was people there that evening.

"They didn't ask me to voice the words on the tape.

"For an injury, you would call the firehouse, not the police. I don't know which one they called. As a matter of fact I did hear that they called Mickey's station.

"[There were] four different pay phones—one at the corner, one up the street at the shopping center, within a mile or mile and a half or two. Or maybe eight phones. At that time most of them were inside stores. 7-Eleven was probably open all night. . . . No, it was [the] other store—open at least until eleven.

"They asked me where I was at and I said, 'At Marilyn's house.' They just asked what time I got there and what time I left—I arrived at eight p.m. and I left at eight a.m. I don't know if they checked with Marilyn—[or] even talked with Marilyn.

"I sure hope you get some answers."

Carl was a friend of the family and spent time alone with Doris, talking about life and taking walks. Without a doubt, he had established a personal relationship with her.

He was extremely familiar with the layout of the house and the address, as he visited quite often. He also knew Doris's children and was friendly with some of them.

One of the daughters told me that Carl owned a gun similar to the one used in the crime; however, during my interview with him he said he didn't own any gun at the time of the murder. He even added, "I didn't even own an air gun at the time."

I learned that Carl was unhappy with his relationship with his own mother and commented that Doris filled in as a kinder, older woman who would listen to his problems. A number of Hoover family members believed he might have been infatuated with Doris.

Carl commented that Doris knew things about him that no one, including himself, had told her. This bizarre statement was made more than once.

"I told Doris I would be back later but I never made it back," he told me.

I wondered why he would be returning at a later time that night and why, if he told her he would come back, he didn't.

"To me he wasn't odd," Debbie told me. "Denise thought [he was]. He was a quiet person. He was very friendly. He would do anything for anybody. He liked me a lot. We dated a couple times in high school. He was good to my kids and husband.

"He was kind of my best friend," Debbie continued. "I could talk to him about the problems with my dad. Maybe he had a crush on my mom. I know he didn't think my dad treated her right. . . .

Monte, my husband, got a dog from the police department, and [my mother] at one time had raised shepherds. Mom wanted to see him [the night she was killed], so I went over, took the dog. Monte took care of the kids. I was there till midnight or later. I left because she got a phone call from my dad and argued."

Debbie said she didn't see Carl that night at the house. Carl couldn't remember if she was there before or after him. Her sisters Laurie and Denise, however, said that they were there together, and that it was quite late. If they *were* there together, it would have had to be after eleven. Carl said he was there from seven to seven thirty p.m. and was going to come back later. Did he return after eleven p.m. with or after Debbie? He said he was there at around seven p.m. and told Doris that he would return later but didn't. But what if he did return? Carl's alibi was that he was a mile away at the home of his girlfriend, Marilyn, by eight p.m. This conflicted with others' recollections of him being at the Hoover house late that night.

There seemed to have been a family confrontation that night. But who was involved is unclear. Some reported that Doris had fought with her husband over the phone. Others told of an argument between Doris and Debbie over Debbie leaving her husband (and possibly for Carl). Carl seemed to be involved in some way or another.

Carl brought up the issue of taking his watch over to Doris to have it fixed. This was a watch she gave him, supposedly for graduation. He said, "It never showed up again." It was highly unlikely that a thief would have chosen to steal Carl's broken watch. It was more likely he was concerned that the watch was in her purse, evidence perhaps that he had returned that night.

Finally, Carl's parents lived nearby and this would be the direction the perpetrator would have been heading after leaving the Hoovers' house, shown by the crayon marks on the sidewalk the perpetrator left after he stepped on them at the crime scene. There was also a convenience store with a pay phone at the end of the Hoovers' street along that same route, the phone the killer used to call the fire station.

* * * *

LAURIE HOOVER SAID she never completely shook off the nagging fear that her father could have had something to do with her mother's murder, that maybe he *had* hired a hit man. It was a feeling that stuck with her over the years.

The police investigation stalled and the survivors waited for years and years for some hope that the case would be reevaluated and a suspect would finally be identified and brought in. A recording of the emergency call disappeared shortly after the murder. And although they hypnotized and polygraphed Laurie, they never interviewed Doris's eldest daughter, Cathy, who lived across the street, or Debbie, who had been at the house that evening, or Doris's two best friends. Nor did they talk to Mickey Hoover's coworkers. They did question Carl.

"It was screwed up," Mickey told me in an interview. "One detective had a daughter who was very ill. He didn't have the time to put into it. Finally, they changed lead detectives. Naturally, I would like to know what happened.

"The police told one of my daughters it was a hit. I didn't hear it from the police. They never questioned me on the hit theory. They questioned my buddies; they never asked me to take a polygraph."

By the time of my investigation, the police no longer had any evidence from the case. They gave the Hoover children a number of reasons for this: it "got lost in the chain of command," "became contaminated," or was "lost in a warehouse fire." It didn't help me that the house where the murder occurred subsequently burned down.

But Debbie—and Carl—appeared to be holding back.

Debbie seemed defensive when we talked about Carl. And, according to Denise, Debbie had been against my being brought in to profile the crime. Was her grief too great and did she not want to dredge up the past, or was there another reason?

Debbie made statements that she and Carl were not romantically involved, yet others believe differently. Carl and Debbie also said that Carl was not romantically involved with Doris, but that also was questionable. What exactly the emotional involvement was among the three of them remains to be discovered.

Mickey, however, fully cooperated in my interview and I found nothing concerning in his answers. He did have questions about Carl, it's worth noting.

"My wife had befriended Carl as a teenager," he said. "Carl, it seemed, had a troubled relationship with his parents, and I don't know whether he was living with them at the time. He never came to the funeral or the funeral home. He said he was at his girlfriend's and the police never went further. My daughter asked me if [Doris] was having an affair. I hate to think that. She had never had any affairs that I had known of."

(Incidentally, Carl told me he *did* attend the funeral and subsequently went with Debbie to put flowers at Doris's grave.)

Mickey was willing to be polygraphed, further decreasing any suspicion about his involvement. I still believed it advisable to request the polygraph anyway. This would serve two purposes. One, since he was willing, why not take the opportunity to leave no stone unturned and be sure nothing was overlooked? Should I be dead wrong in my profile, this was a reasonable way to be sure the killer of Doris Hoover didn't escape attention. Should Mickey have difficulty with the polygraph, then a door of investigation opens. If he passed it without problem and a police interview with him aroused no new suspicions, then Mickey could be dropped low on the suspect list, further narrowing the focus of the investigation to other suspects.

Carl gave me mixed messages about his relationship with Doris and the family. On one hand, he tried to sound nonchalant, like he was just a casual family friend without strong connections to the victim.

Then, during his conversations with me, he made statements suggesting a strong intimacy with the family and Doris in particular. He was eager to be helpful. He didn't even seem upset that he had been considered a suspect. He said he hoped the police solved this crime and that I should call him anytime, yet he purported to have little information to offer of other possible suspects.

It was my feeling that the crime may have been one of passion, at least what most people call a crime of passion. Crimes of passion are really actions that an individual would not object to carrying out should he be provoked. What causes some folks to feel guilty about these crimes is when the crime goes further than expected. If Carl did it, he might not have planned to kill her; he might only have wanted to scare her, maybe appear desperate to her.

He should have been asked if he ever actually engaged in any sexual conduct with Doris. I believed that they may have had a physical relationship and that Carl was uncomfortable with it. I didn't buy his assertions that the relationship was just a friendship. He said that Doris couldn't have sex—how would he know and why should he know? He was confused as to why the police got pubic hair from him when "she couldn't have sex." Perhaps he tried with her—consensually or not—and she found it too painful (following a hysterectomy). Perhaps she told him that as a way to fend him off. Either way, it seemed to me he knew too much about this for a daughter's male friend to know.

He also said Doris knew things about him he had never told anyone. Was he suggesting she was psychic? Regardless of the confused meaning of this, it infers yet more intimacy.

When I completed my profile, in addition to thinking that the police should reexamine Carl, I also concluded that the police should have talked with Debbie. According to her story about when she was at the house and who was there with her, her stories were inconsistent with those of her sisters.

After I handed in my profile to the police, I suggested that they use the Hoovers' appearance on the daytime TV show to see if Carl would talk more about the night of the murder. I suggested they give Carl a ring, tell him that tips had been coming in after the show aired (I had gotten some, but unfortunately they were all from psychics), and they now needed to talk with him.

The detective liked the idea.

The prosecutor didn't.

And nothing was ever done.

CHAPTER 9

MISSY
A CHILD'S NIGHTMARE

The Crime: Sexual assault, homicide
The Victim: Missy Jones
Location: Southwestern United States
Original Theory: Her father did it

As you're driving into this small town in the Southwest, there are signs on the side of the road that say WARNING: HITCH-HIKERS MAY BE ESCAPING PRISONERS.

The town has only two industries: a prison and a mental institution. You either work at one or the other. And then there was the sheriff's department, which put you either in the prison or the mental institution. It's a pretty scary place.

The sheriff's department did an excellent job of investigating Missy Jones's murder, and they had the forensics, photos, and notes to prove it. They wanted my take, and if I came to the same conclusion, they wanted me to encourage the family to finally cooperate with the investigation. They wanted me to convince the family that Missy's own daddy killed her.

Missy's mom was incensed.

"The sheriff is crazy!" she insisted. "What father would rape and murder his own daughter?"

But by the time I finished profiling the crime and researching the background of Missy's dad, Orville, they had come around and their anger wasn't targeted at the sheriff's department anymore. As we sat in a circle on the front lawn of the trailer home, Missy's uncle spoke on behalf of the family.

"Hell, yeah, we'll cooperate," he said. "We're ready to put a bullet in the bastard's head ourselves."

MISSY DIED ON April 25, 1992. The Jones family brought me into this case about nine years later.

They were upset because the police had focused on Missy's father as the prime suspect. The family could not believe that her own father would do something like that to her when there were better choices out there:

- Tommy Hime, the twenty-eight-year-old man down the street who befriended twelve-year-old Missy and was close to another teenage girl who disappeared six weeks after she had a baby and was never found;
- Ron Lewis, who was at the house Missy visited that night. He grew pot and later escaped from a chain gang.

But Orville? Why would the sheriff be looking at him but not be interested in Tommy or Ron?

Instead, the sheriff insisted the only suspect in Missy's murder was Orville Jones, her biological father.

Orville, who was a self-employed carpenter, earned an associate's degree in criminal justice while attending community college, so he considered himself quite the junior investigator. He was always giving information to the police as to who they should be looking at and how the man down the street, Tommy, was trying to be Missy's boyfriend but he was a lot older than her. He also noted how, in the house she was visiting, the boy living there, Ron Lewis's brother, tried to have his way with her once before. I found that amusing. And you, *her father*, let her go back there to play anyway?

Orville was full of stories; he had an answer for everything. Orville, in the long run, comes off as a classic psychopath who likes to run the whole show, and yet his demeanor following his daughter's death shows a total lack of understanding of what's appropriate and what's inappropriate. Or how people will view you. Psychopaths are so busy manipulating people and trying to control the game in their own mind, they don't realize how they come off.

IN ORLANDO, FLORIDA, a girl named Caylee Anthony made national headlines in June 2008 when she disappeared. The story grew disproportionately large primarily because her single mother, Casey Anthony, gave a ridiculous story as to how the babysitter kidnapped her daughter. Meanwhile Casey spent her nights partying in bars.

The public was shocked when, on July 15, the press reported that Caylee's grandparents—who couldn't get a straight answer for weeks from Casey about her daughter's whereabouts—picked up Casey's car from a towing lot and were revolted by the smell emanating from the trunk.

"There's something wrong," Cindy Anthony said in an emergency call to 911. "I found my daughter's car today and it smelled like there's been a dead body in the damn car." Later, apparently to protect her daughter, Cindy claimed the smell came from pizza that Casey had left in the trunk.

That seemed to parallel what happened in Missy Jones's case sixteen years earlier.

There was *definitely* a nasty smell coming from the old sedan that Orville drove. It was something the police honed in on, investigating whether Missy had once been in the car trunk—and just as we later saw in the case of Caylee Anthony, her decomposing body was relocated to a wooded area after a period of time, leaving a smell far worse than rotting pizza.

We often wonder why people bother to put bodies in trunks, but the simple fact is they are convenient, enclosed locations you can lock and keep people from opening. They are also usefully attached to a motor vehicle that allows you to then transport a corpse out of sight of prying eyes. But trunks also keep a lot of good evidence, as well, so unless a killer really does a good job of making sure nothing escapes from the body into the trunk—a really good double or triple Hefty bag wrap for starters that keeps bodily fluids and gases contained—eagle-eyed investigators and the forensics team should easily detect clues there.

Investigators used the latest gas technology in the Caylee Anthony case, which they did not have available in the Missy Jones case.

Missy was missing for two weeks before the body was found. The family brought me in nine years later because, while the police suspected Missy's dad, the family refused to buy into that theory. They were sure that somebody else killed her, but the time line in this case did not support that. Who was available to be involved in the crime? What things made sense in the time line? Who had the ability to commit the crime?

ON THE NIGHT she disappeared, Missy's mother, Miranda, drove her to Rhonda Lewis's home around six p.m. to hang out and sleep over with her friend. Missy was excited about a family trip planned for the next day. She was going to go home in the morning, pack, and take off with her parents and brothers.

Orville and his wife, Miranda, went out drinking that night, came home, and went to sleep.

At some point in the night, the phone rang twice. The first time Miranda heard the phone ring, she was in the shower. Miranda said Orville answered it and told her it was Missy wanting to come home. Miranda told him to tell her to wait until breakfast time.

Miranda thought the phone rang again. She recalled Orville telling her it was a hang-up. She didn't remember anything more. The liquor knocked her out and all she remembered was waking up when the sun was already shining in the window.

Over at the Lewises' house, Missy was watching television when Mrs. Lewis came down around 2:20 a.m. and said, "What are you doing down here?"

"I have a stomachache," Missy said. "I'm going to go home. I already called home and asked them to come get me."

"Okay," Mrs. Lewis said, "but turn the television off, because we don't watch television at this time of night."

Missy, who was fully clothed, did as she was told and Mrs. Lewis went back to bed. When she woke up the next morning, Missy was gone. The Lewis family assumed Missy went home with whomever came to get her.

They assumed incorrectly.

"Between eight and nine a.m., I made a call to my sister's house and decided not to make the trip," Miranda Jones said. "Orville began to make coffee and fix breakfast. It was Sunday morning and no one was in a hurry. About ten a.m., Missy still hadn't come home. I sent my youngest son over to Rhonda's to tell Missy to come home. He came back saying she wasn't there. I then went over to talk to Rhonda's mother, Eva Lewis. Eva said that Missy was up in the living room sometime around two a.m., saying she wanted to go home, she was going to call her mother. Rhonda's house was only about 150 yards through the small wooded area between [our] two houses. I think Eva stated that Missy was complaining about a stomachache. I never received a call or saw Missy that night." (Miranda changed her story here about the phone call most likely because she didn't want to admit she didn't go get her daughter or that her husband actually might have.)

There were five people in the Lewis house at the time that Missy disappeared, and no one saw her leave.

"I went back home and searched the neighborhood," Miranda continued. "Missy's dad called the police and sometime around eleven a.m. to eleven thirty a.m. they arrived. (I can't remember where Missy's dad was at this time; I think he was at the house waiting for the police to arrive.)

"My oldest son was called at work to come home; I think I went to pick him up. When the police arrived they brought a search dog. The officer with the dog and I went through the wooded area between the two houses (the Lewises' and mine) where the kids played. I had given some of Missy's clothes for the dog to get her scent. When we arrived at the Lewis house (up to this point the dog had not picked up Missy's scent) I was asked to stay outside, but I could see through the screen door.

"The dog went crazy when he came to the chair where Missy was last seen sitting. The dog followed her scent to the living room door and stopped. He could not pick up her scent outside the house. [*It was said that maybe so many people walking around may have hindered the dogs' ability to pick up her scent.*] The dog was led around to the back of the house, where Missy and Rhonda had picked berries the day before. He was able to pick up her scent again there, but it led nowhere."

EVA LEWIS CLAIMED Missy was waiting for someone to pick her up. Two phone calls came in to the Jones household just about the time Eva said Missy had contacted her family.

None of the Joneses—Orville, Miranda, or any of the kids—heard any car start up outside their trailer home. Nobody heard anybody drive away. But then again, there was only a two-minute walk between the two homes.

Missy was killed by somebody in the Lewises' home or she was walked out of their home in the middle of the night and somebody else killed her; or someone from the Jones house came over to pick her up and they knew what happened to her. Something happened at that point in time, because she was at the Lewises', and then she was not.

I agreed with the police that the witnesses and their statements eliminated all but one of the suspects. After Missy made her phone call, someone should have been coming to get her. Orville, the dad, said he never talked to Missy and she probably started walking home in the middle of the night, even though Missy was not the sort to do that and she wasn't feeling well. "Tommy probably killed her."

Tommy Hime managed a restaurant and he did live close by, but it would be pretty coincidental that Missy made a phone call home and Tommy showed up. Where did he come from? The Lewis place was not on the way from Tommy's house to her house. It couldn't be that Tommy was just strolling by at the time, although he would have finished work around midnight. He would have to make a specific journey over that way and run into her at the exact same time she gave up waiting for her dad to come. (Tommy, incidentally, passed the lie detector test.)

Back at Missy's home, the time line produced the same result.

Orville never said, "I went to get her, and she wasn't there."

What happened to Missy after she told Mrs. Lewis that someone was coming for her? When did she vanish?

It was highly unlikely at that point that she would have left with anyone else, as she knew someone was coming to get her. It was also unlikely that someone in the household would at this exact moment attempt to abduct and rape Missy, as a parent was only possibly minutes away from arrival.

The most likely scenario was that the father walked over to the Lewises' to get her and something happened on the way home. Orville had been drinking earlier in the evening and maybe he decided it was easier to walk rather than take the car. Maybe he already had the squirrelly idea in his head that he could bring Missy into the woods and have his way with her. It's worth noting that later, the police dogs did not follow Missy's scent from the door. It's possible the father picked her up and carried her. She was a twelve-year-old girl, kind of small, certainly tired. It's also possible the dogs just weren't any good.

She disappeared, but according to police, the person who did the least to help find her was her dad. While everybody else was out searching for Missy, he didn't even bother. He stayed home, hanging around the house.

Orville didn't act appropriately. Just two days after Missy went missing he started making comments like, "You are looking for her body" and "She's dead."

These remarks indicated he believed his daughter was already dead. He knew what happened to her. He made a similar comment to a little girl who lived next door and another to a TV news show. He referred to his daughter as "the body." He said that the search was a waste of time. Sitting in his recliner with a smirk on his face, he looked over at his son and said, "Chuck, you killed Missy, didn't you?" What kind of father says things like that?

His daughter had gone missing and no one knew what had happened to her. She could be a runaway—that's how the police initially classified her because she was twelve years old and her father didn't think the police should waste their time looking for her. Real fatherly behavior, right?

After she was found murdered, Orville went on a local TV news show and said he didn't know if Missy was killed out of "meanness or carelessness." The girl was found partially clothed, her hands tied with a sock and another sock stuck in her mouth, the latter of which caused her death. That could be the mark of a serial killer, a rapist, a child predator. Where would Daddy come up with the notion that it was meanness or carelessness?

ALL THESE BEHAVIORS that Orville exhibited after the fact were peculiar, which is why the police said, "There's something fishy about this guy."

They already knew Orville pretty well. He lived in a small town, and Orville wasn't terribly liked by the police there. He agreed to a polygraph, which was inconclusive. He said he contacted a psychic who told him Missy was in a dark place, probably the car trunk that he knew she was in. He spouted theories of Satanism.

Where was she for two weeks? Why couldn't they find her?

Eventually, an anonymous 911 call came in—it was not recorded because of technical difficulties—telling the police that Missy could be found in one of three places. She was found in one of them, between the two houses, the Jones house and the Lewis house, underneath a honeysuckle bush. She wasn't there before; the area had been carefully searched and searched again. Her hair was matted and stood out from her head. Her skin was black all over except for her legs, which were orangish above the knees. She was laid down in the bush with her body pitched downward and her feet up, wearing a

T-shirt decorated with kittens. Her tennis shoes, the shoelaces tied in a knot to keep the shoes together, had been tossed onto the bush and were hanging from a branch. Missy was not known to tie her shoes in that manner.

Her hands were loosely tied with one of her socks. The other sock was stuffed in her mouth and had hardened there. Missy's black jeans and underwear were wadded up and lying under her. Her shirt was on her torso but it, too, was rolled up. No bra, but she didn't wear one. It appeared to be a sexual assault but there was no visible evidence of it.

If she were there for two weeks, searchers would have found her, because they clearly searched between the two houses.

"A few days before Missy's body was found," according to Miranda Jones, "Rhonda Lewis's oldest sister picked berries at that spot and said she saw nothing. My mom and I searched that area, too; we stood next to the honeysuckle bush where her body was later found and we saw nothing.

"Everyone is in agreement that Missy was not there at that time, that she was killed somewhere else and her body was brought back." It wasn't until later that they brought in cadaver dogs and came across her body. Where did her body come from?

If she got tired of waiting to be picked up and walked home and somebody raped her on the way—like Tommy from down the street—he probably would have just left her there and run.

If somebody abducted her and dragged her off to a vehicle, she wouldn't be there at all. So why did the body end up back by the house? Why wasn't it there to begin with?

Earlier, Orville reportedly told Rhonda that she shouldn't walk between the houses because bad things happen to little girls who walk in that area.

There was a theory that Orville may have actually brought Missy home and done something to her in the house, but I found that kind of unlikely. My theory is that he did something to her in those woods and then didn't know what to do about his dead daughter lying in the middle of the patch. He had to do something with her body—after all, he might have left evidence on it—so he quickly carried her to his house and put her body in the trunk of the car; he would slip back inside and into bed and deal with "the problem" later. He hid the car keys to make sure no one else would borrow the vehicle and decide to put some groceries in the trunk.

Eventually, the car was moved. I think it was moved around quite a few times because he didn't know what to do with it. One of the reasons her body may have ended up where it did, dumped back in the woods to be found two weeks later, was that he got tired of it all. We find this often happens with people who are involved with the killing of a family member. That's one of the reasons we look back at the family when we see something like this. We look at the husband, the parents—whoever the victim had a close relationship with, because these people have to live day in and day out with the search, and at some point they get frustrated by it. They tire of the questioning and the wife or the husband or whoever constantly looking for the missing person and spending their entire lives doing this. They want to move on. *That kid's dead, I want to forget about it. I want to start doing stuff. I don't want to sit here and dwell on this.*

The killer will bring the body back and dump it in a location where it will be found and they can get that part over with. *There's the body. We found her. Now can we move on?* Of course, they don't think ahead to the next part, which is that the authorities will actually investigate the homicide. The perpetrator doesn't think that far ahead.

Orville didn't seem terribly surprised when he got the news that Missy's body was found right near the house in the woods. He said, "Huh." That someone might have brought her body back and dumped it in the bushes would not be a big surprise to Orville if he was the one who put it there. It is most likely that he kept Missy in the trunk until he had an opportunity to move her to another location for hiding. There was speculation that he hid the body in his mother's barn. But, at some point, my theory continues, he wanted her to be found, and so he put her back in the trunk and brought her back to the woods by the house. He carried her body to the bush and dumped it.

Then he went back to the car, looked in the trunk, and realized the shoes were still there. He grabbed them, tossed them into the bushes, and took off. The body was found, and by that time the police were looking at him.

One of the interesting things is that his wife told me that he kept spraying his car trunk with insecticide. He was apparently having a little bit of a fly problem. That's why his wife noticed an odd smell and an insecticide odor as well.

The family, in spite of Orville's squirrelly behavior, did not think he had anything to do with the crime. They just thought he was a quirky fellow.

I see this happen with many families. People around Missy, her teachers and her Girl Scout leader, thought she might have been sexually abused. They believed something was not right in her life long before she was murdered. Missy's behavior had changed in recent months, she seemed sad and distant. Yet they had trouble believing that someone they knew was responsible for this horrific act.

I WENT BACK and looked at Orville's history and there was no shortage of interesting details. He told his first wife that he had had a sexual relationship with his sister, and his sister was killed running in front of a car—away from him, perhaps.

We don't know whether it's true that he had sex with his sister, but he said that he did, which is an interesting admission.

I also learned that another family member had reported that she had been molested by him. When we get to Missy, it's not terribly surprising to learn police suspected he had sexually assaulted her as well.

The information was adding up and Orville was scoring all the points. The time line made no sense for anybody but Orville to have committed the crime. Everything pointed to him: his peculiar behaviors, his lack of interest in looking for his daughter, and the claim that she was already dead, so why bother looking? This guy was awfully confident that he knew what happened to Missy.

The family was blind to these behaviors; they wouldn't and couldn't believe it.

I MET WITH the police, studied all of their materials, and examined the crime scene. I believed that the police were absolutely correct, that Orville must have been involved in the sexual assault and murder of his daughter.

But I came to a slightly different theory about where it happened and how it went down.

The police did not have enough evidence at that point in time to go to court. They wanted the family's cooperation, but they weren't getting any because the police focused suspicion on Orville.

When I made my independent analysis, which pointed to Orville's involvement, I told the police that I would sit down with the family and ask for their cooperation. We had a fascinating meeting outside the house. We all sat in chairs with a beer and relaxed. Miranda was there, as was Missy's uncle, and it was quite a group. Orville was not living there at the time; he had already fled the family coop and was in prison serving time for an unrelated charge that occurred when his new girlfriend called the police on him. They had been arguing over a new man in her life and Orville said he was going to hurt the other boyfriend. When the police arrived on the scene, he shot at them, they shot back, and he went to prison.

I explained Orville's entire history. I explained how his sexual experience with his sister demonstrated sexual deviancy before they ever met him. He was not an honest man and he was a major manipulator. I went through every detail of his background. I explained how they got wrapped up in this, why it was confusing, and how they might have difficulty recognizing the truth in all of this.

When I finished, they looked at me with sad, glazed-over expressions and I realized that this was one family that could handle the truth, even as ugly a truth as this one. Families often fight back against the truth, and they say, "No way," no matter what I tell them. This family did not do that. Instead they said, "What do you need us to do? How can we help?"

I put in place a plan to try to draw a confession out of Orville, and I started by communicating with him. There were letters coming from him, so full of garbage it was just amusing. The family worked with me, so Missy's uncle, Miranda's brother, sent a letter saying, "Orville, we have this great private investigator working with us who believes Missy's death was an accident."

I wanted Orville to think I was on the family's side in supporting him and that the family did not want this going to court. They believed it was an accident because the criminal profiler told them that. This was my ruse: I believed that Orville was drunk when he picked up Missy and, on the way back, they got into an argument, and he accidentally killed her, and he didn't know what to do. I thought the police were wrong that it was murder and that the worst charge he faced would be manslaughter.

The uncle told Orville that I helped the family understand it was an accident, that the family was comfortable with that and wasn't angry at Orville, that if he would plead guilty to that, he could get a manslaughter conviction and get a few years in prison and get out.

It was a pretty good setup. The sheriff liked it, too. I was playing the role of the dumb blond profiler doing the worst case of profiling you ever saw.

I thought Orville would buy this. I thought he would find it terribly amusing and make him think he was manipulating me. Plus, he would believe his family were chumps, too, and he would hardly serve any time if he confessed to accidentally killing Missy.

I wrote Orville a nice letter when I started working the case to get information from him, and he wrote me back all kinds of fanciful theories. Then, after the family meeting, Missy's uncle wrote his letter and I wrote one to match. Finally, when the prosecution stopped the planned visit the sheriff and I were to make to Orville, I wrote him one last-ditch-attempt letter, hoping to spook him. Here are excerpts from it.

OCTOBER 18, 2001

Dear Mr. Jones,

Think carefully about what you are reading, Mr. Jones.

Missy may be dead but her body and her clothes can still speak volumes. Mitochondrial DNA (MtDNA) can link a suspect with a crime by a minute speck of saliva or hair fiber. This new methodology far exceeds the old testing and is being used across the country in getting convictions in cold cases. Expect the investigator on your case to be court ordering your DNA for comparison very shortly. . . .

The family will have to hear all the horrible details and who knows what information will be made public to support the prosecution and what other witnesses will come forward to tell what they know. The person convicted of this crime will have to spend his remaining life among inmates labeled as a child rapist and killer.

The family wishes to believe that this was a crime of carelessness or drunken anger. This profiler believes this may well be true and would support this conclusion in cooperation with a plea bargain for manslaughter with the DA. Once the testing is complete and immunity is given, this case will then have to be prosecuted as a crime committed by a man who has no guilt over what happened. By refusing to plea this down to an unfortunate accident, this person admits to his family, this profiler, and the court that the crime was intentional.

Time is short, Mr. Jones. Use it wisely.

SINCERELY,
PAT BROWN
DIRECTOR/INVESTIGATIVE CRIMINAL PROFILER

Orville was in jail for another crime, so the sheriff and I could have gone down there to talk to him. In this last letter, I let Orville know that Missy's body would be exhumed. I told Orville they were looking for more sexual evidence and some other things that would put him in a death penalty situation. But if he confessed, we wouldn't have the body exhumed.

I added in scientific methodologies, hoping to make him fear that more might be found, so pleading out might be a better deal. Then we would have a confession that he committed the crime.

That's what we were aiming for, but unfortunately the prosecution shut us down. One of the things I've learned over years of profiling and working with police departments is that often there are things that can and will be done, and everybody is on the same page until we get to some level of politics that throws a wrench in our plans. I never got an explanation in this case as to why the prosecution wouldn't cooperate and I probably will never know. If it is frustrating to me, imagine how hard it is on the family to see an investigation suddenly come to a jarring halt with no reason given.

Prosecutors come and prosecutors go, and many are political appointees. If the sheriff and prosecutor aren't buddy-buddy, we might not get any kind of cooperation from the prosecutor. The prosecutor may be looking at his win record. He might say, "This is too tough a case, I don't even want to deal with it."

Sometimes, they won't tell you directly what the politics are, because they can't admit to it, or they will get in trouble if they do. I can't tell you how many cases are ruined by politics. The Anne Kelley case was one. People usually think that it's underhanded, like the suspect in the case is really the police chief's brother. That's not usually what it is. It's more likely something completely unrelated to the actual crime. It's either a time factor, the possibility that they might lose the case, or it could be the specter of negative publicity for the town. Prosecutors may refuse to take a case because they don't want to bring out the community's dirty laundry, especially if that laundry is sitting in some bigwig's basket. If it's a tourist destination, they will especially resist tackling a prosecution that will scare tourists away from visiting their once quiet hamlet.

People think that when a person is murdered there is a requirement by our legal system that the person who committed the crime be prosecuted. There is no such mandate in our country. The state is only required to prosecute crimes it feels like prosecuting, that are in the "interest of the state." That's it. The victim has no rights, the family has no rights, and citizens' only rights are voting the people they favor into office. It is the state's determination whether it chooses to proceed with a case or not. They don't even have to investigate a case. They don't have to prosecute a case.

If the prosecution becomes too expensive or unwieldy or it could possibly lose, it simply may not move ahead. Not even if the state knows who did it and there's a solid pile of evidence, it just won't do it. Prosecutors have so many cases on their plates that they decide which ones they'll take and with which cases they won't bother. If there are easy cases and hard cases, they'll take the easy cases.

The police tend to be frustrated with this, too, and that's why sometimes they develop a negative attitude. They will work hard on a case for two years, thinking they have ample evidence, and the prosecutor won't take it to trial. And if that happens to them enough times, they get cynical, and they say, "Why bother next time? Am I really going to sit here and kill myself investigating this stupid case when nobody will ever take it to court?"

These days, if the police don't have a bucket of DNA and a videotape of the crime going down, they may lose confidence their investigation is worth doing. If they get handed a difficult crime that requires confessions or huge amounts of legwork, or if they have five other cases pending, they'll just dump the most complicated one and go with the other four.

WE OFTEN FIND that predators will wait until a child reaches prepubescence before abuse begins. They don't like having sex with a six-year-old, but once she reaches nine or ten, she's cute, having started to grow breasts and appearing more teenagerlike. That can be attractive to a sexual predator.

A lot of men who are considered child predators are not pedophiles. A pedophile is somebody who has an obsession with having sex with children, with childlike children, little children. A pedophile is not necessarily a sexual predator, because some pedophiles don't do anything about it, they just think about it a lot.

A child sexual predator is someone who assaults children for sex or uses sex as a method of power and control over children. Sometimes a sexual predator would prefer to rape women but he is too chicken to go up against an adult so he picks on the most vulnerable of the population: kids.

I don't believe Orville Jones was a pedophile. But he may have been a sexual predator who homed in on teenagers and prepubescent girls because they're easy—first his sister, then his daughter.

A lot of sexual predators call themselves "teachers." A person of interest in the sexual homicides of three girls in Virginia considered himself a professor of sex. I communicated with him on the Internet, posing as a fourteen-year-old girl named Veronica. He wanted me to do things to myself with various objects and hurt myself. That was what sexually excited him, and he called it teaching. He said, "I'm going to teach you the art of sex. Better me than some young boy who doesn't know what he's doing. I'll teach you what pleases a man. I'll teach you what feels good."

In their own sick, twisted minds they become professors. And of course they want to start with a girl who's a virgin, because they want her taught right. They will pick on a girl who's nine to thirteen years old, just becoming a woman, and they love the idea that they will be her first. That's part of the power trip—that nobody's had that girl before. Once they start introducing her to these things, of course, she's embarrassed, she's humiliated, and sometimes, unfortunately, sexually stimulated. She becomes confused, and she doesn't know how to tell anybody. And then, of course, there is the possibility that he threatens her. *You tell anybody, I'll hurt you,* so she doesn't.

Police told me that they believed Orville was sexually abusing Missy before her murder and that she was going to tell on him. It is possible that she could have fought back. He could have gone further than she was willing to accept, as she was already sick of being abused, and this particular time she was sleepy and not feeling well.

My hypothesis is that her father carried Missy, as she was tired, ill, and very lightweight. She was in her stocking feet—her shoes, tied together by their laces, grabbed up by Orville and carried along with his daughter. It was in the middle of the route through the woods that I believe Mr. Jones, under the influence of alcohol, did decide to sexually assault his daughter. I believe he did not intend to kill her, but when she resisted he became angry and his attempts at control ended in her death. She fought back and it got her killed. Perhaps she screamed; I believe that the sock was pushed into her mouth to stop her from making noise, because it was just a two-minute walk between houses and while it's a wooded area, a scream can still carry in the dead of night. Missy's shoes were not on her feet, making her sock easy to pull off her foot. Offenders often do what is easy and pulling off a sock and stuffing it in her mouth would be a quick and easy answer to shutting Missy up.

Whether or not I believe Orville killed his daughter, I don't think he planned to kill her. The hyoid bone in the neck was not broken. Usually, when someone is strangled, that's broken, but Missy's was not. The autopsy report said she was asphyxiated, but if she wasn't choked, then someone or something suffocated her. I believe it was the sock in her mouth that cut off her air supply. When he realized what he had done, he had two choices. Leave her there in the woods and have her found the very next day or place her in the trunk of an unused vehicle in the yard and have her become a missing person. The latter choice would buy time, and in his panicked state, Orville most likely felt this was the better idea. After placing her in the trunk of the vehicle, he slipped back into the house, his family never having realized he had left.

There is a theory that Missy actually arrived home and her father assaulted and killed her in her bedroom. I find this to be an unlikely scenario for two reasons. The likelihood of Missy arriving home with no one noticing, a brutal attack going unheard, and the removal of a body without being noted or heard in a small trailer with two boys asleep in the living room, which Orville would have to enter or exit, is unlikely. Also, Orville commented to Rhonda that if she went into the woods bad things could happen to her. I believe Orville was reliving the actual experience of the rape and murder of his daughter.

Orville had been drinking earlier that night, so it was possible he wasn't careful, as he said. I believe he was indeed describing what he did to her, because I do not believe it was an intentional homicide. I believe he was sexually assaulting her and shut her up to control her, because Orville was quite a mean fellow—as he told the media the killer might be. It was an accident but it was still murder, because he killed her during the commission of a crime. When he realized she was no longer breathing, he knew he was in big trouble. I do believe, after studying his history, that he would have liked to have kept Missy around. She probably would have been a nice, useful sex partner for him for the next six years. That plan ended when she fought back.

I HOPED POLICE could use my profile to prosecute Orville, but sadly that did not happen. A profiler can go so far in a case and suddenly get the door slammed in her face. You're so close to making a real difference, *boom*, and you can't do any more, so you have to walk away.

The family will ask, "What now?"

I often find it is difficult to get justice for the family.

Once a case goes south, what do you do about it? Go talk with a reporter from the town newspaper? You might and you could get a story or two written about it. But what do you do then? All you can do is start fighting. You go to the town council and rail at the police, the prosecutor, the town itself. Usually nothing ever really amounts to anything. The family fights on and usually fights alone, and most of the time, they don't win.

Sometimes, the family will come back to me and say, "Have you heard anything?" but eventually they give up contacting me because they realize I can't do anything more. My job is profiling. I did my job, and I left. I'm not part of a law enforcement organization and I am not a victim's advocacy organization that does long-term support. My job is profiling, and that's what I do. I prefer to have the cooperation of the police department and the prosecutor so we can do the best job together. If I don't have that, I can do only so much.

I do my job, and whether a case gets prosecuted or not, that's not my call.

Does a profiler solve cases? No. A profiler profiles. That's it. The police department officially is charged with solving cases; the prosecutor chooses which cases to prosecute.

AND THERE THE case of Missy Jones sits. Nothing more has been done.

Orville was never charged with his daughter's rape and murder. If the system puts Orville back out there, he will likely go after someone else's twelve-year-old daughter.

CHAPTER 10

JIMMY
WITH FRIENDS LIKE THIS

The Crime: Homicide
The Victim: Jimmy Conway
Location: Home of his friend, Southwestern United States
Original Theory: Shot in self-defense

People often wonder whether profilers go to the actual crime scene or if they don't always bother and, in truth, I always go if I can. I can learn a lot by being there, standing on the spot where the victim and perpetrator once stood, absorbing the environment.

For example, you might think that some guy could toss a fellow off a particular bridge because the pictures you are looking at make that seem plausible. This happened to me on a case in Minneapolis. One of the theories was that the victim, who had been drinking at a local bar on Halloween night and been thrown out for being too inebriated, was walking over that bridge when he ran into another young man his age who tried to rob him. When he resisted, the guy pushed him over the railing. Well, that *could* make sense, except when I actually stood on the Hennepin Bridge at the point where it crossed the Mississippi River, I wondered how this shorter, smaller, less muscled attacker could have accomplished this. The railing was so high that the robber would have had to pick him up off the ground and heave him over it. If I hadn't gone to the scene, I might have erroneously believed that action was possible. When you go to the location, you can see the neighborhood. You can see possible escape routes. You can analyze why someone would go that way and not this way.

Of course, sometimes crime scenes change, developers plow through them with a bulldozer, and then it's gone, it doesn't look anything like it did before, and then I do have to rely on the pictures.

But I learn a lot in person. I can interview people, and I can do a lot more because I can get the feel for everything. It's not always economically reasonable to do so, in which case I have to rely on the photos and reports and hope that they will be good enough to do the case justice.

Working pro bono, as I always do (unless I am working for a defense attorney—and they don't like me that much so it is a rare event), the family is not paying for my expenses or anything else.

In this case, the Conway family said, "We think that Jimmy was murdered. We don't think it was self-defense, we think his friend shot him in cold blood." They wanted me to look over the case and sent me the files, which they had because the case was closed. (If the case remains open, the family usually gets nothing.) I had access to all the photos of the crime scene and all the details in the police reports, so I could review the case quite thoroughly, even from a distance.

THE CONWAY FAMILY provided me with a solid amount of information, although the photos from the scene were lousy.

But one of the lousiest held the key.

It was one of those off-the-cuff pictures that people take. The police arrived, took a quick picture of the dead man at the scene, and it turned out to be the most valuable piece of evidence in the case file. It was a Polaroid photo that contained a blood spatter evidence pattern that convinced me that Jimmy's "friend," Earl White, was lying.

* * * *

THIS VALUABLE OPPORTUNITY early in my career taught me the importance of photography.

When a murder is fresh, the police sometimes make snap decisions at the scene as to what they think the case is about.

In another Minnesota case, in 1998, a young man was found hanging in his bedroom. Gregg Meissner's death was ruled a suicide at the scene and the police took no fingerprints off objects in the room. They didn't even seal off the scene because, as they told Gregg's mother, "This isn't television." The detective on the case actually allowed Gregg's distraught friends to enter the crime scene.

The family didn't think it was suicide, I didn't think it was suicide, but the tests were never run. The family fought like tigers to prove Gregg was murdered, and finally, a man named Shawn Padden, one of the friends allowed into the crime scene, was convicted of killing him. However, the lack of certain evidence allowed only a manslaughter charge and not Murder One. Gregg's family was convinced the crime was premeditated, but because the evidence wasn't protected, the state could only prove manslaughter, and Padden might get out to kill again.

I often find this is also true for alibis, that if you make an assumption somebody is not involved and you don't ask for an alibi, you can't go back four years later and say, "Oh, by the way, where were you on May third?" If you're innocent, you can't protect yourself, because there is no way in heck you or anyone else can remember where you were on May 3. An innocent person can't provide himself a decent alibi. A guilty person, well, he's got an excuse not to provide himself a decent alibi, because he will say, "How the heck would I know where I was four years ago on that day?" or "How do you expect anybody to remember where I was?"

The innocent person can't defend himself, and the guilty person can laugh and say he's got an excuse not to remember and not have an alibi.

Like getting alibis, photography is sometimes not methodically and carefully done. If the detective thinks he knows what happened on the scene, he may not be concerned about what those detectives will have to do two, four, or ten years from now.

The detective is at the scene, seeing everything and talking to everybody. If he thinks he has solved the case, he doesn't feel compelled to pursue any more information. But then something goes wrong. The case doesn't get prosecuted, or it is closed as an accident or suicide, but later on, if somebody questions the veracity of that conclusion and a new sheriff reopens the investigation, where is the evidence? Now a profiler is brought in and I am looking at a report file so thin I know no interviewing was done and few tests were run. I may have an autopsy on one page that doesn't actually say more than that the victim is dead (known as a "tailgate autopsy" because all the coroner does is drive up in his truck, drop the tailgate, put one foot up on it, light his cigar, and say, "Yep, she's a dead one").

If the photos are so limited that I can't see if anything is odd in the next room of the house or if there was blood dripping off the porch or not, I will not be able to analyze the case accurately.

I've actually had a good laugh at some cases. Sometimes they bring me seventy boxes of notes, and I think, "Good job, guys, you've got typewritten interviews." In others, I am handed a small box with a few sheets of paper and a napkin from the local eatery, on which are scribbled some unreadable words. "Oh goody, I've got diner notes!"

In talking with police detectives today, I tell them what I know is true of case notes: just because you think you know what your note means now, believe me, in four years, you won't have a clue what you once meant, and neither will the next detective reading your notes. If a cold case squad or a profiler comes on board ten years from now, they won't have notes that clearly state what happened and explain whatever you were thinking—and if you don't have quality crime scene photographs, they will have nothing useful with which to work.

BACK TO JIMMY Conway.

If it weren't for that one picture in the Conway case file, I might not have come to the conclusion I did.

I received police reports, the autopsy report, autopsy photos, and the crime scene photos from the family. The crime scene photos were of poor quality and did not clearly show the scene, nor were proper close-ups taken. Autopsy photos were limited and no photos of the full body of Jimmy Conway were included. Only two photos of Earl White exist that were taken that same day. No photos of Earl's girlfriend, Heidi Mills, were taken at any time in spite of the fact that she claimed to have been severely assaulted by the deceased. There was limited processing of the scene, no gunshot residue tests were done, and no fingerprints were processed on the baseball bat or shotgun, the weapons used in the crime. The dimensions of the crime scene were never drawn.

Interviews were limited to one-time statements by Earl, Heidi, and Earl's son, Joey. No statements were taken from Earl's brother, whose house Earl went to right after the shooting. None of the neighbors were ever contacted either. No further interrogation was done and there was no polygraph testing.

There is a question as to when the actual homicide occurred, though it was between eight thirty and nine thirty p.m. There was not a big problem with this vague time frame, as those involved may not have paid attention to the exact time.

All agreed Jimmy arrived before Earl's teenage son, Joey, and entered through the back door in the kitchen. Earl and Jimmy talked in the kitchen. Joey entered the house and went past Earl and Jimmy and got his clothes from his bedroom. Then he went to see Heidi in the bedroom she shared with Earl and asked her to care for his animals, as he was going away. Earl was not in their bedroom during this time because he had no knowledge of Joey asking Heidi to do this. Jimmy and Earl apparently remained in the kitchen the entire time Joey was in the house.

The investigators made one of those critical mistakes where they take a picture of something—a bloody footprint on the floor—but the crime scene investigators didn't document where the footprint *was*. Which room was it in? Which way was it going? Was it headed east, west, north, south? I had no clue.

I took all of the photos in this case and looked at the bottom of each, trying to identify in some cases where the pattern was on the floor and what the green object might be in the corner. Was it the corner of a refrigerator? I took it like a jigsaw puzzle and rebuilt the house so I could determine where those bloody footprints were.

I did this by reconnecting the photos, discerning the floor patterns, and identifying the bottoms of the furniture. Once I accomplished that, I approximated where the footprints would have been and which direction the owner of the bloody feet was heading. This helped me put together part of the scenario of what happened.

But there was one more photo, an otherwise crappy Polaroid picture. I have to say CRAPPY in big capital letters. It *was* crappy. It was blurry. It was junk, but somebody took it and tossed it in the file. My first impression was "Boy, what a shabby picture." But later on I returned to it and realized it was key to the entire crime. The photo said to me that these people who claimed innocence were lying. One picture made the difference.

When detectives work their cases, I urge them to take the best pictures they can, take way too many pictures, shoot a video of the scene, take close-ups of everything, draw diagrams, document as much as possible, collect all their interviews, record all the alibis, write all their notes and explanations legibly, because they never know when one piece of stray information will make all the difference. They might not catch it, and their partner might not catch it, but somebody might eventually notice. It could be the secretary in the department who one day picks up that photo and goes, "Hey, guys, look at this . . ." Because they had that picture, a person was able to identify something crucial.

JIMMY CONWAY WAS forty years old.

His paycheck was usually $4,000. But one payday, somebody at the company inadvertently added a zero to Jimmy's check, giving him $40,000, and he was like, "Cool, I've got a $40,000 check here!"

You and I know that what he should have done was go to the company and say, "You made a mistake."

I made that same mistake myself. Every week I paid the woman who cleans my house $40 via an electronic payment. But one time

I left the decimal out. I put $4,000 in for $40. I hit the button, and the woman received $4,000 for her services. The woman's husband called me up and said, "We think you made an error." I thought, *Oh, my God, I've hired an honest person.* I was both relieved (really, really relieved) and impressed that this person was so honest.

As for Jimmy? Not so much.

When his employer added the zero onto his check and his $4,000 turned into $40,000, he said, "It's my lucky day!" He intended to keep that extra $36,000.

Jimmy didn't have a bank account, according to his sister, because he didn't have a valid driver's license. He told a lawyer friend what happened and said, "What should I do about this? Do I have to return it, or is it mine?"

The lawyer said that he could put it in the bank and if it stayed there for a month and he hadn't heard from the company, then it was his. I guess Jimmy didn't have too many ethical friends.

In addition to not having a bank account, Jimmy had a few other problems, which is why he didn't hold a valid driver's license. He went to his buddy Earl White, who he'd known for years, and who was related to the Conway family by marriage, for help. Earl opened a bank account and Jimmy signed the check over to Earl, who deposited it.

Before the thirty days passed, Jimmy heard back from the company:

"We want our money back."

Jimmy went over to Earl's house on February 4, 1999, and he said, "I need my money back. I have to return it."

And that's where the story gets interesting. According to Jimmy's family, Earl told him, "That's a problem, Jimmy, I spent more than half of it."

Earl used $20,000 of the money Jimmy received by accident to fix up his home. When Jimmy heard this and realized he was in deep shit, he and Earl got into an angry fight.

When Jimmy showed up at Earl's house, Joey was heading out, leaving Jimmy there with Earl and his live-in girlfriend.

A shot rang out. Joey later told Jimmy's sister, "Your brother must have been dead by the time [I] reached the stop sign."

Did Joey hear a shot after he left the house?

THE POLICE WERE called to investigate the incident.

They did not shoot a video, which would have been valuable because it would have shown from many angles what the place looked like. Video evidence gives the viewer a spatial feeling for the house—how long the hallway is, where things are positioned in the room—and it relieves the investigator from going *click, click, click* on a thousand little pictures. The video will capture all kinds of objects and things that might later be important to an investigator. Video is becoming much more routine these days, but some departments still don't use it in *every* homicide investigation.

Actually, along with the video, the investigator should *click, click, click* as many photos as does the crime scene justice.

Video and photos taken care of, the next item needed is a diagram of the room where everything should be mapped out with proper measurements to scale so the detective knows later where the evidence was relative to the body. This was not done. Somebody took a set of crappy pictures with a camera, and there weren't even many of those.

Based on those pictures, I had no idea where anything was and had to guess which rooms were which.

And then there was one snap with a Polaroid.

Some people wonder why Polaroids are even used anymore. In the old days, before we had electronic cameras, we printed everything out. The Polaroid was used just in case something went wrong with the standard camera and the investigator ended up with no pictures whatsoever.

Nowadays, with digital cameras, we can see right away that things are going well, and we can download them immediately to a computer for distribution and storage. The digital advantage is that we can take huge amounts of pictures, so I tell the police, "Snap away. You won't have to print those suckers out and it won't cost you a lot of money, because you will put them on a CD. You may not even necessarily need to waste your time looking at all of those pictures, but at least they're there just in case."

Of course, amateur shutterbugs can still take useless, blurry close-ups.

The police interviewed Earl and his girlfriend, asked them what happened, and that was that. Earl said it was self-defense. He said that Jimmy was enraged and planned to shoot him. Jimmy attacked, pummeling Earl and his girlfriend. They feared for their lives, so Earl pulled his sawed-off shotgun out from under the bed and shot Jimmy to end the rampage.

That was his story.

The detective said, "Sounds plausible to me." And that was it. Case closed.

Why did they accept the story so easily? Was it because Earl's family was well known in town, and the police didn't want to challenge them? Was it because Jimmy was considered a crook? Admittedly, it's hard to care about certain people, so maybe they didn't want to waste their time.

If Earl did shoot him, and it wasn't self-defense, who cares? Let's just close it down.

Maybe they were inexperienced cops. But they didn't do an investigation of any reasonable sort. They took statements from Earl, his girlfriend, and his son. They did the bare basics but no follow-up or analysis. If they had, they would surely have recognized the multiple inconsistencies in their witness statements.

The first inconsistency that struck me was the claim that Jimmy was beating the couple and that he smashed Earl's girlfriend into a window. Earl stated that Jimmy attacked him and Heidi in the bedroom, and he described a violent assault.

"Jimmy was hitting Heidi," he told the police. "I could hear her screaming. . . . I heard glass breaking. I saw Jimmy push Heidi into the bedroom window."

But there was no evidence of a broken window. And there wasn't a single picture of the supposedly brutalized Heidi. Despite the "beating" she says she sustained, Heidi did not go to the hospital.

Unless the police were incredibly sloppy, she probably did not seem injured.

Then I looked for photos of Earl's bodily injuries. How damaged was Earl?

There were two pictures of him. One was a front-facing photo. Earl had his shirt up so you could view his upper body for any damage. I could see none on his chest. There was a slight scrape on the bridge of his nose and a slightly dark spot under his eye. That's it.

Earl also signed a release declining to go to the hospital.

Jimmy, by the way, was a big guy, six feet tall, 220 pounds, and probably drunk.

Earl, by contrast, was a little guy, about five foot five, 130 pounds. And this disparity of force is where he could have had a credible defense. Earl could have said, "We were scared to death of this big guy who was attacking us, and I had to save my girlfriend's life. I had to protect her." His excuse for shooting Jimmy was good, but where was the proof that Jimmy did anything to them? There was no sign of a fight or even a struggle. All we saw was Jimmy dead on the floor with a shotgun wound to his chest.

Before Jimmy was shot, Earl's son, Joey, was there. Joey saw Earl and Jimmy chatting in the kitchen before he left. Joey went past them in the kitchen, went to his bedroom, picked up a change of clothes, and talked to Heidi in her bedroom, the bedroom that Heidi and Earl later said they were attacked in. He asked if she could take care of his animals, because he was going away for a while.

In recounting what happened, Earl said that *while Joey was still in the house*, Jimmy went into Heidi's bedroom and started yelling at her.

But Joey didn't say a word about it in his statement.

Earl and Heidi claimed that there was an escalation between the men in their argument. Then their story became confusing. Earl said that Jimmy charged back into the bedroom after some papers, but Heidi said she brought those papers to Jimmy in the kitchen, so they already weren't making sense, because I believe they weren't telling the truth.

* * * *

THIS IS WHAT *I* think happened:

I don't think Heidi was ever in the room. Heidi stated that she went to the bathroom when Jimmy supposedly started punching Earl. She said that when she came out of the bathroom and entered the bedroom, the altercation was already going on. But Earl said Jimmy attacked him and Heidi in the bedroom. He indicated Heidi was already in the bedroom when the physical violence began. I believe Heidi was never in the bedroom, which is why she seemed to have no bruises on her.

Earl decided Heidi had to be in the bedroom, too, so he had somebody to protect. Earl probably pressured Heidi to support his story, so she reported, "Yep, I was in the bedroom, too, and he attacked me, too."

That made her a witness and a victim as well, giving Earl cover for committing this act of murder.

I believe Heidi was probably in the kitchen when Earl shot Jimmy. I think he coached her to say what she said. They both claim Jimmy said these exact words: "You think you are going to shoot me, motherfucker? I have a gun in my car!"

This was kind of weird, because if Jimmy says, "You think you are going to shoot me, motherfucker?" you would think he was being threatened with a gun at the time. And if he was being threatened with a gun at the time, it's kind of a strange thing to say. "I've got a gun in my *car*." It's not going to do you a lot of good if your gun is not in your hand. How can you threaten a person with a gun that's not even around? It's a stupid statement.

It didn't make sense, but I do think it's possible that such a statement was made in the kitchen. If Earl threatened Jimmy and said, "I could shoot you, buddy," and Jimmy said, "You think you are going to shoot me, motherfucker? I have a gun in my car! Yeah, you get your gun in the bedroom, I'll get mine in my car!" But they probably were just saying stuff, and I don't think Jimmy believed Earl was serious.

I think Earl went to his bedroom, and I think Jimmy followed him in to talk to him.

Here's where it gets fascinating:

After Jimmy was shot in the chest, both Heidi and Earl said he fell onto the bedroom couch. This was true; I could see blood all over the couch, so the police photographs confirmed that, yes, that did happen.

Then Heidi stated that after Jimmy clutched his chest and fell facedown on the couch, she beat him with a baseball bat. Yes, she felt it necessary to hit a defenseless, dying man in the head with a baseball bat that she conveniently found in the corner, where she was trapped. According to her account, she was in the corner of the bedroom, saw Jimmy get shot in the chest and as he fell to the sofa, she thought, *That's not enough, let me hit him in the head with a baseball bat, because I'm scared of him.*

I don't know about you, but if I just saw somebody get blown away with a shotgun, I'm not worried that they will be coming after me at that point.

Except . . . I believe Heidi is trying to make some point about this baseball bat. There is a reason for that, and I'm coming to it.

Heidi claimed not to remember how many times she hit Jimmy. In one report, she supposedly told somebody twenty to thirty times—but Jimmy didn't even have the slightest concussion! No damage to his head at all!

She also said that after she hit Jimmy on the head, he got off the sofa and fell to the floor, then never moved again.

Jimmy was found on the floor next to the sofa. He was dead right there, that's for sure. But what she said was curious: "He never moved again."

Earl said that Jimmy fell on the couch and then straight to the floor. He also said that Heidi hit Jimmy with a baseball bat *after* he got to the floor, so their stories didn't quite agree.

At that point, they both checked on Jimmy and then they left the house. That was their claim.

I say that Heidi was never in the bedroom at all. It is my belief that Heidi *never* touched the baseball bat, *never* struck Jimmy, and was merely repeating a story given to her by Earl to account for *his* use of the baseball bat on Jimmy.

Here's where the photos made such a difference to the plausibility of their stories. There was only one set of bloody footprints leading from the bedroom into the kitchen. *One.* Of course, the police never said to whom those bloody footprints belonged. They should have been able to look at their feet and make an easy match, but that was never in the notes. There was one foot that stepped into the blood but, I wondered, if there were two people running around going crazy, beating people with baseball bats and checking on the dead guy on the floor, then why were there not two sets of footprints leaving? It seemed obvious to me that Heidi was never, ever, there.

Earl said that when Jimmy fell to the floor and was dead, he and Heidi left the premises. No mention was ever made of coming back to check on the dead man.

Heidi, however, maintained that she and Earl came back with a handgun and went to the bedroom and saw that Jimmy hadn't moved at all. She said they went back to check after they got a handgun. The guy was shot in the chest and beaten twenty times with a baseball bat, but Heidi thought they needed another gun to make certain he was 110 percent dead.

Earl, on the other hand, didn't mention returning with another gun.

Was Jimmy really dead when they claimed he was?

However, one photo showed that there was blood from Jimmy's body all the way from his right side to the entrance of the room.

This was blood that spread out from under his body after he was shot; but it was not just a solid, expanding pool of blood. Something had come in contact with that blood. The photo showed smeared blood, and a dead man doesn't smear blood. If he had lain there and hadn't moved, there would be no smearing.

The picture of the blood going to the right side of the room was one of the regular pictures. But it was the Polaroid that linked it all together. In the spread blood, you could see two interesting things. There were four lines parallel to each other through the blood, and then there was kind of a muck mark, a spot where a palm pressed on the floor. I looked at that and thought, *Hmmm.* I looked at his fingers, and there was blood on them. It looked like somebody's hand dragged through that blood, like a person trying to push himself up, trying to get off the floor. Was that indeed what I was looking at?

A little bit further down in that blood there was something else interesting. There was a crescent, a bloody area with a little crescent moon shape missing out of it. I wondered, *Where did that go?* It was lifted out of there somehow. Why was that spot of blood missing?

Something had been in that blood and then was pulled off it. I looked at that. The extra Polaroid picture showed Jimmy lying on his stomach on the floor. There were other pictures, better pictures showing Jimmy on the floor, but this was the only picture that showed his shoe. This picture showed the bottom of Jimmy's right shoe, and it showed Jimmy's heel. At first glance, one would think there was no blood on his shoe. And there shouldn't be, because, after all, the guy fell and was lying on his stomach, so the blood would not be on the soles of the shoes. But then I looked closer and I saw it, blood; blood on the bottom of Jimmy's heel. There was a small crescent of blood, a curved area of blood on his heel that matched exactly the missing part in the pattern on the floor.

This evidence contradicted the accounts of Earl and Heidi.

I believe that Jimmy was not dead on the floor. He lay on the floor, alive, and tried to get up. He dragged his hand through the blood, put his palm down, got his knee up underneath him, and stepped in the blood. There was some blood spatter on the door. I think he picked up his hand and cast off the blood onto the door, and that's as far as he got when somebody or something made him step back, fall down, and never move again.

That somebody was probably the returning Earl, who came back with the baseball bat, pushed Jimmy with it, and knocked him down.

But when Earl and Heidi both said, "He never moved again," that was probably a lie, because I believe the photo shows that Jimmy moved.

Continuing with my hypothesis, I believe the two of them left the room thinking he was dead, and then they heard Jimmy moving around. *Oh crap, Jimmy's alive and he's getting up!*

One of them went for the gun and one went for a baseball bat. And they both thought, *That guy better be dead.* But he wasn't dead. He was dying. I don't think they had to do more than push him, and then he collapsed and never moved again.

As for the bat? If you hit somebody with a bat twenty to thirty times, wouldn't you have blood spattered all over that bat? But there wasn't any blood on the bat except for where it looked like someone laid the bat in some blood and rolled it around.

It's also possible that Earl asked Heidi to hit him—Earl—in the nose with the baseball bat just enough to look like Jimmy caused some damage to support their assertion that Earl was assaulted. Maybe Earl did it to himself.

It reminds me of the husband who said, "The robbers came into the house and they shot my wife six times in the face, and they shot me in the shoulder. It was painful." In other words, they killed the wife, but they left the husband alive and only gave him a flesh wound in the shoulder.

Really?

Did Earl bop himself in the face with that baseball bat just enough to cause some damage and pretend he was attacked? I guess he couldn't bring himself to hit his girlfriend in the face with a baseball bat and damage her.

What I saw clearly from the photos in this case was that this was no case of self-defense. Most likely, Jimmy was shot while sitting on the couch complaining. It was a downward shot to Jimmy's chest, so it looked like Earl reached under the bed, pulled out the gun, and shot down at Jimmy, who then fell to the floor.

After he was dead, I believe Earl and Heidi concocted the story about how they were both assaulted. But their statements and the pictures did not match. Their statements were inconsistent. They didn't match each other's. They didn't make sense. They didn't match the elements of the scene. There was little evidence of self-defense.

This was a homicide; the police should have investigated the crime scene for at least second-degree murder. It didn't seem like it

was premeditated because the fight erupted after Jimmy confronted
Earl. But it is important to remember that premeditation can be a
plan you work out just a minute or two before the murder, something like, "Son-of-a-bitch, I am going to have to repay Jimmy! Or I
can kill him." Then it would be murder in the first degree.

I SENT MY profile to the Conway family in 2005.

The manner of death in this case should not have been classified as
a justifiable homicide, and the case should be reopened and properly
investigated. There was no evidence here that anyone in the house was
in danger of death or extreme bodily harm by Jimmy Conway.

Earl White had a clear motive to kill Jimmy Conway. He had
been involved with Jimmy in an effort to bilk Jimmy's employer of a
considerable sum of money and had spent a good portion of what
he was supposed to be holding for Jimmy. Jimmy wanted the money
back so he could turn it over to the company but the money no longer existed.

Clearly, there was reason for bad feelings on the part of both
Jimmy and Earl. Certainly Jimmy could have threatened Earl that
night but we have no evidence that he did other than the cockeyed
word of the shooter and his girlfriend. Based on this information
only, the stories of these two should be carefully checked and analyzed against the evidence and not taken as the unvarnished truth.

The family of Jimmy Conway deserved more than a cursory glance
at the events of that night. A full investigation into the murder of
Jimmy Conway should be undertaken by whatever law enforcement
agency is willing and equipped to do the job.

CHAPTER 11

DONNELL
A QUESTION OF MOTIVE

The Crime: Double homicide
The Victims: Frank Bishop, Renee Washington
Location: Midwest
Original Theory: Drug dealers sought vengeance against Renee's son by killing her

Motive is tricky.

Analyzing motive properly really counts at the beginning of an investigation in order for the right suspect to be identified and investigated.

On December 10, 2002, when Donnell Washington's mom and her boyfriend turned up dead in a basement apartment, the police thought his mother was the target of a drug gang the son pissed off. But Donnell's family thought the boyfriend was killed because he was going to turn state's evidence.

Donnell, thirty-two, knocked repeatedly on the door of his mother's boyfriend's house, but no one answered. Worried, he kicked in the door and found the boyfriend, Frank Bishop, lifeless on the sofa, a dozen stab wounds to his head and neck. Donnell ran to the back bedroom and found his mother, Renee Washington, on the floor, her throat cut. He lifted her onto the bed and attempted to give her CPR. He was too late.

The case stalled and no one was arrested. Months went by, then a year, and the police and Donnell's family were still arguing about who killed the couple. The police said it was someone taking revenge on Donnell over drug territory and for robbing their illegal gambling joints, but Donnell's family believed the mom's boyfriend, who was turning state's evidence, was the target of the crime.

I spent a week in town poring over the evidence. By the weekend, I had an answer as to who I thought was right and who was wrong. Nobody was right and everyone was wrong.

ONE OF THE compelling aspects of this case was how people tend to form a theory and then fit the case to the theory. This happened both with the families and the police detectives, because it's a natural human response to go for what seems most likely.

If we find a mutilated naked body, we assume it's a sexual crime. Why would a body be shorn of its clothes if sex wasn't involved? We don't think it could be something else. If we find a man shot in the head in an alley and he was wearing gang clothing, we say, "It must be a gang hit." Of course, it may have nothing to do with a gang. It may just be that he wears gang clothing because he finds it fashionable and, in reality, his girlfriend shot him.

But people will go to the most likely solution first, and sometimes this can cause trouble, because when you focus in on one particular avenue, you often ignore the other possibilities. It's like watching a magician who distracts you from the real sleight of hand so what he does appears to be genuine magic instead of a highly practiced trick. By the time you figure out that you were staring intently at the wrong hand, you have lost the opportunity to witness what the other hand was doing (with the evidence, in a crime) and this, I believe, is what happened with Donnell Washington.

* * * *

I WAS BROUGHT in to study this case by members of the Washington family two years after the double homicide because they believed the police department focused on the wrong motive for the crime.

Two people were murdered, Renee Washington, fifty-two, and her boyfriend, Frank Bishop, fifty-three, and they were killed at Frank's place. They had been in a committed relationship for a while. They were looking forward to the family Christmas just a couple weeks away and had their Christmas tree up and decorated, presents beginning to collect underneath the limbs.

Renee had last been seen the evening before the murder when she visited with her mother until she left to spend the night—as she did most of the time—at her boyfriend's house. Frank was known to be already at home.

At seven in the morning, Renee's son, Donnell Washington, went by the house because he was supposed to take his mother to a funeral. He arrived at his mother's boyfriend's home and knocked on the door. Nobody answered. He knocked again and again.

That's crazy, Washington said to himself. *They have to be in there. She's expecting me.*

He went back to his car, where his own son was waiting to be driven to school.

"Why don't you go up and knock on the door?"

So the son got out and knocked on the door.

"Dad," he said, "I heard a thump, but I didn't hear anything else."

"If you heard something in there, maybe I should break the door down."

But Donnell didn't break the door down and instead called his mother's sister—his aunt—and said, "What should I do? She's not answering the door. She should be there, because I have to take her to a funeral."

The aunt said, "Why don't you call the police?"

"No," Donnell said, "I'm going to knock the door down."

But he didn't do that. Instead, he took his son to school and finally returned—at ten a.m.!

He used his cell phone and called his cousin, Lamont, to come over. When Lamont got there, Donnell had already kicked the door in and ran out of the apartment and told him, "They're dead!"

Lamont told his girlfriend to stay in the car, went in, and saw Frank dead on the sofa and his aunt lying facedown on the bedroom floor. He said he freaked and left right away. Donnell later said he didn't know Frank had been stabbed because the body was so bloody he thought he had been shot. Then he ran the five steps into the bedroom, because his mother wasn't in the front room, and he found her lying on the floor in a nightshirt and panties, similarly bloodied, and he attempted to revive her. He put her on the bed and applied CPR, but didn't succeed in bringing her back.

This is where—to use a technical term—some of the story points don't hold water.

Washington's cousin, Lamont, said he saw the dead woman on the floor but Donnell said as soon as he found his mother he moved her to the bed and gave her CPR. If he did the CPR when he said, how was it that Lamont said he had seen the woman still lying on the floor? When Lamont arrived, Donnell ran out of the apartment, told him that his mother and Frank were dead, the implication being Donnell must have already completed the CPR. Yet Lamont saw the woman on the floor. Had Donnell given CPR at that point? Something didn't add up.

But others who arrived on the scene witnessed Donnell giving his mother CPR. Next, Renee's sister, Charmaine, arrived on the scene, went into the apartment, saw Donnell trying to give his mother CPR, and then ran to a neighbor's, banged on their door, and told them to call 911. There was no landline at Frank's apartment.

The police came on the scene and completed a routine crime scene process. Donnell was still doing CPR.

Donnell didn't do CPR when it might have been useful—in the first few minutes after he found his mother. Instead, he waited until his aunt and the police arrived. Was Donnell's CPR just a show?

The police focused in on the fact that Donnell was a violent felon who had a history of bad behaviors. He had just served seven years in prison for battery, and he told police he had just stolen forty pounds of marijuana from drug dealers.

Sometimes, you look at the last event that occurred in somebody's life. "What's the most recent thing that made somebody mad at Donnell Washington? What happened in the last few days?"

The police concluded that the double homicide was a retaliation hit in which they went after Washington's mom to get back at Donnell, and they took out the boyfriend as collateral damage.

Not a bad theory.

Except that there were several curious things about the case. One was something that Donnell said. This happened to be an African American community, and he said, "In our community, nobody goes after somebody's momma. If they want me, they are going to go after me. They know who I am. They'll come after me. They won't take out my mother."

Culturally, that is correct in my experience. It is rare that in an African American community a bad guy would attack somebody's mother in retaliation for something that her son did. But that was the angle the police pursued.

It was the Washington family that disputed this theory.

"I think the police have this wrong," said Charmaine. "First of all, this was not her apartment. This was her boyfriend's. I think somebody was going after *him*. Renee stayed at her boyfriend's home often, but she could have been at her own place. But her boyfriend turned state's evidence in a drug case. We think they were after the *boyfriend* and *she* was collateral damage."

That was actually a pretty good theory, too.

Which theory does the investigator work on? Again, the problem with many theories is that people are fitting the available evidence to the theories they like best, ignoring any evidence that will blow their theory out of the water. The evidence should guide you to a theory; you should not be allowing the theory to guide the evidence upon which you focus.

Did anybody stop to look at the actual evidence to see what exactly happened in the home that day and then reconstruct all the available information to determine the culprit and nature of this particular crime?

We knew, without a shadow of a doubt, that somebody definitely stabbed that man and that woman to death. There was no question about that, and it was a very violent crime. Frank was stabbed numerous times, far more than was needed to kill him. Renee fought her attacker but ended up with her throat cut.

The police told the Washington family that Renee had human blood under her fingernails, having scratched her attacker. But if they knew whose blood it was, they never said.

We also knew that a knife was not found at the scene. We don't know where the knife came from or where it went, so whoever did this took the knife away with him or her. We knew that.

We also know that the man—because of the blood spatter pattern and from the blood that was tested—was killed first, and the woman second. Therefore, the attack began in the living room with the man, and the second attack was on the female in the bedroom.

Of course, that doesn't tell us who the target was; it just tells us that somebody came into the home and killed the man in the front room. Was he killed because the murderer was on his or her way to get to Renee and he had to get through Frank first, or was Frank killed and then somebody heard Renee in the bedroom and had to kill her, too? Therein lies the question.

I took a look back at exactly what happened over the preceding twenty-four hours.

The night before he died, Frank returned home by seven thirty p.m. from visiting a friend.

As for Renee, she was at her brother's home until six thirty p.m. She left by herself and visited her mother until nine thirty p.m., knowing that if she was going to spend the night at Frank's, she had to be there by ten or he wouldn't let her in. Frank was stubborn about this. Her mother lived ten minutes away from Frank.

The time line itself was pretty intriguing. Donnell said that his son heard a thump in the living room, which upset Donnell. He told the police that he thought, *If I had broken that door down earlier, perhaps I would have been able to stop this.*

We could look at some physical evidence and find out whether Donnell was correct about that. Was there rigor mortis? Was there livor mortis? Rigor mortis is the stiffening of the body after death; livor mortis refers to the blood that settles in the body after death. If you're facedown, it settles to your face and stomach; if you're on your back, it settles to your back as gravity pulls it toward the earth. A smart investigator can identify this and sometimes tell how long a person might have been dead. It depends on how quickly the body is found, too. Then a forensic scientist, coroner, or medical examiner can tell the investigator the probable time of the person's death.

There is also circumstantial evidence for when a person died, and what makes sense.

The Washington family said there were two interesting points that the police didn't seem to consider. One is that the boyfriend, Frank, would never open his door to anybody if he did not know who it was. Whether his drug-dealing past had made him paranoid or he just didn't like to open the door to people he didn't know, he would not open his door to just anybody. And after ten p.m., he wouldn't take a chance on anyone, not even his girlfriend—at least that is what the Washingtons claimed.

Frank was involved in some serious drug dealing; a year before the murder, he was caught in another city, in possession of marijuana valued at more than $150,000. A judge gave him probation and he was reported to have turned police snitch against his boss to avoid serious prison time.

Frank had taken the opposite path in life of his brother, Barry. Barry was the general foreman for the city, by all reports an upstanding citizen. Some speculated that the police didn't solve the murder because it would shine a light on Barry's brother's unsavory activities.

When he died, Frank was trying a do-over in his own life, attending barber school in an attempt to learn a legal trade.

Donnell came over at one a.m. the night before to borrow his mother's car because he did not have one; he was going to come back and pick up his mother for the funeral in the morning. He called the house that night and he said nobody answered, so he went over in person and knocked on the door. At least this time, Frank answered the door. And despite the late hour, he obviously did let Donnell in. Donnell borrowed the car and went on his way. Donnell was the last one to see them alive.

I looked at what was going on in the home in the hours before the double homicide. There was no breakfast on the table, no plates set out, no dirty dishes in the kitchen. Dinner was gone—if it had ever been prepared and eaten in the apartment—and it didn't look like anybody had had breakfast yet.

Frank was on the sofa. He was dressed. He had on a pair of jeans and an undershirt, a long-johns type of shirt, and some soft slippers. He didn't look like he was going out at that moment. It looked like he was hanging around the house.

Renee was dressed in panties and a silk nightshirt, and her sister, Donnell's aunt, said, "My sister always laid out her clothes for the morning. That's one of the things she always did. She laid out the clothes, what she was going to wear, everything ironed and ready to go. She was going to a funeral in the morning. If she had gone to bed, she would have definitely laid those clothes out."

The most pressing question was no longer who did it but when did the murders actually happen? Did it happen in the morning after they had all gotten up, or did it happen before they went to bed?

Donnell was there sometime in the middle of the night. . . .

I considered the possibility that the crime occurred when Donnell's son said he heard a thump in the living room. But it is unlikely to be the time it happened. Still, even if it had, some rigor mortis would have set in. The fact remained that neither Frank nor Renee seemed like they had been to bed yet. This is circumstantial evidence, but I needed to think about its implications.

The next thing I wanted to do was check out everyone's stories; where did they agree, where did they conflict? How accurate were their individual reports?

Donnell said when he returned to Frank's home later in the morning, he busted in the door. This is one of the reasons I go to the scene of the crime whenever possible and see what I can still see. So I went to the boyfriend's basement apartment.

To reach it, you had to go through a locked outside screen door and then walk downstairs and gain access through a sturdy locked door.

The apartment door itself had not been changed since the crime, and I could see absolutely no evidence that it was ever kicked in. I had pictures of the door from the scene, and I saw no evidence in those that the door was any different. What door did Donnell kick when he "broke the door down"? Where were the signs of damage?

Nobody paid attention to the fact that Donnell said he broke the door down, and yet the door was just fine and dandy. That lit a bulb in my head.

Next I wanted to see the interviews Donnell did with the police. One concerning issue was the CPR. He told the police that when he did CPR on his mother, he knew he shouldn't have done that because he disturbed the scene.

"I knew I shouldn't have done it, but I couldn't help myself," he said.

I thought, *What a strange comment.* Most people would think doing CPR was the right thing to do. If you thought there was a chance in hell of saving someone's life, not much would get in your way. It would not have been wrong to move your mother's body under those circumstances. And you probably wouldn't say the words, "but I couldn't help myself." What an odd statement. I kept that statement in the back of my mind, because I thought it peculiar.

There was another very damning set of statements about the CPR issue. Donnell said as soon as he found his mother lying face-down on the floor, he picked her up, turned her over, and put her on the bed. Then he proceeded to give CPR. But Lamont said when he arrived Donnell had run outside to tell him his mother and Frank were dead and when he followed Donnell back into the apartment, he saw his aunt "facedown on the floor."

Seems to me Donnell didn't exactly rush to give CPR to his mother. He waited until his aunt and the police showed up!

* * * *

PEOPLE TEND TO have problems coming up with stories that sound truthful when they have to explain what happened (and they can't be entirely forthcoming). One method often used is to take an episode that really happened and move it to another point in time. This way the storyteller runs through the events as he saw them and need not continually fabricate details. The result is a fairly honest-sounding tale, which it is, except that events didn't happen when the storyteller claims they did. The emotions one felt at the time can also be described and come off as sounding truthful because they *were* truthful at that earlier time.

Donnell made a number of statements that could have related to different actions that occurred at an earlier time than when he found his mother dead in the morning.

The first interesting statement was the one about Donnell doing CPR on his mother: "I knew I shouldn't have done it, but I couldn't help myself," he said.

What if that statement wasn't about CPR, but about murder? What if he murdered his mother? If you roll that statement back to an earlier time, say, to the time Donnell might have murdered his own mother, the weird statement makes a lot more sense. *I know I shouldn't have done that, but I couldn't help myself.* He shouldn't have done that. He shouldn't have *killed* her, but he couldn't help himself. Why couldn't he help himself? Because something got so out of hand that he had to do it?

Donnell made another statement that bothered me: "I don't mind that my mother's dead," he said. "I just don't like the way it went down."

He didn't care that she was dead. That showed a person with a lack of empathy, which is a sure sign of a psychopathic human being. Also, given his criminal history, it was not unlikely that he might have been a psychopath. He had no empathy for the victim, even if she was his mother. He didn't care that she was dead; he just didn't like the way it went down.

If he was involved in it, I guess he *wouldn't* like the way it went down, because he ended up killing his mother, and chances are he kind of liked having her around. She was useful, and maybe he didn't mean to kill her. Maybe he *had* to kill his mother.

What was really going on? Did Donnell Washington tell the truth?

LET'S STEP BACK a bit.

The family said Frank Bishop, the boyfriend, was the target of this crime. It wasn't the mother. Could they be right? Why would Frank Bishop be the target?

First of all, the attack occurred at Frank's residence. That makes sense in supporting the boyfriend as the target theory. Usually, if a person wants to kill somebody, they go to where the person lives. Renee Washington, Donnell's mother, stayed there sometimes, but she didn't always, so if they wanted to kill Renee, why not go to her own house and kill her there and leave Frank out of it?

Donnell picked up the car after midnight and brought it back at seven a.m., so unless the killer was actually watching the residence, he would not know Renee was even there that night, because her car wasn't there.

No one was permitted in the house unless they called first; Frank didn't open the door to strangers. If some crazy person from a gambling joint, or a drug gang, were after Renee, Frank wouldn't know them and would not have opened the door.

Renee was not dressed at the time she was killed. Frank was. She was in the back room in her nightgown, and he was killed first. So whoever came to Frank's home was let in by Frank and attacked him. He also received the more violent attack, even though he fought back less than Renee did. He had almost no defensive wounds on him, despite a shockingly violent assault. He was stabbed and stabbed. She was stabbed just enough to kill her. Usually when you see major anger released on a victim, that's the person the killer was after.

I found evidence that there was a show of anger before Frank was attacked.

The table in the living room was tossed, and it seemed like Frank wasn't expecting things to turn volatile. He was just sitting docilely on the couch, the table was thrown, and then the attacker went after him.

It all brings us back to the common knowledge that Frank wouldn't open his door to someone he didn't know. The murder scene suggests that Frank was having a conversation with somebody he knew, that somebody got mad, picked up a table, and heaved it out of his way. It hit the Christmas tree and knocked ornaments off it.

The killer was angry. If we were talking about a hit man, he wouldn't do any of this; he would be an unemotional professional who could come in quickly and cleanly nail everybody. And it wasn't a gang of thugs because there wasn't *enough* turmoil in the apartment.

The perpetrator here was somebody who was obviously pissed off. He went after Frank like crazy and stabbed him without mercy. After that, the person went into the room where Renee was. There was a cell phone lying there. If she was in the back room and she heard this assault occurring in the front room, she most likely would have called 911.

Why did she get stabbed to death? I believe it's because she was *about* to call 911, and she was going to rat on who did this. That's when Renee became collateral damage.

The target of the crime was Frank. Renee was just in the way at the time and about to make that phone call.

Donnell said, "I didn't mind that she died, I just didn't like the way it went down." He also said, "I knew I shouldn't do it, but I couldn't help myself." But what if he wasn't referring to CPR but to murder? As in, *I knew I shouldn't have killed her, but . . . I thought she was going for the telephone. She was going to call the police. Couldn't have that happen.*

THERE WAS OTHER information that corroborated when the crime probably occurred:

- A neighbor reported hearing loud "fussin'" between one and three in the morning. She didn't hear anything break, just arguing.

- There was light food in Renee's stomach that should have been gone by morning had this attack happened at seven a.m.

Someone attacked Frank sometime after midnight. Who was there early in the morning? The only person I know of was Donnell Washington. Donnell admitted he was at Frank's home. Donnell was someone Frank would have let in. And he was the last one known to see his mother, Renee, and Frank alive.

At seven a.m., when he returned to Frank's home and knocked on the door, Donnell pulled some shenanigans—like a fast-talking con artist. He called relatives and told them, "I can't get in!" But what if that was all a con?

It took him more than two hours to come back and finally kick the door in—if he actually did that, he must have had the gentlest touch in America—at ten a.m. Then he attempted to give Renee CPR.

This is one of those cases where, if you look at the physical evidence, it tells you a sure thing. And the statements of the people who were interviewed, when I paid attention to the right key points, gave us information that matched the physical evidence.

It's one of those cases where the family could have shut up and not said so much, but by saying more and more, it seemed to me they implicated Donnell in the crime.

Donnell was extremely concerned about establishing the time of death. He wanted the police to believe it was seven in the morning. That was important to him. Why? Because we know where Donnell was at seven in the morning and he had his son as his witness. He was knocking on the door—but didn't enter then. He even thought the killer might have been there at that time, because he saw a gray Cherokee parked outside, and somebody sped away. He implicated other people in the crime.

In his police interview, Donnell made a point of saying that he was never on time. But this particular day, oddly enough, he showed up exactly on time! He even got there early! On this date, he was methodical and did everything exactly correctly.

"When I kicked the door in," he said, "I saw Frank on the fucking couch, dead. I knew my mom was fucked up, dead or something. I went in there; I panicked. I picked her up, turned her over, I tried to give her CPR. I knew; I just, I just couldn't stop is what I did. I put her on the bed. I couldn't leave her on the floor, so I picked her up off the floor. I knew I was fucking up, I knew I was fucking up when I did that. When I grabbed her, I couldn't control myself."

He tried to overexplain what occurred. He said he started CPR immediately on his mother, and then he moved her to the bed and continued CPR. His CPR statements were all out of context. Rigor had already set in. Can you imagine doing CPR on a person with rigor mortis? I don't think so. And if the person was really stiff and their eyes were open and staring, you wouldn't want to be doing CPR on them. That doesn't make a whole lot of sense. But you might fake doing it for a minute if you were trying to pretend to be saving her life.

Interestingly enough, he also said that he picked his mother up off the floor. But Renee had been stabbed heavily, and there was blood all over her. She was a mess. He said he did CPR, then picked her up, moved her to the bed, and performed CPR on her again. Before he moved her to the bed, he came out and leaned on his cousin's car. But no blood was found on his cousin's car. And neither the cousin nor the cousin's girlfriend recalled seeing any blood on Donnell.

It had also been snowing, so bright red bloody footprints would have been easily spotted.

He also told the police that after trying to revive his mother, he knocked on a neighbor's door. There was no blood on *that* door, either. How did a man who handled his bloody mother, held her head and pushed on her chest while he was doing CPR, have no blood on him and leave no blood anywhere he went? That was impossible.

Based on what I saw, Donnell never touched his mother until after his cousin left the scene. It was only when Donnell's aunt and the police arrived that he moved his mother's body to the bed and started CPR.

* * * *

AT TEN A.M., Donnell Washington was at the house for the third time in less than twelve hours and it was the second time in that period that he was in the residence.

None of this made a lick of sense.

I think that when the aunt arrived, followed by the police, Donnell tried to show himself as a distraught son. He did CPR on a very stiff stiff.

Donnell made yet another interesting statement.

He actually said that after he saw the slash on his mother's throat, he started looking "for the motherfucking knife." Most people, when they are at a crime scene and see somebody's been killed, don't usually look around for the murder weapon. That's just not the first thing in a person's head. Why would you be looking for the knife? Was the knife left there the night before? Because after the cousin was in the room with Donnell, the cousin suddenly jumped in his vehicle and fled. One of the questions I had was, did Donnell return at seven a.m. because he realized, *Oh, my God, where is that goddamn knife?* Did he then find it, call his cousin, and hand the knife off? That would explain why the cousin disappeared so quickly from the scene. That was one of the possibilities that I developed in the profile.

A person who commits a crime must manufacture a fact-based statement of events, finding a level of truth that fits the crime without revealing a truth he doesn't want told. I believe Donnell wanted to come up with a fake story, but he had none. He borrowed liberally from the truth and tried to reconstruct it to a later time, a later place. It came off sort of true, because parts of it really did happen. I just didn't believe it happened when he said it happened.

I TOOK ALL the statements that Donnell Washington made about coming to Frank Bishop's home in the morning when he came with his son to pick up his mother and moved them back to one a.m., when he came over to get the car.

Donnell said, "I got out of that car, and I banged on the door. I was banging hard as hell, because I'm like, what the fucking hell, she knows I'm here."

Is that what happened at seven a.m., or is that what happened when he went to pick up the car at one a.m.?

Clearly, Donnell was mad and getting madder. He got crazy about how he would have to kick the door in. He ranted and raved about kicking the door in. Why, if it was seven a.m., didn't he just kick the door in if he thought something was wrong? His mother might be hurt, dying, or dead on the other side. Why didn't he kick the door in? Why did he just *talk* about kicking the door in?

The answer seemed to me to be that he wasn't worried about what was going on inside, he was just mad that nobody opened the goddamn door. He was pissed off because he was being refused entry—and it probably was sometime after the hour that Frank didn't like to open his door. It probably wasn't the first time he had been refused entry.

SUPPOSEDLY, DONNELL CALLED his mother when he wanted to come get the car and told her he was on the way. But if that was true, when he got there, why did he have to bang and bang on the door? At some point, Frank relented and let him in, maybe because he didn't want him waking up the whole neighborhood.

"*What took you so damned long to let me in?*" Donnell *might* have asked Frank. "*Why didn't you answer the phone when I called earlier?*"

Donnell was known to have problems controlling his anger and it was possible that Frank threatened to call the police if Donnell didn't calm down, because Frank had done it before when Donnell's temper flared up.

Donnell wanted his mother's car keys. He wanted to be let in; he wanted what he wanted. My hypothesis is that Donnell went over to get the car, and they were too slow, so he became pissed off when Frank wouldn't let him in, lectured him after he did, and threatened to call the police on him if he didn't calm down. So Donnell killed them.

Here's another thing Donnell said in his police interview: "I know she was fighting, man, I know she was trying to hold on. I know my momma, man."

He might have known she fought her attacker because he *was* the attacker. Maybe he watched her struggle. Frank went down without a fight but his mother, he knew, lasted longer.

In the early rounds of Donnell's police interrogations, when they asked him about his mother and Frank's relationship, he had nothing bad to say. None of the relatives had anything bad to say about Frank, either. But the longer the interview went on, the fewer nice things Donnell said about Frank. At one point he called him a coward. Why would he say that? Somebody killed his mother. Frank was the only one there, and Renee was dead, so it was Frank's fault. He didn't feel a bit sorry for Frank. He said Frank was the cause of it. Maybe he was telling the truth there.

Oh, and there was another great statement: "Frank was just a cool guy. All this shit I'm telling you now is shit, is just coming to me. I'm making this shit up."

Donnell said he spit on Frank on the way out of the crime scene. Yet he told the police that Frank was a nice guy who treated his mother well. Why then would he think that this nice guy got his mother killed, and why would he spit on him?

I think he despised Frank because he felt that if Frank hadn't antagonized him, none of this would have happened, and his mother wouldn't be dead. In other words, Frank pissed Donnell off, Donnell killed Frank, and then he killed his own mother, and it was Frank's fault.

Donnell also said, "I'm not fixing to go to prison behind this shit."

Say what?

If you didn't have anything to do with it, why would you be fixing to go to prison "behind this shit"? How was that possible? Donnell may have told the police that he could handle his mother's death, but of course if he killed her, he wouldn't have been too happy that her death was putting him in a bad situation. He said, "I'm trying to deal with this shit, and it's hard dealing with it when I know what the fuck went on. I panicked. I just couldn't stop. It's what I did. I knew I was fucking up, I knew I was fucking up. When I grabbed her, I couldn't control myself."

These are statements about CPR he made, but that didn't sound like a CPR statement. It sounded like murder.

And yet Donnell was never an official or unofficial police suspect.

I DON'T BELIEVE the police ever analyzed the double homicide crime scene.

An investigator has to go in and reconstruct a crime. Find out what happened first, second, third, and fourth. Look for inconsistencies. Discern whether all the evidence matches and not make assumptions. The detective possesses some information, he thinks it's true, and decides to move on. Some establish a theory and then ignore or don't listen to the evidence that fails to support that theory.

The police decided that since enough people were ticked off at Donnell Washington, one of them certainly killed his mother. So when Donnell was talking, they didn't listen. They just let a victim's family member talk. They did the interview, and that was the end of it.

It seemed like everybody involved had some form of drug involvement and they were all squirrelly.

This was a wonderful opportunity to put Donnell away. The police did not like Donnell. They wanted Donnell off the streets. He was a problem in their community, no question about it. He was a menace.

I honestly think they decided that this was a hit on the mother because of Donnell's drug involvement and they simply did not thoroughly analyze the evidence or what Donnell said.

It seemed to me that the evidence was almost overwhelming that Donnell was involved in this crime. I read the interviews and to me they read like a confession. But if a detective gets his mind set a certain way, he won't notice that. He simply won't hear it or see it.

Most of the time, the police do hard work trying to track down the people they think are involved and gather the appropriate evidence, but if we forget to stop and analyze the crime, we'll be wasting time, because it has nothing to do with what we are looking for. We can work hard—but for no reason.

This crime did not take me tremendously long to analyze. It was a fascinating case. There were a lot of details in it, but a week was the most I needed to profile it. I gathered all the physical evidence, went through all the interviews, and right away, these things jumped out at me, starting with Donnell's police interviews.

The police did a great job interviewing him, because they got a huge amount of information from him that demonstrated to me that he was involved in this crime.

The downside of reaching such a conclusion was that by the time I got the case, law enforcement lost a year's time and the knife was nowhere to be found. The police may have had a surrogate confession from Donnell but not a true one. Any blood evidence that might have linked Donnell to the killings, evidence at his place of residence for example, would be long gone. I suggested that they interview the cousin and see if they could get him to talk. When I left town, the case remained unsolved.

I NEVER TOLD anybody I was coming to town to investigate the Bishop and Washington murders. That's one of my rules. When I go in, I want to work with the police and leave.

In this case, the family must have said something to the press because I heard that a reporter contacted the police: "The family told me there was a profiler in town. Did she help you?"

They said, "No."

By the time I came up with my profile, the police probably didn't have enough evidence to go forward with anything, so they let it lie. There was no sense—in their view—to admit that maybe they should have analyzed this crime better a year earlier. That's one of the reasons I feel so strongly about police training.

When my profile was done, I said, "You should be looking at this guy."

I expected them to say something like, *"We still like the drug thing, but boy, you've made some points. . . . We never saw this*

confession thing. We better get Donnell back in here. We better get
that cousin back in here and find out if he can corroborate anything
that Donnell says. We need to find out why he drove off so quickly
and if Donnell gave him a knife to dispose of. We better find that
knife."

Had that happened, they might have solved this crime. Instead, the case remained open. They told me they were still looking for drug connections. They were still looking for somebody other than Donnell Washington.

Sometimes, when I hear a police department say that they're not looking at my suspect, I think, *Did I really analyze this crime correctly?* But there was an astounding amount of information that pointed to Donnell, and he walked away.

Here are the key elements of the profile I wrote about this case:

1. The attack occurred at Frank Bishop's residence.
2. While Renee Washington often stayed overnight at Frank's home, she did not do so all the time.
3. Renee's car was not at the residence between the time Donnell picked it up (sometime around midnight) until he brought the car back at seven a.m. Unless the killer was very familiar with Renee Washington's habits and was watching the residence, the killer would not know if she was there that night.
4. No one was permitted into the house without calling first. After ten p.m., Frank Bishop did not open the door to strangers. And sometimes not even for relatives.
5. Renee Washington was not dressed at the time she was killed. Frank was fully dressed and had his slippers on. He was in the front room. Renee was in the bedroom.
6. Frank was killed first.
7. Frank received the more violent assault in spite of the fact he fought back less than Renee.
8. Even if Donnell Washington had angered certain people, it would have been highly unusual for those people to take this kind of action. Rather than kill Washington's mother, it was more likely they simply would have killed Donnell. Donnell left

alive would continue to be a problem. Killing his mother would make him *more* of a problem. Furthermore, it was not within the cultural mores of Donnell's community to go around killing people's mothers.

If Frank Bishop *was* the target of the attack, what was the motive? Frank had been involved in drug activities and there were rumors that he may have turned or was about to turn state's evidence. However, there was no proof that anything immediate was going to happen. Frank appeared to have been well liked by family and acquaintances. No one, at that point in time, seemed to have a grudge against Frank or have made any threats. It was unlikely that any of Frank's business dealings were the cause of retaliation.

It was also unlikely that a hit man would use the methods of killing I saw at the scene. The tossing of the table and the sudden, violent attack on Frank would seem to be born of extreme anger, not a planned killing. The attack on Renee seemed to be more of necessity than anger. None of Renee's blood is in the living room or on Frank, but Frank's blood is mixed with Renee's. It would seem an argument erupted between Frank and his killer and Renee was then eliminated because she was a witness. Only one person appeared to have been involved in the killing.

The time of death was also crucial in determining whether this crime was a stranger homicide, a hit, or a killing of a personal nature. While Frank Bishop was fully dressed, he was not in clothes one would expect for a man planning to attend a funeral that morning. Renee Washington was dressed for bed, in a nightshirt, panties, and a cap to cover her hair while she slept. Frank Bishop had nothing in his stomach. Renee had a yellow substance and a white meat substance and green pepper. Renee's family has stated that Renee was not a big breakfast eater, but when she did eat, she would have cooked and eaten with Frank, not alone. There was no evidence of dishes or pans being used that morning. Renee most likely consumed an omelet late in the evening before coming to Frank's place. The state of dress and the food remaining in Renee's stomach put the time of the deaths relatively early in the morning. Add to this the statement of a neighbor that she heard "fussin'" sometime between one and three in the morning, and it was not a homicide that occurred at seven a.m.

Since Frank would not have permitted anyone access to the house that he did not expect, we could safely determine that this was not a stranger homicide.

We know of only one person who was there late that evening/ early morning: Donnell Washington.

My hypothesis is that Donnell was responsible for the deaths of Renee Washington and Frank Bishop. Because I saw no bloody footprints or blood spatter in the hallway, on the door frames, on the doors, or outside, it was possible that Donnell simply did not get that much blood on him during the murders. He may have grabbed a towel and wiped off enough to be able to leave without a trail of evidence. It *was* possible this *was* why no blood was found in Renee Washington's car. It was also possible that he did not leave in her car but left with friends who brought him. He may have picked up his mother's car later.

I'd love to hear that the detectives finally paid attention to my profile and actually brought Donnell in. This was a well-documented case and the police did a good job with the physical evidence. They had good photography. The autopsy report was great. Everything about the case was handled well, except for the fact that they did not do a crime reconstruction or profile the case. That was all left undone. The doing part was done well; it was the thinking part that was missing.

In my opinion, Donnell was a violent person who needed to be locked up for life.

Drug dealers didn't kill Frank Bishop and Renee Washington.

Incensed gamblers didn't kill Frank Bishop and Renee Washington.

I believe Donnell killed Frank and Renee.

He had just wanted the damn car keys.

CHAPTER 12

SABRINA

THE MIND OF A TEENAGE GIRL

The Crime: Teen suicide
The Victim: Sabrina Oliver
Location: Home
Original Theory: Suicide

One of a criminal profiler's most difficult jobs is telling a family that their child really did commit suicide.

I received an e-mail from a mother whose daughter, Sabrina Oliver, was found by her uncle Rufus:

A friend gave me your e-mail address. I don't know if you can help or maybe direct me to another source. My 14 yr old daughter was supposedly found hanging from her bedroom wall by her uncle. He was the last one to talk to her and the only one to see her hanging. Reasons for doubt:

1. No damage at all to her throat.
2. Egg size knot above her right brow with bruising.
3. Small hammer found next to body when I entered the room.
4. Error filled records, from EMT's, hospital, medical examiner, 911 tape, and police report. (Funeral director wrote letter

stating facts about knot on head, but did no good.) Example of errors with records in my possession: EMT received call at 4:05 a.m. (their record), 911 call made at 4:11 a.m. (police record), body found at 4:15 a.m. (police report).

5. Uncle that found her went off the deep end about two months ago and is now in a mental institution (no history of mental illness).

There is so much more, but I'm trying to make this brief. The sheriff's department will not help. They say there is no evidence. WRONG! They just want to wash their hands of it.

My daughter was pretty, talented, smart, and had made future plans as well as weekend plans. Is there anything you can suggest that I do?

Thank you for taking the time to read this.

Penny Oliver

PROFILERS GET CALLED in on suicides more than any other kind of death, including homicide.

These are especially difficult cases to deal with, because sometimes the family is right. A person who commits a homicide may stage the event as a suicide and do a pretty good job of it and actually fool people. Certainly, a few of those do slide by. But what I've found as a profiler is that the majority of them are exactly what the police said they were—suicides.

Why does a family doubt suicide even when the police are thoroughly convinced? There is usually an overwhelming amount of evidence proving suicide. But quantity and quality doesn't matter to a family in shock; they just won't believe a loved one opted out of life.

Families have a difficult time accepting suicide. They can't believe that they didn't know that a loved one wanted to commit suicide or that they couldn't stop their loved one from committing suicide or, even worse, that they contributed to their loved one wanting to commit suicide.

In the aftermath of such tragedy, they feel a heavy weight of guilt that they did something wrong and pushed a family member over the edge. *I wasn't a good enough mother (or father or wife or husband)! I didn't love her enough. I didn't show her enough caring, and therefore she killed herself.*

They prefer to think that the person was murdered.

For the people whose children commit suicide, guilt sits on their chests like an elephant's foot, and they'd rather have almost any other answer than accept that their loved one killed herself.

SABRINA OLIVER WAS a fourteen-year-old girl who was found hanging in her bedroom. She had looped her raincoat belt around her neck and hanged herself on the curtain rod; and, considering how many children die playing choking games, it's sadly not an unusual suicide route for a child to pick anymore. Hanging is a fairly well-known way of committing suicide and quite simple. It doesn't require a special weapon, it doesn't require drugs that might be hard to obtain, and it doesn't involve having to do something terrifyingly scary like leaping off a bridge.

Most people haven't given it a thought, but you don't have to step off a chair to commit suicide; you can die by wrapping something around your neck and a stationary bar, then bending your knees and letting gravity do its job. The blood vessels will constrict, your brain won't receive enough oxygen, and you will pass out and die. It's not all that uncomfortable or terrible, you just get sleepy, pass out, and that's it. It's not a violent death. Sometimes elderly people use this method, because they are lying in a hospital bed and they want to commit suicide, but they can't figure out what to do, so they'll take the belt from their robe, tie it on a bar of the bed, and lean their head down over the side so it constricts long enough for them to pass out. It's not unusual that a fourteen-year-old girl might pick this type of exit.

Although her mother later claimed she was a happy child and was fine the night she died, Sabrina clearly was having problems in her life. She had just been kicked off the basketball team and kids at school were being mean to her because she didn't have fashionable enough clothes. Uncle Rufus found her hanging. He took her down and called 911. The family took turns on the telephone talking to the 911 operator trying to direct the ambulance to their home, which turned out to be a difficult location to find, and that delayed the paramedics.

The autopsy reported that Sabrina died of ligature strangulation. The medical examiner found no evidence of any kind of bruising to her head, nothing else that would have caused her death, and the police agreed.

But the Oliver family could not believe that Sabrina killed herself.

As Penny Oliver indicated in her e-mail to me, there was a hammer found in the room, and the family believed Uncle Rufus hit Sabrina over the head with it and then hanged her. A rape kit was done, but the actual testing never was performed because the police were certain Sabrina committed suicide. It is wise to at least be sure that the rape kit is completed, so if there comes a time when there is a question that the victim was sexually assaulted, the evidence will be available.

At the funeral home, Penny said she saw a bruise over Sabrina's eye. The next day, she claimed, it was even bigger, which was impossible, because when you're dead, you don't bruise, and bruises that are already on the body don't get bigger. But there was nothing ever noted in the autopsy report or by the hospital. No one else documented a big abrasion or swelling or anything else on Sabrina, so I was not sure what the family thought they saw. It's possible they saw some discoloring caused by decomposition, which they mistook for something else.

Penny said, "We believe Rufus committed this crime."

I said, "Why? Why would he do this?"

When Sabrina died, Penny's husband, Steve—Sabrina's stepfather—was also at home. He and Rufus were both there with Sabrina for some time before Penny arrived home from work that night.

The stepfather said he saw Sabrina shortly before she went to bed. For Penny's belief to be true, Uncle Rufus would have had to rape Sabrina, hit her over the head with the hammer (which the investigators denied seeing in the room), and kill her before Penny got there. By that theory, maybe he raped Sabrina, she screamed, he panicked, and he hanged her.

Because I could see some logic in this, I agreed to take on the case. I wanted to see if there was a possibility that Rufus did these things.

The autopsy report proved nothing of the sort. No hammer hit Sabrina, according to the medical examiner; there was also no evidence of any kind of a trauma to her head.

But Rufus still could have hanged her.

Then I listened to Rufus's call to 911.

"Please someone get over here, please, hurry, please, please, hurry, she's not breathing, she's not breathing, for God's sake, please."

Calls to 911 are fascinating. Something traumatic just happened, and these calls record a fresh response from the people involved. The first thing I noticed was that Rufus was hyperventilating so badly he could barely get the words out. He found his niece; he was an absolute wreck. I thought, *That's one fine acting job if you are acting here, buddy, because man, you sound totally, completely, out of your mind distraught.* It didn't sound to me like a cold-blooded psychopath who had raped and hanged his niece. That was one of the most telling things.

But then I learned of the clincher—and this is where normally rational families go into such huge denial over their children's emotional state and well-being.

Sabrina actually left an incredibly long, detailed, three-page suicide note. In it, she bid good-bye to everyone in her life, and she said how much she loved the people who cared for her. Then she went on to explain why she needed to leave them.

"I was a mistake," she wrote, "and everyone knows it, or at least I do. I know I'm not wanted here or anywhere else I go to, so I'll leave, and I'll have nowhere else to go, so I'll rot in hell if I have to. For everything I've ever done or said to anyone that's caused them pain, I'm so sorry. I hope you don't end up like me."

She went on for three pages, describing how much pain she was in, how things people said to her hurt her deeply.

"Every insult and every comment I've ever received has left a deep hole inside my heart. I'm a person who takes everything seriously. I am the mistake you can't fix. You can't give me advice. No one seems to understand the emotional stress and pain that I have been going through. I wrote this letter to everyone, all my friends that I have. I didn't and don't want you to feel bad for me. Be happy you won't have to deal with me any more. I'm an emotional person forever."

This was the tremendously sad suicide note of a girl with incredible teenage angst.

She used the term "Jehovah" quite often, which led me to believe she might have had some association with Jehovah's Witnesses. There is a beautiful land that Jehovah's Witnesses believe people will go to when they die, kind of like Heaven, but this is the new world, and that's a beautiful place to be. We inhabit a hopeless world because of so much drug use and drinking and sex and violence that it's hard to remain good. Sabrina believed she had to stick close to Jehovah.

After her daughter was dead, Penny decided that her brother Rufus—who tried to tell her it was a suicide—actually wrote the long suicide note.

The poor uncle. Essentially, there was never any problem between the uncle and the niece, because I asked the family that question.

Everyone said the same thing: "No, they got along fine."

I said, "Was there any suspicious activity?"

And again, the answer was no; he lived there with them and everything was fine. He was just the unfortunate schmuck who found her.

I studied the suicide note that she thought Rufus forged. She sent me another sample of Sabrina's handwriting, insisting the suicide note was not in Sabrina's handwriting. And yet when the police and I analyzed it, we both came to the same conclusion: it was exactly the same handwriting. She had a loopy, teen girl's handwriting style, and she even drew a heart in the letter just like one that she had drawn on her hand. A teenage girl's thought process is clearly evident in the language and narrative of the note.

At the time, my daughter was the same age as Sabrina, and I, as a profiler, couldn't even come up with that good a replica of a teenage girl's suicide note. It would be an astonishing ability for a grown man to write a believable suicide note in the voice and handwriting style of a teenage girl.

On top of that, if someone were to stage a crime, they would not write anything with the level of depth and emotion Sabrina expressed in that note. Generally speaking, most suicide notes that are written by those who kill themselves are fairly short, because it's hard to write a long one when the foremost thought in your mind is *I've had it. The world sucks.* That would have been a note I might have believed the uncle forged. That might have made sense, because he could have sat down and worked hard to make sure that "the world sucks, I'm out of here, Sabrina" matched her handwriting pretty well. But to actually write a three-page good-bye note, that's pretty darn difficult.

Uncle Rufus was completely tormented by what happened, and by discovering his niece. He ended up in a mental hospital. The family claimed the reason for that turn of events was because he felt such horrible guilt about killing her. *I* believe Rufus ended up in a mental hospital because his own sister, Penny, accused him of killing Sabrina. Can you imagine losing your niece and then having your sister say that you raped and murdered her?

Rufus became paranoid after Sabrina's death, thinking that everybody was out to get him, and it was terribly sad. And this was all because of how difficult it is to believe that your child could commit suicide.

WHEN I PROFILE suicides, I always write back to the family in a gentle way with my conclusions: "I know how much you are suffering from this . . ." I explain to them how we can't always know what our children are thinking, how so many of us wouldn't know the difference between a child exhibiting normal teenage depression and a teen in serious emotional distress who suddenly kills himself the next day. Sometimes teenagers make rash decisions that we can't see coming. I point out to families that it's not unusual for them to not know, so they shouldn't feel guilty that this came out of the blue and blindsided them, that they didn't necessarily contribute in any way to it. Some people, especially teenagers, don't necessarily communicate what they're going through. Most of the teenagers who complain and cry and say they hate everyone and their lives never attempt suicide and get through those years. We can only do so much, try our best to help our children, relatives, and friends, but sometimes they just do what they want to do and it ends up tragically.

I always naïvely think that if I can logically explain the crime to the family, detailing exactly what happened so that they can understand it, and stress that they were not responsible, they will accept it and move on. But to this day I can say that, for all my attempts to communicate these points, I've had almost zero acceptance after I'm done. The family will inevitably come back and argue that I'm wrong; they will say that I don't know how to profile, that I don't understand what's going on.

When people cannot accept suicide, they go to the next most likely conclusion: the person who *found* her is the person who *killed* her. I believe Rufus ended up in a mental institution because his whole family turned on him and assumed he was a murderer.

All the evidence in the world would not change the family's opinion of their daughter's death, their conclusion that her uncle killed her, or of that idiot, Pat Brown, who calls herself a profiler.

CHAPTER 13

BRIAN

WHO PULLED THE TRIGGER?

The Crime: Suicide
The Victim: Brian Lewis
Location: Western United States
Original Theory: Suicide

A s a profiler, I find crime-scene role-playing a useful tool.

In the courtroom, it's increasingly common to see a crime-scene reenactment during which the prosecution or defense attorneys will take the judge and jury through an alleged crime. Sometimes, they'll do it with 3-D pictures; sometimes they'll make a video.

If a gun was shot, they'll want to show the trajectory, so they'll tack strings from wall to wall showing the exact path the bullets took, demonstrating whether they could have hit the victim and at what angle they had to be shot.

Not every police department has the money for all this fancy stuff or they don't see that it is necessary. But sometimes it really should be done, even if in a simpler, less expensive way, like through role-playing. This is something I often do in order to test out a theory as to how a crime went down. I set up scenarios that are similar to what occurred. I have to be fairly careful, because I don't want to do something that is based on vague guesswork.

One time, the police theorized that a man had transported his wife in the trunk of a particular vehicle. My question was, would she fit in this car's trunk? Trunks come in all different sizes. The month before, I drove a nice little sports car out in California. If the convertible top was up, the tiny trunk allowed me to fit in my briefcase and my handbag. When I put the convertible top down, I couldn't even get my purse in there. I did manage to lay my suit jacket carefully inside, and when I clicked the ragtop into its open position, my suit got a nice pressing. Certainly, no body would squeeze into *that* trunk. Even if I put the roof back up, only the body of an infant would fit in that tiny space.

The car the police suspected might have been used in the crime had a bigger trunk than that sports car. I found a vehicle of the same make, model, and year parked outside of a shop I was in with about eleven minutes left on the meter. I walked outside and waited for the driver to show up.

"Excuse me," I said when a young couple arrived at the car, "would you mind terribly opening the trunk of your vehicle so I can look in it and see how big it is?"

They looked at me kind of funny, so I said, "I'm a criminal profiler, and I'm working on a case. I know it sounds a little odd, but I want to know if a body would fit in your trunk."

They just laughed—wouldn't you?—and said, "No problem."

They opened it up, I checked out the size of the trunk, and then said, "Thank you very much."

Since the victim I was dealing with was a bit on the overweight side, I had to make sure that this wasn't a trunk for anorexics only. The lady would have fit in the trunk.

On occasion, if the police found a body in a certain position, I might wonder, "Could that body be in that position in the trunk?" In that situation, it's not going to be good enough to look in the trunk. I'm going to say, "I'm about the same size as that woman. Guess who's going in the trunk?"

Could an alleged perpetrator climb through a given window if, for example, the window seemed kind of small? I have to find somebody the same size and try to shove him through it. I can't just guess.

The Virginia detective who nailed the cat burglar turned serial killer dealt with this issue in one of the murders he investigated. He said, "That was a pretty small window that guy had to use to get into the house. He had to be a certain weight to slither through that one." A 210-pound man couldn't get through it, but a 140-pound man might.

If a weight limit isn't definitive, I have to analyze how the weight is distributed on the body. Maybe a guy with a big butt can't get through, but a guy with big shoulders and a small butt could wiggle through. I play devil's advocate and try different things to prove what is true and what is not true.

It can be rather amusing as well.

"Mom is stabbing me again!" my daughter once told her friend on the other end of the phone line as I circled her with a fake butcher knife.

A YOUNG AMERICAN enlisted man stationed in Japan was found hanging naked by a belt in his closet. He was on his knees; the police determined it was an autoerotic death. The family, however, went ballistic and blamed his death on the Yakuza—the Japanese mafia. "They murdered him!"

What dealings he might have had with the mob in Japan and why they would want to do him in was quite unclear, but motivated families are like detectives, and they explained how the Yakuza hung around military bases and could have tried corrupting their son. They came up with every imaginable story that might link their son to being murdered.

And when that failed to convince, they simply rejected accidental death, outright. His mother said, "First of all, he would not put that belt around his neck because it would be so uncomfortable."

Just because we're profilers doesn't mean we've experienced everything in the world and can instantly determine whether something is true. In a case involving a sexual predator, I needed to find out if dripping hot wax on someone's body was simply sadistic or if there was some pleasurable erotic component to it. I always found that warm wax, like you get when candles melt, was fun to play with, warm and squishy, like a fancy Play-Doh. So I got a candle and dripped a few drops from up high onto my leg. *SON OF A BITCH!* Okay, the man was a sadist.

Now, what about a belt around the neck? Was it uncomfortable? If you're hanging yourself with a belt, and you're trying to achieve autoerotic pleasure, that strategy prevents the blood from going back to your brain. In theory, at least, you put the belt around your neck, bend your knees, and then while you masturbate, your brain is deprived of oxygen. But as soon as you have an orgasm—because it is supposedly much better when you have less oxygen to your brain, which is why you're doing the hanging thing—you must remember to push up on your knees, stand up straight, and the pressure of the ligature ends. The blood rushes back to the brain and the masturbator is okay.

The problem comes when the masturbator doesn't! If the fantasy isn't good enough, it takes too damn long. That means the blood isn't returning to the brain soon enough, there is not enough oxygen, and the person passes out. That's when autoerotica becomes accidental hanging, and that's when the person dies. The masturbator needs really good fantasy material. Otherwise, he'll be dead.

Maybe, I thought, whatever fantasy he was using didn't work for the young soldier. Sometimes, if a person involves himself in autoerotic sex too often and too many times, he finds it harder and harder to get aroused quickly enough to stay safe.

His mother said, "My son cannot stand things around his neck choking him. He would not do this."

I wanted to find out for myself what it would feel like so I called my daughter over.

"Honey, can you come into the bathroom? Mom has to hang herself."

"Okay," she said, knowing she's seen me try worse.

When using myself as a prop, I always have someone "spot" me, stand next to me in case I get myself in trouble. Say, for instance, I am testing out the usefulness of a particular belt for hanging myself in a small closet space. I don't want to accidentally reenact the whole scene successfully and then have another profiler analyze what happened to me.

"I'm going to put this belt around my neck and bend my knees and do what the soldier did, minus the fun part," I told my daughter. "And just in case anything goes wrong, be here and grab my body and push it back up so I don't pass out."

I put the belt over the towel rod, wrapped it around my neck, and bent my knees. I took it to the point I could feel a constriction and a light-headed feeling start to occur. I didn't stand with my knees bent until I was near to passing out; I only needed to test the feeling of the belt on my neck.

"That doesn't feel bad at all," I said.

My daughter rolled her eyes, eager for the experiment to be over.

I did not feel like I was choking. It did make me slightly giddy. But now I knew, firsthand, that when any parent said to me, "They wouldn't do it because they would be choking," I could say with authority, "No, it doesn't feel that way. You do not feel like you're choking. Actually, it makes you kind of happy; that's why they do it."

I proved the police correct on that aspect of the case.

On the wall in front of this young Japanese man was a little bit of shaving cream. The Japanese police claimed he was using shaving cream to masturbate. Was this true?

His mother claimed this, too, was a lie.

In the autopsy photos, on one hand, the young man had a tiny bit of white material. It was not semen, but it was some bit of dried white stuff, in the webbed area of his right hand between his thumb and first finger. It was not seen anywhere else. If he really used shaving cream, why would it be only in that one little spot? Wouldn't we see a white film on more of his hand?

The family thought so. "That's right. Somebody just dabbed a bit of foam on his hand to make it look like he was doing that. He would have had it all over his hand if he were really using it."

I used a black light, two fingers of my left hand (as the young man's penis), and my other hand to reenact the situation. When I finished and turned on the black light, the only place that I found shaving cream was in the web of my hand. I proved that he must have been masturbating, and hearing what I did makes the cops I tell crack up laughing. I didn't have anything else to work with. I'm sorry! What can I say?

THE BRIAN LEWIS case taught me a lot.

Brian's mother was adamant that her son had been murdered, but the police ruled it a suicide.

He was found sitting in the front seat of his car, an old 1977 Cadillac, with a shotgun up under his chin. It was a sad, sad case with horrifying crime scene photos. The damage caused to the head and face by a shotgun with its barrel pressed against the chin or placed in the mouth is horrific and grotesque.

This poor family had to see their beautiful son not looking anything like they remembered him because there were huge gashes distorting what remained of Brian's face. It was a brutal thing for anyone to witness.

Brian worked nights at a grocery store and had appeared to be in a good mood to those who saw him that last night. After work, he bought some beer. Then the next morning, the family got the phone call that changed their lives. Brian's car had been found in a remote mountain area with his body in it. He was dead of a self-inflicted shotgun wound.

The police closed the case pretty quickly. They looked at the crime scene and felt no need to do much in the way of evidence analysis or investigation. "It's a suicide," they reported. Brian was in an isolated location, alone in the car with a shotgun in his lap, and nothing indicated that anyone else had been with him at the scene or any crime happened. It looked like a suicide, so it *was* a suicide.

The family felt that the police rushed to judgment and failed to perform a proper investigation. They didn't even test for fingerprints on the gun or the beer bottle between his legs. The family thought somebody staged that. They wanted the beer bottle and gun tested for fingerprints and they wanted people interviewed, but none of this was done. The family fought long and hard to prove that Brian would not have attempted suicide. They insisted he wasn't depressed or upset or having any problems in life.

They came to me and said, "Can you look into this case and bring us some peace?"

One thing I learned right off was that "experts" often disagree with each other. At the beginning of my career, I wasn't all that familiar with what happens when you shoot yourself with a shotgun, what happens to your head, what happens with the blood, in what direction the pieces go, and what happens to the wadding in the shotgun. I wasn't a ballistics expert, so I sought out people who were. The original person I approached gave me information that turned out to be incorrect, and I had based a good portion of my initial profile on that.

In the beginning, I agreed with the family. I thought the blood looked like it was going in the wrong direction. But that was an error on my part, because I believed what the first expert told me.

I eventually sought out a different expert, but something still seemed wrong with the picture.

A third ballistics expert brought yet another conflicting opinion but one that came with a much better explanation. That's how I learned that I shouldn't blindly believe an expert; I need to find out *why* they believe what they do. We often see a courtroom expert who will give an opinion, but nobody bothers asking him exactly how he came to that opinion. Just because an expert says "In my professional opinion . . ." doesn't mean you should automatically believe he is correct. The courts are a great example of this. How is it that the prosecution expert and the defense expert almost always give opposing opinions? They can't both be right.

A profiler should always have a thorough explanation of each point in his profile so that anybody, whether a police detective or a victim's mother, can understand exactly why we believe what we write. Any forensic expert should have a thorough explanation as well. I learned in this case to require any expert who analyzes any portion of a case I am working on to do the same.

The Lewis family believed that Brian did not pull the trigger on the gun that killed him. Someone else must have been responsible.

If you shoot yourself and the trajectory is going in a certain direction, it will continue in that direction. The family and private investigators they brought in looked at the blood spatter. Brian was shot sitting in the driver's seat, and the shotgun muzzle was up against the right side of his neck, just under the jawline. They expected that the blood would go backward toward the backseat or maybe the back part of the driver's window. But the blood in this case was mostly over the front half of the driver's side window and on the roof of the car toward the front. It looked like the shotgun blast went up under his chin toward the back left door but then the blood U-turned and came out through the front of his face. The family and its expert thought the back of Brian's head should have been blown off, but not his face. *Wait a minute,* I thought. *Geez, that is pretty weird.*

If I took a wire starting at the butt of the gun and threaded it down the barrel, wouldn't it blow off the back of the victim's head? Why did the front of his face get blown out?

If you don't understand how a shotgun works, you might misinterpret the blood spatter evidence. Most of us are much more familiar with how a handgun works. Usually, when you shoot a handgun, the bullet sails out in a straight line.

Brian, however, used a Remington 870 Express Magnum twelve-gauge shotgun. He used a shell that contained dove and quail shot, lots of little pellets with a bunch of powder propelling them. Basically, instead of a bullet tearing through the head in a straight line, a bomb is launched into the brain. Once that is accomplished, it explodes, and blood gases come into play. They expand, just like a bomb, and the gases move more easily against the places of least resistance. The skull is pretty strong, but the nose and eye sockets are permeable cavities, so Brian's face exploded but his skull remained intact.

This ballistics issue was one of the things that confused everybody. The family didn't understand this, and I didn't understand this, not having a great familiarity with shotguns and shotgun blasts early on in my career as a profiler. Oddly, the first shotgun expert I approached didn't appear to understand the physics of shotgun ammunition, either. Fortunately, I found a much wiser, more experienced ballistics expert, and he thoroughly explained it.

Now I was contending with determining from where Brian could have been shot. Could he have shot himself in that position? The family believed the shooter might have been in the backseat. That, they believed, was how blood traveled toward the front. The police never addressed the issue.

I purchased the exact same shotgun from Walmart. The next day, I was planning to take a trip, and I was in a luggage shop trying to buy a new bag, and they wouldn't accept my credit card.

I called the credit card company while I was in the store, and they said, "There were some unusual purchases with your card. Did you go to Victoria's Secret?"

"Yes."

"And did you purchase a shotgun yesterday at Walmart?"

They must have thought Bonnie and Clyde were on the run again.

I HAD TO find a car with the same dimensions and seat heights as Brian's. Luckily, I had a big old car in my yard that did fine as a stand-in.

You have to reach really far to pull the trigger on a shotgun. Sometimes people use their toes to push the trigger when they kill themselves; some people use a stick. Brian would have had to pull the trigger with his own hands. Could it be done while he sat behind the steering wheel with the gun on the seat?

I'm five foot seven. Brian was four inches taller than me, five foot eleven.

I was able to reach the trigger on the gun I bought at Walmart and was able to push it with my thumb. That proved to me right away that Brian could have, but it didn't prove that he did. It also showed me that when I went to push the trigger on the gun—because of the way I had to reach—my head was in exactly the right place for the blood spatter pattern shown in the crime scene photos. Another very important clue had to do with where the wadding inside the shotgun shell ends up. While pellets may disperse, the shotgun wadding will continue on its trajectory, in a straight line. The shotgun wadding was in the left parietal lobe, in the posterior region of Brian's brain. In order to push that trigger, I had to turn my head to the left and lift my chin in order to get in a position where I could stretch my body and arm enough for my thumb to contact the trigger. And sure enough, if you put a rod along the barrel of the gun that ended under my chin and you pushed that rod straight through my head, the rod would pierce the parietal region of the brain exactly where the wadding ended up on Brian. More fascinating, my face shifted up and a little bit toward the driver's side window, which was exactly where the exploding blood gases caused all the blood coming out the front of Brian's face to land.

It sure looked—if he was sitting in that seat—like he could have pulled the trigger, and the wadding in Brian's head and the blood spatter proved it.

But I wanted to make really, really sure that there still couldn't be another angle at which the gun could be held, by someone else, that could explain the blood and wadding evidence.

I wanted to hold the shotgun up to somebody's head in that car and see with what angles the shooter worked, so I said to my son, "David, do you mind coming outside and getting your head blown off?"

And he said, "Okay, Mom."

(Of course, the gun was definitely not loaded.)

We looked around and hoped nobody was watching. I had a boarder at the time and naturally, he returned home at exactly the time I was in the car holding the shotgun to my son's head.

"Don't worry," I said, "nothing's going on here. I'm calm. I'm just blowing my son's brains out."

I climbed in the backseat and aimed the gun in different directions, trying to get his head in the right place. I immediately had trouble getting the gun over the top of the backseat to put it in the correct line. I tried getting him to look back at me like he was saying, "Hey, guys, what's up back there?"

I tried all kinds of methodologies, moving my son's head in different directions, and found that there was no realistic way from the backseat that I could get that shotgun to line up properly with the evidence.

I went around to the front seat and sat in the passenger side, which was the only other possibility. I tried from that side, and found it was possible to do it from the front. Brian would have had to have been asleep, passed out or so drunk that his head was just lolling against the headrest and he wasn't paying a bit of attention, and the person with him in the front seat would have had to hold the shotgun in a funny fashion, the passenger door open and his right elbow sticking out in front of him. But he *could* do it. It was possible, but only if Brian's head was *waaaay* back and he didn't have time to push the gun away.

I made a mental checkmark that maybe it could have happened that way. But *did* it happen?

BRIAN HAD BEEN hanging around with a couple of no-good characters. They were involved in Dungeons & Dragons stuff and other role-playing fantasy games. That, in and of itself, didn't mean anything, but they were into negative, evil, dark things, and Brian had talked about moving on from the group because they weren't healthy for him to be around.

One of those guys said something strange later on when a private investigator hired by the family talked to him. He knew what Brian was wearing the night he died; he even purported to know what music was playing in the car when Brian died.

The family was convinced these friends took Brian into the mountains and killed him. But this would have required two cars, because obviously they left the scene, which was a remote location. I wondered why, if they wanted to kill somebody, they would drive two vehicles to a site so far into the hills. It would be easier just to drive his car down the block, shove him out, and blow him away. Furthermore, it was clear Brian drove himself up there. He was in the driver's seat of his own car. His body wasn't placed in the vehicle later, even though the family had this idea that somebody had changed his clothes, put someone else's shoes on him, and put strange tobacco in his pocket— things that made no sense in the crime. No one would do that, but families, when they see some oddity about a crime, something that they don't equate with their child, will deny what's right before their eyes. The Lewis family said, "That wasn't the chewing tobacco that he used," "He would never leave his pocketknife at home," and "Those aren't his shoes."

They thought they knew everything about their child, but nobody who stages a crime would change the victim's shoes or put their own shoes on him. There was no reason to give Brian a different brand of chewing tobacco; it would be smarter to have him have his regular brand. If someone were staging a suicide, he would want everything to look as normal as possible. The family's arguments were attempts at stirring the pot, not impressive for proving a homicide had occurred.

In theory, one could say that someone put a gun to his head and made him drive up there, but that beer bottle between his legs was interesting. The family was convinced somebody put that bottle there.

"What guy is going to think of that?" I said. "Especially after Brian's head has already been blown off, and there's a lot of blood all over the place? Would someone really crawl across the seat to put a bottle between his legs?"

Probably not. Chances were that Brian was drinking beer from that bottle. Did somebody abduct him at gunpoint, force him to drive into the mountains, and then give him a beer? We may see it happen in a Western, where a condemned man is given a final smoke, but it didn't seem terribly likely for somebody who was about to be murdered in cold blood.

Nobody had a real, credible motive for killing Brian Lewis, not even for a rage-induced homicide, where somebody got mad and did something stupid. That would have happened in Brian's home, where he kept the gun. Or if they went out for any reason, maybe he'd be shot somewhere nearby and the killer would have thrown his body into a ditch or left him in the car where he shot him. But to go up to the mountains to shoot him seems premeditated. And yet, if it was premeditated, why did Brian drive up there and have a beer?

None of the nonsuicide theories made sense.

There were two interesting pieces of evidence, one of which convinced me that Brian probably wasn't killed by somebody else.

The other one, however, made me wonder if somebody was there with Brian.

There was some flesh from the shotgun blast found on the passenger's seat. There were three pieces where a person would be sitting, so I had to think, if somebody was sitting there and they shot him, how did these three pieces of flesh end up on that seat? That evidence couldn't be there if something blocked it. Therefore, nothing blocked it. There was nobody shooting Brian from the front seat because then the flesh couldn't have landed there.

Also missing was a transfer pattern—smears—in the car. When something like this happens, we'll see smears from a person's hand or some other part of the body that might have had blood on it. As they moved around in the car, opening and closing car doors, we would see evidence. Except for one location on the side of the driver's seat by the door, I didn't see any of that, either. Even that blood pattern was a bit questionable as it was not clear from the photo if spatter just landed in such a position or it was transferred from someone's hands. Sometimes photos just aren't totally clear, and they aren't three-dimensional, so some determinations simply can't be made.

It still seemed like Brian was alone in the car.

The passenger door was locked, too. If you blew somebody's brains out, it would take a lot of thought to lock the passenger door behind you. We would have a very clever killer if that were true.

The odd piece of evidence that messed up everybody's confidence in suicide was a little piece of flesh discovered in the driver's doorjamb. How did that happen? In the photos of the car taken when Brian was found, the doors were closed. But if the doors were closed when Brian shot himself, how did the flesh get in the doorjamb? Somebody had to have disturbed the scene! There had to be somebody else involved! Brian couldn't have killed himself and then opened the door! Either the door was open when he got shot and the flesh went there and then the door slammed shut, or somebody innocently opened the door, not yet seeing that the front of Brian's face was blown off because his head was hanging down. When they pushed his head back toward the seat, they were startled and horrified—"Oh my God!"—and during that moment some flesh flew backward and went into the doorjamb. They slammed the door and ran.

Oh, but then we have the wrench thrown into even that theory. That one photo was taken *after* the boy was removed from the car. Here again we have the problem of not taking photographs properly or not taking enough photographs. A photo should have been taken of that doorjamb and then another a few feet back from the doorjamb and another a few *more* feet back from the doorjamb. If I see the flesh in all the pictures and Brian's body in the one that is far enough away to capture his image as well, then I know the flesh was in the door when the police got to the scene. But all I have is a picture of a doorjamb with flesh on it and I don't know if the medical technicians bumped Brian's body against the doorjamb when they removed him from the car. If that happened, then that flesh isn't part of the crime scene.

So Brian was likely alone at the crime scene. If somebody else actually was there, he or she still didn't kill Brian.

There were subsequent indications that Brian was more emotionally upset with his life than his family knew or could admit. There were also indications of depression and possible suicidal ideation.

Brian could and did commit suicide, but the family still demanded an official investigation. The police were right about the manner of death, but they still should have taken better photographs, done basic evidence analysis, and interviewed Brian's friends. Because they didn't, the family won't stop hounding them; I bet now, looking back, they realize that it would have been a little extra work to double-check the manner of death but it would have saved them a whole lot of grief.

THE AVERAGE PERSON thinks that the scientific method is strictly performing chemical tests in a lab. We can, of course, scientifically prove DNA and fiber matches. But using the scientific method in criminal profiling is all about being methodical about the analysis, and coming up with a theory and then deliberately trying to strike it down. I spend a great deal of time and energy generating potentially valid explanations for murder—or suicide—and then knocking those very theories out until I can't come up with any other explanation but the last one standing.

That's what I did with the shotgun in the Brian Lewis case.

Could Brian shoot himself from the driver's seat? Could somebody do it from the backseat, either the left or right side, or the passenger seat? There were four inside positions. And could someone shoot him from the outside?

I went to each one of the positions with the gun, trying to prove that it could or could not be done, and as I eliminated each of the possibilities, I was left with only two.

One was that Brian shot the gun himself while sitting in the driver's seat. The other possibility was that someone else shot Brian from the passenger side.

The flesh on the passenger seat was a piece of scientific evidence that ruled out anyone sitting in that seat.

This was the case that showed me that I had to be able to rule everything out. If I had just looked at the pictures, I might not have figured out the same things that I did with the shotgun in hand.

CHAPTER 14

BOB AND CHRISTINE
DOUBLE MURDER

The Crimes: Double homicide
The Victims: Christine Landon and Bob Dickinson
Location: Midwest
Original Theory: Pedophile committed aggravated murder

I returned to the Midwest. This town was so small that when I asked for a good place to eat, I was told to go back to wherever I came from.

The sheriff's office was in the nearest "big" town. The sheriff had the same look on his face as the detective in the Hoover murder.

"Don't tell me," I guessed. "Problems with the case files?"

The sheriff was disgusted. "The judge won't release them."

"What? But isn't it an open case?"

"I know. It's ridiculous, but he sealed them."

Politics. Had to be politics.

Luckily, I had access to a few police reports and interviews and one autopsy out of two. But no photos, no evidence reports, no forensic reports.

At least I had a really nice sheriff. And a fascinating case.

* * * *

ON JULY 5, 1986, a lazy summer night in a tiny Midwestern town, Marshal Bob Dickinson was sitting in his easy chair when he got a late-night call from a panicked man, Hugh Marshall, Christine Landon's boyfriend. "Get on down to Christine's house! I was talking with her and she started screaming! Hurry!"

Stuffing his feet into his slippers and slapping on his gun belt, the marshal took only half a minute to make the three-block drive to Christine's house. The phone rang again as soon as he left.

"Tell Bob we're on the way!" the sheriff's office advised Bob's wife. But it was too late to stop Bob.

Ten minutes later, patrol cars screamed into the eight-block town to the front of the Landon residence. The house was dark. Dickinson's car was parked haphazardly at the curb, the driver's door hanging open. No one answered the door. Around back the police officers discovered the sliding door open. Entering the house, they saw Christine Landon on the kitchen floor, half-naked, tied hand and foot, a dozen stab wounds to her chest, and her throat slashed.

They called out to Bob; no answer. The house was eerily quiet. Moving up the stairs to the second floor, they found the marshal, folded over at the top of the stairs, shot to death with his own gun.

Horrified police officers and citizens tried to come to grips with the brutal double murder in their peaceful town. They vowed this killer would be brought to trial. Wanting to go the extra mile, the sheriff's office reached out for expert assistance, something few police departments are willing to do.

What started as an exemplary effort by the local law enforcement to ensure justice for the victims of these vicious homicides soon careened out of control. Big egos, ambitious politicians, and a desire to win without regard for the truth aborted the rules of fair play and the law, tearing apart the town and the lives of all who became involved; all except the real killer of Landon and Dickinson.

The players in this story stopped at nothing to achieve their goals. FBI agent John Douglas, the criminal profiler and a twenty-year agency veteran who was then working at the National Center for Analysis of Violent Crime at the FBI Academy, profiled the crime as a sexual homicide and identified Curtis Cox, the babysitter, as the suspect. Though there was no physical evidence linking Cox to the crime, Curtis Cox was arrested. The prosecutor believed he could get a conviction using the FBI profiler's testimony and psychological profile. A police psychic was brought in and he came up with details of the crime, and the man he said did it looked and acted just like Curtis Cox, an unpopular character in town. The families were comforted that there was no question as to who killed Bob and Christine, and the right guy was going to trial. Oddly, when I read over the police reports, some of them were word for word what the psychic had claimed. Either that psychic had visions of the police reports or someone had slipped him the files.

Without a shred of evidence, the sitting duck suspect, Curtis Cox, was arrested. The defense attorney raised hell, complaining to the judge that the case ought to be thrown out because there was zero physical evidence and the entire case was based on the egregious use of criminal profiling, presenting psychological and behavioral theories of the crime and then claiming Curtis Cox was a sexual psychopath and therefore must have done it. The judge dismissed the case and then—for reasons unknown to me—sealed the case files.

For fifteen years, the case remained untouched by law enforcement.

One day, the daughter of Bob Dickinson tried once again to honor her father by bringing his killer to justice. She contacted me and I went to the town to review what information existed at the sheriff's office. I interviewed and investigated some of the key players, profiled the crime, and disagreed with John Douglas.

The murderer was not Curtis Cox.

It was not even a sexual homicide.

The defense attorney was right; Cox was railroaded.

DICKINSON'S DAUGHTER CALLED me because her family wanted me to confirm that Curtis Cox was guilty, and that the FBI profiler was right. But there were doubts.

Cox was a bit creepy. He was a skinny, effeminate fellow, very soft-spoken, who had never married. He liked to make friends with women who had young children. He was a friend of both Christine Landon and her ex-husband, Craig, and they frequently allowed their two young daughters, ages eight and eleven, to visit him at his home. He also came to their home quite often to babysit the girls. Christine gave him a key to the house.

Cox had access to the home, he was comfortable there, and he was weird. But he had no record. So did he commit this crime and, if he liked children so much and was a suspected pedophile, why would he choose to attack a grown woman?

The police report includes this description of Cox's actions while babysitting the girls:

When visiting Cox the girls would play among themselves or with Cox, occasionally shop at the drugstore across the street from Cox's home, and once traveled with Cox to a K-Mart in another town. Cox and the girls played several different games, including the "rug game," in which Cox would wrap the children up in a rug, tie a rope on one end and drag them around the floor. In a variation on hide-and-seek, a person was tied and had to get loose in order to find the other players. Cox would untie the girls if they were unable to do so themselves.

Some of Cox's other activities with the girls were of an overtly sexual nature. On at least one occasion he showed X-rated videotapes, and explained to the girls what was happening in the films. At times while watching the videos, Cox's hands would be down his pants. On other occasions, Cox would walk through his house in a bikini swimsuit or bikini underwear, and would sometimes have his hands down his pants. Cox also showed [them] *Playboy* magazines, and allowed the girls to make audiotapes of themselves uttering sexual language. There has been no testimony that Cox ever touched the girls in a manner which constituted sexual contact.

The sheriff gave me what he still had in terms of police reports and the autopsy of Marshal Bob Dickinson. The sheriff tried his best to get the crime scene and autopsy photos released to me, but they remained sealed by the prosecutor's office and thus unavailable for inspection. The evidence should have been accessible. The sheriff's department couldn't fight whoever was in the power seat.

I visited the actual house where the murders occurred. Strangely, Christine Landon's estranged husband, Craig, had kept it and moved back in as soon as the police tape was down, eventually raising the couple's two daughters in the house where Christine was murdered. He eventually remarried and continued living there with his new wife.

When Craig came over from the side of the yard to meet me, the lawnmower backfired and he pretended to stumble as if he were shot. Then he laughed.

He brought me into the house and proudly showed me pictures he took of the crime scene after the police let him back in. The blood was still there on the kitchen floor, as were all the fingerprint powder and bullet holes in the walls. His pictures helped me reassemble that scene. Why he gave them to me still mystifies me.

WITH THE INFORMATION available, I came to the following conclusion: the likelihood of Curtis Cox committing the double homicide of Landon and Dickinson was extremely low.

There was no physical evidence tying him to the crime, so the focus on Curtis Cox as the killer in this double homicide was based on erroneous conclusions: first, that the motive for the crime that resulted in the death of Christine Landon was sexual and, second, that Curtis Cox's fantasies would lead him to the behaviors exhibited during the commission of the crimes of that evening.

My view is that the killer or killers had no intention to commit a sexual crime on the premises. The only crime that I believe was supposed to have occurred at the Landon residence was the abduction of Christine Landon. There was no way to prove motive of anything but abduction from what I saw at the crime scene. Even the court trial record from Curtis Cox's almost-prosecution stated:

The murder scene contained no direct evidence which indicated that the killings were sexually motivated. Landon's body was found clad only in a shirt, but there is no dispute that the attacker surprised Landon after she had quickly emerged from the shower to answer the telephone. Landon's body was not sexually mutilated.

So there was no conclusive proof at the scene that this was a sexual homicide. There was semen found in the vagina of the victim but it turned out to be that of her boyfriend, with whom she had spent the evening. The FBI profiler claimed that the stab wounds to Christine's breast area were sexual in nature, but if you want to be sure someone is dead, you stab them in the heart, and for women, the heart just happens to have a breast covering it. The only true possible support for this being a sexual crime would be the ropes tying Christine's hands and feet. This could be a sign of bondage, but I couldn't jump to this conclusion. I would have to see how all the evidence fit. I needed to do a thorough crime reconstruction and "see" what actually occurred that night at the Landon residence.

There were three possible suspects—Curtis Cox, Craig Landon (alone or with assistance), and an unknown suspect (alone or with assistance)—that I could theorize as responsible for the deaths of Landon and Dickinson. I examined each without benefit of access to proper crime scene information.

THERE WAS NO solid evidence that I knew of that connected Curtis Cox to this crime.

The prosecution and police cited the following reasons as probable cause for the arrest and prosecution of Cox in the murders of Landon and Dickinson.

1. Access to the house. This was the strongest element in the prosecution's case. I was told that Cox did have access to the house.
2. Cox acted in a strange manner. This was not evidence. This was simply interesting.

3. A witness identified Cox. This was questionable, as the witness did not have a clear view of the man seen and there was also reason to believe the identification was not particularly reliable.

4. Cox had an alleged history of sexual deviancy. This information was actually not proven. When I studied the police records I found that this information was elicited from Christine's estranged husband, Craig. Right after the crime he was brought in for questioning and during the interview, he and his children told the police of disturbing behavior by Curtis Cox when he was around children.

5. If Craig Landon's and his children's stories about Cox have any validity to them, Cox would be even less likely to have chosen an adult female as the target of any attempted crime or sexual encounter. Cox would have an interest only in children as the objects of his sexual endeavors. True pedophiles do not change sexual preferences from children to adults. *If* the information that I received from those who knew Cox was accurate, he was too weak and lacking in confidence to approach an adult, especially a fully functioning (physically and emotionally) adult. If Cox were a pedophile and the stories about him were true, he would have used a totally different MO. He would have enticed children, then slowly introduced them to sexual activities with him, all in a nonviolent manner. Whoever attacked Christine Landon was aggressive and violent. It should also be noted that some of the stories of Cox's behavior came from Christine's children, who may have been coached by their father or someone else prior to their interviews with the investigators.

6. The "Power List." There was a piece of paper found in Cox's trash that had the names of some of the women in town, their husbands, and their children, and Christine Landon's was among them. One of the women's names had a sexual comment next to it, but what that comment was or meant, I had no idea. But no words were written next to Christine's name, so there would be no way to say Cox was targeting her. The FBI profiler imagined what this paper might mean to Curtis Cox and

decided it was a list of women over whom he would like to have power. The prosecutor and the FBI profiler claimed this was an indication of Cox's ideation and plan for the abduction and sexual assault of Christine Landon. There was no proof that the list had any such meaning except in the creative minds of the profiler and prosecution.

7. Cox's disappearance and faked suicide. Cox's life had definitely taken a bad turn. The woman for whom he babysat was murdered, the police were hounding him and insinuating he had something to do with it, and he was growing tired of caring for his sick father. One day he drove his car to a lake and left a suicide note stating he couldn't deal with anything anymore. His body, however, was not found in the lake but just down the road in a cheap motel—still moving about quite well.

8. The prosecution claimed this was evidence of a guilty conscience, but all this bizarre behavior proved was that Curtis Cox was a weak man who couldn't handle pressure. Cox burned some materials at a campfire while he was "on the run," before he was found at the motel. The district attorney claimed he burned evidence, although he couldn't come up with what the evidence was. It was possible Cox had another reason to have put material, kindling, and wood together. Many people do that. It is called building a fire.

There was zero evidence to support a theory that Cox planned or carried out any crime against Landon and Dickinson. There *are*, however, a number of reasons to believe that he did *not* commit the crimes:

1. Cox had an unusual interest in children, even being accused of being a pedophile.

2. In abducting and killing Christine, Cox would have severed his connection to the children and thwarted his own desires.

3. Cox would have had to exhibit an incredible change of behavior to go from an ineffectual individual to one who had the guts to abduct a full-grown woman, violently assault her, and also shoot a police marshal.

4. Christine Landon immediately screamed when she saw the offender in her house. The fact that Christine knew Cox well and had no noted fear of him indicated to me that even if she saw Cox, suddenly standing in front of her with a rope and a knife, she would be more likely to respond with disbelief as in "What the fuck are you doing?" The immediate scream indicated to me that Christine was frightened of her attacker.

5. Cox had no history of violence (of which I was aware). The crime scene showed a man who did not hesitate to take violent action. The offender either had a history of violence or was extremely angry at his victim, or both.

There was also little evidence to label the assault on Christine as a sexual crime.

While I previously said I didn't believe this was a sexual homicide, there were several reasons why the prosecutor called the death of Christine a sexual homicide:

1. Christine Landon was naked from the waist down. Nakedness does not necessarily indicate motive of a crime. Some victims are simply found in this state when the crime begins. In other cases, offenders remove clothing to delay identification or to eliminate evidence. In this case, I believe Christine was not fully dressed because she was showering and preparing for bed.

2. Christine was tied up. Tying up a victim does not necessarily indicate sexual intent. In bondage scenarios, yes, the victim would be tied. However, the limited restraints on Christine do not indicate a well-developed bondage scenario of a sexual sadist. The restraints on Christine were more indicative of control—control of the victim while removing her from the premises, control while placing her in the trunk of a vehicle, and control by keeping her restrained in the vehicle while driving.

3. Christine was stabbed in the breast area. The location of the stab wounds may make it appear that the assault was sexual. However, the heart is located underneath the breast and the

breast can be just in the way when the offender attempts to kill the victim.

4. Semen evidence at the scene. Semen evidence proves only that the victim had a sexual encounter with somebody.

I believe the only crime the attacker intended to commit inside the residence was an attempt to abduct Christine Landon. The abductor wanted Christine to appear as though she never arrived home, or that she went back out again.

Since there were no other vehicles noted by Christine that concerned her, no vehicle noted earlier by the neighbors, nor was any vehicle seen leaving the scene after the murders were committed, the only car available for transporting a bound person was the victim's own car. And since a sex crime or a homicide could be committed most easily in the victim's house, there had to be a good reason to remove her. This was most likely so that the offender would not be identified as having some kind of relationship with Christine and so that a stranger might be suspected of abducting and attacking Christine elsewhere. The abduction would also have served to delay the discovery of the crime so that the body and other physical evidence would not be found too quickly. The delay in discovery would also aid the offender in establishing an alibi. Lastly, it was also possible that the abductor did not want the house to become a crime scene or "get messed up" with blood and other unpleasant emissions.

Christine had had company over on previous evenings so there was no way for an abductor to know if she would have company with her when she arrived home. It would therefore be unlikely that the offender would have hidden in the house awaiting her arrival. It would be far safer to observe the house from a safe location (in an abandoned residence next door or from another nearby secret location). The offender would be able to clearly observe the arrival of Christine in her car and to note that she was alone. The offender may have waited a bit longer just to be sure no one else followed her home. It was also possible that the offender arrived after Christine came home and, seeing no other vehicles or visitors, quickly entered the residence. If the offender had hidden in the house, it would be extremely unlikely he would have allowed her to get out of her clothes, take a shower, and, especially, answer the telephone call from her boyfriend before attempting to abduct her.

There were only two entrances into the house: through the front door and through a sliding glass door in the back. Entering the house through the front door could be accomplished either by knocking or with a key. Christine did not tell her boyfriend when he called that she had opened the door to anyone since arriving home, so the killer entered the house without her assistance. She had installed a chain lock on the front door. It would make sense that when she arrived home, she would have placed the chain back on the door. There was blood on the chain, indicating some possibility that the killer removed it to allow the marshal in.

Also, the killer would not want the neighbors across the street to see who was entering the house. This makes entering the house through the back more desirable. If someone had a key to the house, he could have entered the house earlier in the day and unlocked the sliding back door. The killer may have relocked the door after entering.

Shortly after her arrival, Christine took a shower in the downstairs bathroom. The phone rang and she left the shower, threw on a sweatshirt, and went to answer the phone. It was not clear whether the phone she answered was in the kitchen or the upstairs bedroom (although the upstairs phone is more likely considering Christine did not hear the offender enter the house nor would it appear the offender knew Christine was on the phone).

The crime scene behaviors indicated that the initial assault took place away from the location where the victim answered the phone, most likely in the upstairs hallway and quickly moving to the first floor.

The caller, Hugh Marshall, with whom Christine had just spent the evening, stated that during the conversation with Christine, he encouraged her to check the house (front and back door) to make certain it was secure. Hugh said Christine said she was uncomfortable with her estranged husband coming and going in the house and believed he had been there earlier that day. Christine put the phone down and went to check the house. She quickly encountered an intruder. She screamed and possibly said something more, but this was not confirmed. Marshall then hung up his phone and called Bob Dickinson. He followed that call up with one to the sheriff's department.

I could not determine if the offender knew the caller was still on the phone when Christine encountered him. However, it would seem odd that, realizing she was screaming for help to a phone that was off the hook and that someone may have been calling the police to help her, the offender would take the time to tie her up and attempt to abduct her. I would expect the offender to either run out of there or immediately kill the victim and then clear out of the house. It was more logical to conclude that when the offender encountered Christine, he did not know she was even on the phone. Not until *after* she was tied up was the phone discovered off the hook and the receiver put back in place. It would also be nonsensical to tie up the victim *after* the murder of Bob Dickinson, because the first murder would eliminate any point in removing Christine from the house. Tying her up and carrying her out would slow down the killer's escape. Christine must have been tied up immediately upon the offender and Christine's meeting. This would mean the offender brought the materials along with the intention of tying up the victim.

Christine was tied up immediately upon encountering her attacker, and she had to be in the kitchen at the time Marshal Dickinson arrived at the front door. At that point, it was likely the abductor was in the process of leading Christine out of the kitchen toward the back door, her feet hobbled, hands tied, and a knife at her throat. The killer stopped to get the keys from her handbag on the desk, evidenced by the items that spilled out of the purse.

Christine was not gagged and she was on her feet at the time she was brutally attacked—demonstrated by the blood found on the bottom of her feet. Why did Christine's attacker start his assault on her then? Most likely, the marshal had just knocked on the door and shouted out, "Christine? Are you in there, Christine?" The natural response for Christine when she heard the police marshal yelling her name would have been to scream for help. It was then the natural response of the offender to put his hand over her mouth.

Continuing with my hypothesis, from this point on, there would be no way to abduct the victim without wasting too much time and allowing the offender to be caught in the act by the police. Christine would need to be eliminated as quickly as possible at that point.

The offender stood behind Christine, with his hand over her mouth; her body faced the west wall and living room doorway, away from the refrigerator. This position explained why more of the kitchen did not have cast-off blood.

It can also be noted that while there were numerous stab wounds in the left upper quadrant of Christine's body, all the defense wounds were on her right arm and hand. If the attacker were facing her, we should have seen wounds on both arms and hands. However, it was most likely that the victim's left arm was trapped against her body as the killer clamped his hand over her mouth.

If Christine had then attempted to push the attacker's arm away from her so she could call for help, her right arm would have been brought directly in front of the left quadrant of her body. I believe her hands must have been tied in front of her body, because if they were behind, there would have been less opportunity to inflict defense wounds unless she obtained them in the process of being tied up, which was again unlikely. However, none of the reports to which I had access stated if the victim's hands were tied in front or in back.

The killer was also most likely right-handed. When Christine finally collapsed, he finished the job by cutting her throat. Again, with the victim's head facing the floor, cutting her throat from behind eliminated any arterial spurt onto the walls and onto the offender (the blood simply pooled beneath her neck on the floor). It is likely that the killer committed this homicide with relatively little blood spraying onto his person. For this reason, he would be able to answer the door without having the police marshal immediately notice something was amiss. He may also have been wearing gloves that he removed before allowing the marshal into the residence. What is clear to me is that at the point he let Bob in, Christine was already dead. He undid the chain on the door, leaving a speck of blood on it, and invited Bob inside.

After leading Bob upstairs to where he said Christine was either sick or injured, the offender grabbed for Bob's gun as he approached the door of the rear bedroom, and after gaining control of it, he shot Bob again and again until Bob collapsed near the top of the stairs. By this point, the sheriff's department was undoubtedly on the way and he may have heard sirens. It is likely he ran into the bedroom to look out the front window to determine if any other police or witnesses were out there. This was where a bit of blood was found on a pillowcase on the bed right next to the window. Even a tiny bit of blood in a room with no other signs of a struggle has a meaning if only we can figure out what it is.

There seemed to be little time between the gunshots being fired and the neighbor across the street stating he witnessed a tall, dark-haired man coming between the Landon house and the vacant house next door with a bag and a five-foot stick or piece of wood in his hand. It made no sense that a killer leaving the scene of a crime would take a long stick or piece of wood with him. This object would make him more noticeable as he tried to run away, slow down his escape, and lack usefulness unless he was removing something with evidence on it. This was unlikely. It is more likely that the long "stick" was a rifle.

Then, according to this witness, the man ran down the street toward town and the abandoned railroad tracks. As a tarlike material was found on the floor tile of the victim's home in two partial impressions, it would have been useful to compare that substance to any coal tar creosote that might have been used as a preservative on the old railroad tracks to determine if there was a match. If there was, then the killer would have had to come *from* the tracks to the home before returning in that direction.

As I have said, I believe this was an abduction gone awry. It is likely that the killer parked his own vehicle some distance from the house, came in on foot, and planned to take Christine bound and gagged from the house in her car, and then dispose of her (or leave Christine dead in her car and leave in his own vehicle). This would have allowed the offender's car to go unseen, allowed him to leave the victim's car someplace unrelated to the offender's home, and allowed the offender to get rid of the body where he wished and still have a way to get back home.

Although there was technically a possibility of two offenders, there was no evidence that established this to be true. If there were two offenders, it was more likely the police marshal would have been killed immediately upon entering the house; there would be little reason to get him upstairs in order to put him off guard and find an opportunity to kill him. It was also unlikely two men would feel the need to hobble a small woman when they could more quickly abduct her without bothering to tie her up. Also, only *one* person was noted running from the scene.

Marshal Bob Dickinson clearly knew his killer, as he willingly walked upstairs, his gun still holstered and the perpetrator behind him. Therefore, it is likely that Christine knew him as well. These were not stranger homicides. This was also a premeditated crime. If we eliminate Curtis Cox as a suspect because he lacked motive and capability, we must look for someone else known to the victims who had motive and capability.

The police investigated Craig Landon as he was upset about their divorce and losing custody of the children and stood to financially gain from Christine Landon's death. My theory that the murder was to have taken place away from the home supports my supposition that it could have been the ex-husband. Craig would not have wanted the house messed up, because he wanted to move himself and the children immediately back into their home. Several people told me that they noticed that his behavior changed dramatically following the crime. He suddenly became *real* friendly to the neighbors—neighbors he didn't have the time of day for before.

Craig also had a history of threatening his estranged wife. The marshal had been called to the residence a number of times to investigate domestic violence complaints when neighbors heard arguments sounding like they were growing out of control. That doesn't prove he killed his ex-wife, but it does mean the police should have looked at him.

Christine would have screamed immediately upon seeing Craig in her hallway, brandishing a knife, and one witness claimed Hugh Marshall told her that after hearing Christine scream, he thought he heard her say, "No, Craig, no!"

Soon after the murders, Hugh Marshall said that he thought Craig was guilty of the double homicide. He was afraid Craig would come after him with a gun. And speaking of guns, Craig would certainly know if there was a shotgun or rifle under the bed.

My own interview with Craig made me wonder about the man.

He seemed to be taking pride in and enjoying showing me the pictures he took of the crime scene and the blood found there.

Craig was the first suspect in this case because, as we have all seen in many, many cases, a woman is usually killed by someone she is romantically involved with—a husband, a boyfriend, an ex-husband, an ex-boyfriend. After the police discovered the bodies and secured the scene, they drove straight to his temporary apartment, which, coincidentally, was not too far down that railroad track, and Craig Landon was a runner. When they got there, they found the engine of his car still hot. They brought him in and found gunshot residue on his hands. He claimed it was just residue from the fireworks he had been shooting off for his children the day after the Fourth of July.

He must have been convincing, or his lawyer and friend must have been since he gave Craig an alibi and said they were together that night. Still, doubts lingered, and in his four-year battle to exonerate his client, Curtis Cox's lawyer in court claimed that Craig was the killer.

THE LAST POSSIBILITY was that neither Curtis Cox nor Craig Landon was involved in the crime.

However, there was little evidence to point to any other party having motive to abduct and kill Christine Landon, or to any other party having access to her house. The only exception to this would have been a hired hit by Craig Landon. Another Craig, Craig Bright, was acquainted with Christine and later convicted of the sexual homicide of a coworker in a state down south. He was someone who should have at least been eliminated as a suspect. Supposedly, Christine had known him for a short period of time due to her work, but Craig Landon reportedly did not have a relationship with this other Craig or even know him.

This case should have been reopened and reinvestigated with open minds and new investigative avenues. I finished my profile and told the sheriff that they should reopen the investigation and take a hard look at Craig Landon just as Cox's lawyer asserted. The physical evidence pointed to him, the behavioral evidence pointed to him, and the motive pointed to him. But the case files are still locked up and the killer, whoever he is, remains free. I can only hope one day justice will prevail.

CHAPTER 15

LAST WORDS

Not every murder in the United States is caused by a serial killer, but there are a lot of them. It used to be that we worried about our sons dying in war or our daughters in childbirth. Now we worry about our children being murdered at college or in the comfort of their own homes.

And the average American feels powerless to do anything about it.

Criminal profiling is a great tool to use in solving murder cases and taking dangerous predators off our streets. The more we understand about how men (and some women) become psychopaths and criminals, their motives for doing bad things, and how they go about committing their crimes, the better off we will all be in recognizing them in our lives. Then we can change our society to prevent our kids from turning into psychopaths, reduce crime, keep from becoming victims, and solve crimes quickly so the perpetrators get put away where they can't hurt anyone anymore.

The night that I first came to suspect that Walt Williams murdered Anne Kelley, I thought, *I'll gather all the evidence, deliver it to the police, and by morning, they will come and arrest him, and he will go away to jail.* That was what I expected would happen. I never dreamed it would take more than that.

When the police showed no interest in the information I brought them, at first I merely couldn't believe it. And because the killer, whether it is Walt Williams or someone else, has never been caught, I had a second thought, one that terrorized me for years: *Oh, my God, the murderer is still out there.*

I first started researching serial homicide and sexual crimes, serial killers and psychopaths, not to become a criminal profiler or to start a national organization, but to play devil's advocate, because I didn't want to suspect someone of a heinous crime for no reason. I was surprised to find that some police investigations were shallow at best, and certainly I was amazed that quite a few police officers didn't understand the behavior of psychopaths or serial killers. I thought, *How is this possible?*

I hit an iceberg, a massive problem in our society: that Anne Kelley could go running one night in my sleepy, safe hometown, past the baseball field where my sons played every day, be brutally murdered, and a week later nobody mentioned her name ever again—how could this be? The newspapers went silent on the subject, the people in town pretended she never existed, her case was never solved, while the killer hopped, skipped, and walked away. And this was repeated over and over in the surrounding communities—in fact, all across America.

In time I was haunted not just by Anne Kelley but by Deborah Joshi, Lisa Young, Vicki Davis, Sarah Andrews, Mary Beth Townsend, Doris Hoover, and hundreds more women nobody knew or cared anything about. My neighbors slept well at night thinking that our system of dealing with serial homicide was smart and effective, that we always caught the bad guys.

The system, however, is broken.

Look across the United States, in your own backyard, and you can start multiplying how many serial killers are running free. For forty years, the Green River Killer in Washington State was able to kill women whenever he felt like it. The man called the Grim Reaper, who slaughtered a multitude of women in Los Angeles, is still out there. Dennis Rader roamed free as a bird for thirty-one years, killing women whenever he felt like it. Finally, he was caught and charged as the BTK strangler for the murders of women in Wichita, Kansas, but there is still a long list of unsolved sexual homicides in police files. If Rader didn't kill them (and he likely did not), Wichita still has one or more serial killers at large.

FOR SOME REASON, I am one of the few people in the United States looking at the big picture and only because I tripped over it. This wasn't the kind of trouble I ever looked for in my life before Anne Kelley.

I believe that I ended up with this information and perspective in order to do something about it. I don't know why Walt Williams came to live in my house and shortly thereafter a woman I never met was murdered near my home. I don't know why I'm the type of person who would actually put two and two together and gather up evidence and take it to the police. Maybe if I hadn't been there, no one would have gone to the police. Most people would have just shrugged their shoulders and erased the crime from their minds.

So why me? Well, why not me, as they say! Maybe I have an inquisitive mind. Maybe I've always been a curious person about certain things. Maybe I'm a logical, deductive person, and I can add things up. But whatever the reason, I was there, it happened in my neighborhood, and I had this suspect in my house.

It was brought to me, whether by destiny or fate, but I felt I could make a difference, and that's what I set out to do, and I've sought to do that ever since.

Twenty years later, I'm just getting to the point where I feel I will be able to influence the changing of the American criminal justice system. That's my goal, and there are still plenty of places I have to go. For starters, I developed the first criminal profiling program in the country outside of the FBI, one intended to provide training for law enforcement officers and future profilers in the United States and in other countries struggling with the same issues.

I want the police to learn how to do this themselves. I want them to have more time and more funds to do it. Sometimes, they just don't have enough hours to focus on each homicide they're presented. They work so many cases, run down so many leads, and spend a good deal of their days in court. They write stacks of paperwork. We should actually consider ourselves fortunate when our police detectives have the luxury to put their full effort into an investigation. Sometimes we are lucky if they do any investigating at all. And when they actually solve a crime and get all their ducks in a row, it's quite an accomplishment under horrible work conditions.

The FBI has a dedicated domestic crime computer it calls ViCAP. It is supposed to assist homicide detectives and investigators and fill in gaps in their knowledge base. But it doesn't catch serial killers. It's a poor system because the inputs are questionable and it is too unwieldy. Some police investigators rush through the form and the information is less than accurate. Other detectives just toss the damn form because it's so long they can't be bothered. The end result is a confusing mess. Some of the information is so vague that it serves little purpose. "The woman was strangled and found outside." Oh, grand! Do you know how many women are strangled and found outside across the United States? Is that going to identify a serial killer? Is that a common linkage between that serial killer's crimes? I don't think so.

There are only so many ways to kill a woman. You strangle, you stab, you beat her to death, maybe you shoot her, but that's it. So when you input that, you've got a whole lot of strangled dead women in the bushes. That's not going to help. The way it is being done with ViCAP isn't winning any popularity contests with local law enforcement.

What they don't have is a suspect bank. I've been lobbying for a system in which a detective doing an investigation could input the name of a suspect or a witness connected to a crime, or toss in the name of a friend, workmate, or relative of the victim, then, *bam,* they could see if that name came up in connection with another crime. It is amazing how often a suspect will be interviewed at different times and by different police departments but nobody knows about that until after the killer is convicted of a homicide.

Suppose Walt Williams moved to San Diego and his female neighbor went missing and soon turned up dead. The police knock on all the doors of the residents on the street and Walt is living in one of the houses. The police have a little chat with him and when they get back to the station, they input all the names of the folks on the street, including Walt's. His name gets flagged!

"Whoa, wait a minute here! This Walt Williams was a suspect in the homicide of an Anne Kelley two decades ago in Maryland!" Wouldn't that be useful to know?

But what actually happens is that a potential suspect moves from jurisdiction to jurisdiction, and while he could be interviewed in five separate crimes, not one investigator will have a clue that he was interviewed in the other incidents unless there is a conviction.

That's the state of affairs of serial homicide in the United States. And that's why, even though I was already over forty years old when I took up profiling, I still believed I could make a difference. I thought the status quo was just not acceptable.

But how does a former housewife change an entrenched criminal and political system, much of which is rather militaristic, almost all male, and well guarded? There are fragile egos and jurisdictional challenges at play. Sometimes it's as simple as balancing well-meaning but divergent views of the same evidence or suspect.

There are plenty of dedicated, wonderful police officers who are overworked and undertrained. There are thousands of men and women who do their best, day in and day out, with limited resources. These deficiencies contribute to the high level of unsolved homicides. Some do amazing work, solve difficult crimes, and are role models for others in law enforcement. But unfortunately, as in every organization, there is always a percentage of people who are simply not that good. There are incompetent professionals in every walk of life. Not every police officer is top-notch, so there will be cases that go under just because the detective working them isn't the brightest bulb, and that's unfortunate.

I HAVE NO issue with where I came from. I don't feel I need to apologize for being a homemaker in my life. I loved being a homemaker, and I think homemaking is a wonderful contribution, one of the finest contributions, to a community and to the family. I'm entirely supportive of homemaking. I think it's fabulous. I don't regret a day that I was a homemaker or a day of homeschooling my kids. I loved being home with my children. I'm not one of those people who wishes I hadn't done it. I loved it and I am thankful I was fortunate enough to have had the choice to stay home.

But I can't walk away from something if I feel that it's my duty as a human being to do something about it.

Some people don't care, some think they can't do anything about the system. They don't feel qualified or competent to act. They just feel that they're not going to make a difference, so there's no point in trying. And there are some who are afraid. They think if they get involved, bad things will happen to them, which is a realistic and logical thing to think. In many circumstances, when you do stick your head out, it gets chopped off.

My belief system requires me to act, damn the consequences.

I am passionate about the things I believe in. I'm passionate about children. I am passionate about women and their right to have a safe and abuse-free life. I believe in justice.

There are twenty or thirty more years of work ahead of me for changing serial homicide methodology and criminal profiling in this country. I'm only at the halfway point. I've got a long way to go, and hopefully I'll live long enough to accomplish the rest of it. My mother turns ninety this year and my father will turn eighty-six and they still ballroom dance, so my genes are pretty good! But I know change is a group project and more people will come along the trail and will take up the work, and I welcome more profilers and police detectives to evolve methodologies and make a difference in our closure rate.

The whole point is to save more lives, because nobody deserves to die like Anne Kelley. No family deserves to have their loved one murdered—their dreams and hopes ruined and dashed. It should make everybody who hears this story so angry that they want to find a way to assist law enforcement and put an end to these senseless killings.

None of these murdering bastards should exist, and if they get away with it one time, we may be able to claim we were caught unaware. But when it happens over and over again, that is another thing altogether. Fool me once, shame on you; fool me twice, shame on me. We should be ashamed of ourselves, because we've been fooled over and over and over by serial and other types of killers. We refuse to open our eyes and recognize what does and does not work and where we need to put our money and support.

Hopefully, this will change.